Our Daily Bread

Devotional Collection

 Discovery House®

Discovery House is affiliated with Our Daily Bread Ministries, Grand Rapids, Michigan.

Requests for permission to quote from this book should be directed to: Permissions Department, Discovery House, PO Box 3566, Grand Rapids, MI 49501, or contact us by email at permissionsdept@dhp.org.

Article by Harold Myra adapted from *The Practice of the Presence of God: Experience the Spiritual Classic through 40 Days of Daily Devotion* (Discovery House, 2017).

ISBN of Navy Walnut edition: 978-1-62707-849-8

ISBN of Iris Purple edition: 978-1-62707-850-4

Printed in China
First printing in 2018

Introduction

You've picked up a copy of the 2019 *Our Daily Bread* Devotional Collection. This book of devotionals is designed to assist you in your time with God. Here are some suggestions for getting the most out of your *Our Daily Bread* devotional reading.

- **Set aside a regular time and place.** Your time will be more meaningful if you can concentrate and establish a regular practice.

- **Read the Bible passage.** Those words from God's Word are the most important statements you will read each day. As you read God's Word, seek to learn more about God, your relationship with Him, and how He wants you to live each day.

- **Note the key verse.** It is printed above each article. You may want to memorize this key Bible verse.

- **Read the article thoughtfully.** Reflect on what the writer is saying.

- **Reflect on the questions or personalize the words of the prayer.** The prayer may be used as a prayer-starter that expresses how you feel.

- **Use the closing "thought" to help you remember the key idea.** The last statement in bold type on each page is what we call the "thought of the day."

- **Write down your discoveries.** For example: What is God saying to you through His Word?

- **Take time to pray.** Talk to the Lord about what you've discovered in His Word and your response to Him.

- **Share the lessons with others.** When you talk with others, share what the Lord is teaching you from His Word.

It is our prayer that in these devotional articles you will find encouragement, hope, and comfort as you draw closer to God and grow in your love for Him. ❀

THE OUR DAILY BREAD STAFF

Thanks-Living

Read: Psalm 23

Surely your goodness and love will follow me all the days of my life.
Psalm 23:6

Wanting to mature in her spiritual life and become more thankful, Sue started what she called a Thanks-Living jar. Each evening she wrote on a small piece of paper one thing she thanked God for and dropped it in the jar. Some days she had many praises; other difficult days she struggled to find one. At the end of the year she emptied her jar and read through all of the notes. She found herself thanking God again for everything He had done. He had given simple things like a beautiful sunset or a cool evening for a walk in the park, and other times He had provided grace to handle a difficult situation or had answered a prayer.

Sue's discovery reminded me of what the psalmist David says he experienced (PS. 23). God refreshed him with "green pastures" and "quiet waters" (VV. 2–3). He gave him guidance, protection, and comfort (VV. 3–4). David concluded: "Surely your goodness and love will follow me all the days of my life" (V. 6).

I'm going to make a Thanks-Living jar this year. Maybe you'd like to as well. I think we'll see we have many reasons to thank God—including His gifts of friends and family and His provisions for our physical, spiritual, and emotional needs. We'll see that the goodness and love of God follow us all the days of our lives.

ANNE CETAS

Dear Lord, You bless me in more ways than I can count.
Thank You for Your love for me.

When you think of all that's good, give thanks to God.

The Perfect Gift

Read: Romans 11:33–12:2

Offer your bodies as a living sacrifice, holy and pleasing to God—this is your true and proper worship. Romans 12:1

The weeks after Christmas are the busiest time of year in the US for merchandise returns as people trade unwanted gifts for what they really want. Yet you probably know a few people who always seem to give the perfect gift. How do they know just what another person values and what is right for the occasion? The key to successful gift-giving is not money; it's listening to others and taking a personal interest in what they enjoy and appreciate.

This is true for family and friends. But what about God? Is there anything meaningful or valuable that we can give to God? Is there anything He doesn't already have?

Romans 11:33–36, a song of praise to God for His great wisdom, knowledge, and glory, is followed by a call to give ourselves to Him. "Therefore, I urge you, brothers and sisters, in view of God's mercy, to offer your bodies as a living sacrifice, holy and pleasing to God—this is your true and proper worship" (12:1). Instead of being shaped by the world around us, we are to be "transformed by the renewing of [our] mind" (V. 2).

What's the best gift we can give to God today? In gratitude, humility, and love we can give ourselves completely to Him—heart, mind, and will. It's just what the Lord is longing to receive from each of us. *DAVID MCCASLAND*

Dear Lord, I'm Yours. I want to offer myself to You—heart, mind, and will—in humble service and in thankful worship for all You have done for me.

The best gift we can give to God is ourselves.

Not What It Seems

Read: 2 Kings 6:8–17

Don't be afraid . . . . Those who are with us are more than those who are with [the enemy]. 2 Kings 6:16

Don is a border collie who lives on a farm in South Lanarkshire, Scotland. One morning, he and his owner, Tom, set out to check on some animals. They rode together in a small farm utility truck. When they arrived, Tom left the vehicle but forgot to put the brake on. With Don in the driver's seat, the vehicle rolled down a hill and across two lanes of traffic before it stopped safely. To watching motorists, it appeared the dog was out for a morning drive. Indeed, things are not always as they seem.

It seemed as if Elisha and his servant were about to be captured and carried off to the King of Aram. The king's forces had surrounded the city where Elisha and his servant were staying. The servant believed they were doomed, but Elisha said, "Don't be afraid . . . . Those who are with us are more than those who are with [the enemy]" (2 KINGS 6:16). When Elisha prayed, the servant was able to see the multitudes of supernatural forces that were in place to protect them.

Situations that seem hopeless are not always the way we perceive them to be. When we feel overwhelmed and outnumbered, we can remember that God is by our side. He can "command his angels . . . to guard [us] in all [our] ways" (PS. 91:11).

JENNIFER BENSON SCHULDT

Dear God, please give me a glimpse of Your power today. Help me to believe that You are willing and able to help me in any situation I encounter.

Things are always better than they seem to be when we remember that God is by our side.

A Multiplied Love

Read: 1 John 4:20–5:5

Anyone who loves God must also love their brother and sister.
1 John 4:21

When a woman in Karen's church was diagnosed with ALS (amyotrophic lateral sclerosis, also known as Lou Gehrig's disease), things looked bad. This cruel disease affects nerves and muscles, eventually leading to paralysis. The family's insurance wouldn't cover home care, and the stricken woman's husband couldn't bear the thought of putting her in a nursing home.

As a nurse, Karen had the expertise to help and began going to the woman's home to care for her. But she soon realized she couldn't take care of her own family while meeting the needs of her friend, so she started teaching others in the church to help. As the disease ran its course over the next seven years, Karen trained thirty-one additional volunteers who surrounded that family with love, prayer, and practical assistance.

"Anyone who loves God must also love their brother and sister," said John the disciple (1 JOHN 4:21). Karen gives us a shining example of that kind of love. She had the skills, compassion, and vision to rally a church family around a hurting friend. Her love for one person in need became a multiplied love lived out by many.   *TIM GUSTAFSON*

How might God use your talents and abilities to serve others in need? Ask God to show you how He wants you to use your gifts for His kingdom.

Love your neighbor as yourself.
JESUS

Listening to God

Read: Genesis 3:8–17

The LORD God called . . . "Where are you?" Genesis 3:9

My young son loves to hear my voice, except when I call his name loudly and sternly, followed by the question, "Where are you?" When I do that, I am usually calling for him because he has been into some mischief and is trying to hide from me. I want my son to listen to my voice because I'm concerned about his well-being and do not want him to get hurt.

Adam and Eve were used to hearing God's voice in the garden. However, after they disobeyed Him by eating the forbidden fruit, they hid from Him when they heard Him calling, "Where are you?" (GEN. 3:9). They didn't want to face God because they knew they had done something wrong—something He had told them not to do (V. 11).

When God called for Adam and Eve and found them in the garden, His words did include correction and consequence (VV. 13–19). But God also showed them kindness and gave them hope for mankind in the promise of the Savior (V. 15).

God doesn't have to look for us. He knows where we are and what we are trying to hide. But as a loving Father, He wants to speak to our hearts and bring us forgiveness and restoration. He longs for us to hear His voice—and to listen.   *KEILA OCHOA*

Thank You, Lord, for Your love and care. Thank You for sending Your Son, our Savior, to fulfill Your promise of forgiveness and restoration.

When God calls, we need to answer.

Someone to Celebrate

Read: Matthew 2:1–12

Come, let us bow down in worship, let us kneel before the LORD our Maker. Psalm 95:6

Many manger scenes depict the wise men, or magi, visiting Jesus in Bethlehem at the same time as the shepherds. But according to the gospel of Matthew, the only place in Scripture where their story is found, the magi showed up later. Jesus was no longer in the manger in a stable at the inn, but in a house. Matthew 2:11 tells us, "On coming to the house, they saw the child with his mother Mary, and they bowed down and worshiped him. Then they opened their treasures and presented him with gifts of gold, frankincense and myrrh."

Realizing that the magi's visit happened later than we may think provides a helpful reminder as we begin a new year. Jesus is always worthy of worship. When the holidays are past and we head back to life's everyday routines, we still have Someone to celebrate.

Jesus Christ is Immanuel, "God with us" (MATT. 1:23), in every season. He has promised to be with us "always" (28:20). Because He is always with us, we can worship Him in our hearts every day and trust that He will show himself faithful in the years to come. Just as the magi sought Him, may we seek Him too and worship Him wherever we are. *JAMES BANKS*

Lord Jesus, just as the magi sought You and bowed before You as the coming King, help me to yield my will to You and to follow where You lead.

When we find Christ we offer our worship.

Our Source of Provision

Read: Matthew 6:9–15

The LORD is near to all who call on him. Psalm 145:18

In August 2010, the attention of the world was focused on a mine shaft near Copiapó, Chile. Thirty-three miners huddled in the dark, trapped 2,300 feet underground. They had no idea if help would ever arrive. After seventeen days of waiting, they heard drilling. Rescuers produced a small hole in the mine shaft ceiling, and that hole was followed by three more, establishing a delivery path for water, food, and medicine. The miners depended on those conduits to the surface above ground, where rescuers had the provisions they would need to survive. On day sixty-nine, rescuers pulled the last miner to safety.

None of us can survive in this world apart from provisions that are outside of ourselves. God, the Creator of the universe, is the one who provides us with everything we need. Like the drill holes for those miners, prayer connects us to the God of all supply.

Jesus encouraged us to pray, "Give us today our daily bread" (MATT. 6:11). In His day, bread was the basic staple of life and pictured all the daily needs of the people. Jesus was teaching us to pray not only for our physical needs but also for everything we need—comfort, healing, courage, wisdom.

Through prayer we have access to Him at any moment, and He knows what we need before we even ask (V. 8). What might you be struggling with today? "The LORD is near to all who call on him" (PS. 145:18).   *BILL CROWDER*

**Prayer is the voice of faith, trusting that
God knows and cares.**

Put Down Your Burdens

Read: Matthew 11:25–30

Come to me, all you who are weary and burdened, and I will give you rest. Matthew 11:28

A man driving his pickup truck on a country track saw a woman carrying a heavy load, so he stopped and offered her a lift. The woman expressed her gratitude and climbed into the back of the truck.

A moment later, the man noticed a strange thing: the woman was still holding onto her heavy load despite sitting in the vehicle! Astonished, he pleaded, "Please, Madam, put down your load and take your rest. My truck can carry you and your stuff. Just relax."

What do we do with the load of fear, worry, and anxiety we often carry as we go through life's many challenges? Instead of relaxing in the Lord, I sometimes behave like that woman. Jesus said, "Come to me, all you who are weary and burdened, and I will give you rest" (MATT. 11:28), yet I've caught myself carrying burdens I should offload onto Jesus.

We put down our burdens when we bring them to the Lord in prayer. The apostle Peter says, "Cast all your anxiety on [Jesus] because he cares for you" (1 PETER 5:7). Because He cares for us, we can rest and relax as we learn to trust Him. Instead of carrying the burdens that weigh us down and weary us, we can give them to the Lord and let Him carry them.   *LAWRENCE DARMANI*

I'm tired, Lord. I bring You my burdens today. Please keep them and carry them for me.

Prayer is the place where burdens change shoulders.

Old Yet New

Read: Revelation 21:1–5

He who was seated on the throne said, "I am making everything new."
Revelation 21:5

In 2014, a sinkhole opened up under the National Corvette Museum in Kentucky, swallowing eight vintage, irreplaceable Chevrolet Corvette sports cars. The automobiles were severely damaged—some beyond repair.

One car in particular received a lot of attention. The one-millionth Corvette, which rolled off the assembly line in 1992, was the most valuable in the collection. What happened to that gem after it was pulled from the sinkhole is fascinating. Experts restored the car to mint condition, mainly by using and repairing its original parts. Although this little beauty was in horrible shape, it now looks as good as it did the day it was built.

The old and damaged was made new.

This is a great reminder of what God has in store for believers in Jesus. In Revelation 21:1, John spoke of seeing "a new heaven and a new earth." Many biblical scholars see this "new" earth as a reno-vated earth, for their study of the word *new* here reveals that it means "fresh" or "restored" after the decay of the old has been wiped away. God will renovate what is corrupt on this earth and provide a fresh, yet familiar place where believers will live with Him.

What an amazing truth to contemplate: a new, refreshed, familiar, and beautiful earth. Imagine the majesty of God's handiwork!   *DAVE BRANON*

Lord, we thank You for this beautiful world we live in—but at the same time we anticipate greatly the new world You have in store for us. We praise You for Your love for us, revealed in Your amazing plans for our future.

Our Creator God makes everything new.

Random Acts of Kindness

Read: Ruth 2:8–13

*Why have I found such favor [grace] in your eyes that you notice me—
a foreigner? Ruth 2:10*

Some say that the American writer Anne Herbert scribbled the phrase "Practice random acts of kindness and senseless acts of beauty" on a placemat at a restaurant in 1982. The sentiment has since been popularized through film and literature and has become a part of our vocabulary.

The question is "Why?" Why should we show kindness? For those who follow Jesus, the answer is clear: To show the tender mercy and kindness of God.

There's an Old Testament example of that principle in the story of Ruth, the emigrant from Moab. She was a foreigner, living in a strange land whose language and culture she did not understand. Furthermore, she was desperately poor, utterly dependent on the charity of a people who took little notice of her.

There was one Israelite, however, who showed Ruth grace and spoke to her heart (RUTH 2:13). He allowed her to glean in his fields, but more than simple charity, he showed her by his compassion the tender mercy of God, the One under whose wings she could take refuge. She became Boaz's bride, part of the family of God, and one in a line of ancestors that led to Jesus, who brought salvation to the world (SEE MATT. 1:1–16).

We never know what one act of kindness, done in Jesus's name, will do.
DAVID ROPER

*Lord, what do You want me to do for another today? Lead me. And may that
person see a glimmer of You.*

It's never too soon to be kind.

Work Together

Read: Romans 8:28–30

We know that in all things God works for the good of those who love him, who have been called according to his purpose. Romans 8:28

My wife makes an amazing pot roast dinner. She takes raw meat, along with raw sliced white and sweet potatoes, celery, mushrooms, carrots, and onions and throws them into the slow cooker. Six or seven hours later the aroma fills the house, and the first taste is a delight. It is always to my advantage to wait until the ingredients in the slow cooker work together to achieve something they could not achieve individually.

When Paul used the phrase "work together" in the context of suffering, he used the word from which we get our word *synergy*. He wrote, "We know that in all things God works for the good of those who love him, who have been called according to his purpose" (ROM. 8:28). He wanted the Romans to know that God, who didn't cause their suffering, would cause all their circumstances to cooperate with His divine plan—for their ultimate good. The good to which Paul referred was not the temporal blessings of health, wealth, admiration, or success, but being "conformed to the image of [God's] Son" (V. 29).

May we wait patiently and confidently because our heavenly Father is taking all the suffering, all the distress, all the evil, and causing them to work together for His glory and our spiritual good. He wants to make us like Jesus.   *MARVIN WILLIAMS*

Read 2 Corinthians 12:9, Philippians 1:6, and 1 Peter 5:10. What encouragement did you find for tough times?

The growth we gain from waiting on God is often greater than the answer or result we desire.

Nothing Hidden

Read: Hebrews 4:12–16

Nothing in all creation is hidden from God's sight. Hebrews 4:13

In 2015 an international research company stated that there were 245 million surveillance cameras installed worldwide, and the number was growing by 15 percent every year. In addition, multiplied millions of people with smartphones capture daily images ranging from birthday parties to bank robberies. Whether we applaud the increased security or denounce the diminished privacy, we live in a global, cameras-everywhere society.

The New Testament book of Hebrews says that in our relationship with God, we experience a far greater level of exposure and accountability than anything surveillance cameras may see. His Word, like a sharp, two-edged sword, penetrates to the deepest level of our being where it "judges the thoughts and attitudes of the heart. Nothing in all creation is hidden from God's sight. Everything is uncovered and laid bare before the eyes of him to whom we must give account" (HEB. 4:12–13).

Because Jesus our Savior experienced our weaknesses and temptations but did not sin, we can "approach God's throne of grace with confidence, so that we may receive mercy and find grace to help us in our time of need" (VV. 15–16). We don't need to fear Him but can be assured we'll find grace when we come to Him.   *DAVID MCCASLAND*

Nothing is hidden from God's sight. Nothing is greater than God's love. Nothing is stronger than God's mercy and grace. Nothing is too hard for God's power.

No part of our lives is hidden from God's grace and power.

Remember When

Read: Psalm 126

The LORD has done great things for us, and we are filled with joy.
Psalm 126:3

Our son wrestled with drug addiction for seven years, and during that time my wife and I experienced many difficult days. As we prayed and waited for his recovery, we learned to celebrate small victories. If nothing bad happened in a twenty-four-hour period, we would tell each other, "Today was a good day." That short sentence became a reminder to be thankful for God's help with the smallest things.

Tucked away in Psalm 126:3 is an even better reminder of God's tender mercies and what they ultimately mean for us: "The LORD has done great things for us, and we are filled with joy." What a great verse to take to heart as we remember Jesus's compassion for us at the cross! The difficulties of any given day cannot change the truth that come what may, our Lord has already shown us unfathomable kindness, and "his love endures forever" (PS. 136:1).

When we have lived through a difficult circumstance and discovered that God was faithful, keeping that in mind helps greatly the next time life's waters turn rough. We may not know how God will get us through our circumstances, but His kindness to us in the past helps us trust that He will.   *JAMES BANKS*

Thy mercies how tender, how firm to the end, our Maker, Defender,
Redeemer, and Friend.
ROBERT GRANT

When we cannot see God's hand, we can trust His heart.

Growing in the Wind

Read: Mark 4:36–41

Who is this? Even the wind and the waves obey him! Mark 4:41

Imagine a world without wind. Lakes would be calm. Falling leaves wouldn't blow in the streets. But in still air, who would expect trees to suddenly fall over? That's what happened in a three-acre glass dome built in the Arizona desert. Trees growing inside a huge windless bubble called Biosphere 2 grew faster than normal until suddenly collapsing under their own weight. Project researchers eventually came up with an explanation. These trees needed wind stress to grow strong.

Jesus let His disciples experience gale-force winds to strengthen their faith (MARK 4:36–41). During a night crossing of familiar waters, a sudden storm proved too much even for these seasoned fishermen. Wind and waves were swamping their boat while an exhausted Jesus slept in the stern. In a panic they woke Him. *Didn't it bother their Teacher that they were about to die? What was He thinking?* Then they began to find out. Jesus told the wind and waves to be quiet—and asked His friends why they still had no faith in Him.

If the wind had not blown, these disciples would never have asked, "Who is this? Even the winds and the waves obey him!" (MARK 4:41).

Today, life in a protective bubble might sound good. But how strong would our faith be if we couldn't discover for ourselves His reassuring "be still" when the winds of circumstance howl?

MART DEHAAN

Father in heaven, please help us to remember that anything that frightens us comes with an invitation to find the strength of knowing and trusting You.

God never sleeps.

Losing to Find

Read: Matthew 10:37–42

Whoever loses their life for my sake will find it. Matthew 10:39

When I married my English fiancé and moved to the United Kingdom, I thought it would be a five-year adventure in a foreign land. I never dreamed I'd still be living here nearly twenty years later, or that at times I'd feel like I was losing my life as I said goodbye to family and friends, work, and all that was familiar. But in losing my old way of life, I've found a better one.

The upside-down gift of finding life when we lose it is what Jesus promised to His apostles. When He sent out the twelve disciples to share His good news, He asked them to love Him more than their mothers or fathers, sons or daughters (MATT. 10:37). His words came in a culture where families were the cornerstone of the society and highly valued. But He promised that if they would lose their life for His sake, they would find it (V. 39).

We don't have to move abroad to find ourselves in Christ. Through service and commitment—such as the disciples going out to share the good news of the kingdom of God—we find ourselves receiving more than we give through the lavish love the Lord showers on us. Of course He loves us no matter how much we serve, but we find contentment, meaning, and fulfillment when we pour ourselves out for the well-being of others.

AMY BOUCHER PYE

When I survey the wondrous cross on which the Prince of glory died, my richest gain I count but loss, and pour contempt on all my pride.
ISAAC WATTS

Every loss leaves a space that can be filled with God's presence.

The Valley of Blessing

Read: 2 Chronicles 20:1, 13–22

If calamity comes . . . [we] will cry out to you in our distress, and you will hear us. 2 Chronicles 20:9

French artist Henri Matisse felt his work in the last years of his life best represented him. During that time he experimented with a new style, creating colorful, large-scale pictures with paper instead of paint. He decorated the walls of his room with these bright images. This was important to him because he had been diagnosed with cancer and was often confined to his bed.

Becoming ill, losing a job, or enduring heartbreak are examples of what some call "being in the valley," where dread overshadows everything else. The people of Judah experienced this when they heard an invading army was approaching (2 CHRON. 20:2–3). Their king prayed, "If calamity comes . . . [we] will cry out to you in our distress, and you will hear us" (V. 9). God responded, "Go out to face [your enemies] tomorrow, and the LORD will be with you" (V. 17).

When Judah's army arrived at the battlefield, their enemies had already destroyed each other. God's people spent three days collecting the abandoned equipment, clothing, and valuables. Before leaving, they assembled to praise God and named the place "The Valley of Berakah," which means "blessing."

God walks with us through the lowest points in our lives. He can make it possible to discover blessings in the valleys.

JENNIFER BENSON SCHULDT

Dear God, help me not to be afraid when I encounter difficulty. Help me to believe that Your goodness and love will follow me.

God is the master of turning burdens into blessings.

Finding Life

Read: John 14:5–14

Because I live, you also will live. John 14:19

The words of Ravi's father cut deep. "You're a complete failure. You're an embarrassment to the family." Compared to his talented siblings, Ravi was viewed as a disgrace. He tried excelling in sports, and he did, but he still felt like a loser. He wondered, *What is going to become of me? Am I a complete failure? Can I get out of life some way, painlessly?* These thoughts haunted him, but he talked to no one. That simply wasn't done in his culture. He had been taught to "keep your private heartache private; keep your collapsing world propped up."

So Ravi struggled alone. Then while he was recovering in the hospital after a failed suicide attempt, a visitor brought him a Bible opened to John 14. His mother read these words of Jesus to Ravi: "Because I live, you also will live" (V. 19). *This may be my only hope,* he thought. *A new way of living. Life as defined by the Author of life.* So he prayed, "Jesus, if You are the one who gives life as it is meant to be, I want it."

Life can present despairing moments. But, like Ravi, we can find hope in Jesus who is "the way and the truth and the life" (v. 6). God longs to give us a rich and satisfying life.

POH FANG CHIA

Dear Lord, I acknowledge that I am a sinner, and I need Your forgiveness. Thank You, Jesus, for dying for me and giving me eternal life. Transform my life so that I may bring glory and honor to You alone.

Only Jesus can give us new life.

Long Shadows

Read: Psalm 100

The LORD is good and his love . . . continues through all generations.
Psalm 100:5

Several years ago, my wife and I stayed in a rustic bed-and-breakfast in the remote Yorkshire Dales of England. We were there with four other couples, all British, whom we had never met before. Sitting in the living room with our after-dinner coffees, the conversation turned to occupations with the question "What do you do?" At the time I was serving as the president of Moody Bible Institute in Chicago, and I assumed that no one there knew of MBI or its founder, D. L. Moody. When I mentioned the name of the school, their response was immediate and surprising. "Of Moody and Sankey . . . that Moody?" Another guest added, "We have a Sankey hymnal and our family often gathers around the piano to sing from it." I was amazed! The evangelist Dwight Moody and his musician Ira Sankey had held meetings in the British Isles more than 120 years ago, and their influence was still being felt.

I left the room that night thinking of the ways our lives can cast long shadows of influence for God—a praying mother's influence on her children, an encouraging coworker's words, the support and challenge of a teacher or a mentor, the loving but corrective words of a friend. It's a high privilege to play a role in the wonderful promise that "His love . . . continues through all generations" (PS. 100:5). *JOE STOWELL*

Lord, help us to remember that while our lives are short, what we do for You now can have an impact long after we are home with You. Lead me today to invest in the lives of others.

Only what's done for Christ will last.

A Treasure to Be Shared

Read: 2 Corinthians 4:1–7

We have this treasure in jars of clay to show that this all-surpassing power is from God and not from us. 2 Corinthians 4:7

In March 1974, Chinese farmers were digging a well when they made a surprising discovery: Buried under the dry ground of central China was the Terracotta Army—life-size terracotta sculptures that dated back to the third century BC. In this extraordinary find were some 8,000 soldiers, 150 cavalry horses, and 130 chariots drawn by 520 horses. The Terracotta Army has become one of the most popular tourist sites in China, attracting over a million visitors annually. This amazing treasure lay hidden for centuries but is now being shared with the world.

The apostle Paul wrote that followers of Christ have a treasure inside them that is to be shared with the world: "We now have this light shining in our hearts, but we ourselves are like fragile clay jars containing this great treasure" (2 COR. 4:7 NLT). The treasure inside us is the message of Christ and His love.

This treasure is not to be hidden but is to be shared so that by God's love and grace people of every nation can be welcomed into His family. May we, through His Spirit's working, share that treasure with someone today.   *BILL CROWDER*

The good news of Jesus is too wonderful to keep to myself, Father. May I live the gospel and share it with others throughout my journey with You, Lord.

Let others see your testimony as well as hear it.

Breath of Life

Read: Genesis 2:4–8

Then the LORD God . . . breathed into his nostrils the breath of life.
Genesis 2:7

On a cold and frosty morning, as my daughter and I walked to school, we enjoyed seeing our breath turn to vapor. We giggled at the various steamy clouds we could each produce. I received the moment as a gift, reveling in being with her and being alive.

Our breath, which is usually invisible, was seen in the cold air, and it made me think about the Source of our breath and life—the Lord our Creator. For He who formed Adam out of the dust of the ground, giving him the breath of life, also gives life to us and to every living creature (GEN. 2:7). All things come from Him—even our very breath, which we inhale without even thinking about.

We may be tempted, living with today's conveniences and technology, to forget our beginnings and that God is the one who gives us life. But when we pause to remember that God is our Creator, we can build an attitude of thankfulness into our daily routines. We can ask Him for help and acknowledge the gift of life with humble, thankful hearts. May our gratitude spill out and touch others, so that they also may give thanks to the Lord for His goodness and faithfulness. *AMY BOUCHER PYE*

Dear heavenly Father, what an awesome and powerful God You are! You created life by Your very breath. We praise You and stand in awe of You. Thank You for Your creation.

Give thanks to God, our Creator, who gives us the breath of life.

Abandon It All

Read: Romans 12:1–8

*I urge you, brothers and sisters, in view of God's mercy, to offer your
bodies as a living sacrifice. Romans 12:1*

When I played college basketball, I made a conscious decision
at the beginning of each season to walk into that gym and
dedicate myself totally to my coach—doing whatever he might
ask me to do.

It would not have benefited my team for me to announce, "Hey,
Coach! Here I am. I want to shoot baskets and dribble the ball, but
don't ask me to run laps, play defense, and get all sweaty!"

Every successful athlete has to trust the coach enough to do
whatever the coach asks them to do for the good of the team.

In Christ, we are to become God's "living sacrifice" (ROM. 12:1).
We say to our Savior and Lord: "I trust You. Whatever You want
me to do, I am willing." Then He "transforms" us by renewing our
minds to focus on the things that please Him.

It's helpful to know that God will never call on us to do something for which He has not already equipped us. As Paul reminds
us, "We have different gifts, according to the grace given to each
of us" (V. 6).

Knowing that we can trust God with our lives, we can abandon
ourselves to Him, strengthened by the knowledge that He created
us and is helping us to make this effort in Him.   *DAVE BRANON*

*Heavenly Father, no one deserves our sacrifice and dedication more than You.
Help us to realize the joy that comes from abandoning ourselves to You.*

There is no risk in abandoning ourselves to God.

Music and Megaphone

Read: 2 Corinthians 3:17–4:7

We have this treasure in jars of clay to show that this all-surpassing power is from God and not from us. 2 Corinthians 4:7

Christopher Locke buys old trumpets, trombones, and French horns and transforms them into acoustic amplifiers for iPhones and iPads. His creations are modeled on the trumpetlike speakers used in the first phonographs during the late 1800s. Music played through Christopher's AnalogTelePhonographers has a "louder, cleaner, richer, deeper sound" than what is heard from the small speakers in the digital devices. Along with being interesting works of art, these salvaged brass instruments require no electrical power as they amplify the music people love to hear.

Paul's words to the followers of Jesus in Corinth remind us today that in living for Christ and sharing Him with others, we are not the music but only a megaphone. "What we preach is not ourselves," Paul wrote, "but Jesus Christ as Lord, and ourselves as your servants for Jesus' sake" (2 COR. 4:5). Our purpose is not to become the message, but to convey it through our lives and our lips. "We have this treasure in jars of clay to show that this all-surpassing power is from God and not from us" (V.7).

If an old horn can amplify music, then perhaps our flawed lives can magnify the goodness of God. We're the megaphone; the music and the power come from Him!   *DAVID MCCASLAND*

Thank You, Lord, that You can take our lives and use them in ways we never thought possible. Help us to be the instruments that convey the music of Your love.

Nothing is unusable in God's hands.

Lack Nothing

Read: Mark 6:7–12

God is able to bless you abundantly, so that . . . you will abound in every good work. 2 Corinthians 9:8

Imagine going on a trip without luggage. No basic necessities. No change of clothing. No money or credit cards. Sounds both unwise and terrifying, doesn't it?

But that's exactly what Jesus told His twelve disciples to do when He sent them out on their first mission to preach and heal. "Take nothing for the journey except a staff," said Jesus. "No bread, no bag, no money in your belts. Wear sandals but not an extra shirt" (MARK 6:8–9).

Yet later on when Jesus was preparing them for their work after He was gone, He told His disciples, "If you have a purse, take it, and also a bag; and if you don't have a sword, sell your cloak and buy one" (LUKE 22:36).

So, what's the point here? It's about trusting God to supply.

When Jesus referred back to that first trip, He asked the disciples, "When I sent you without purse, bag or sandals, did you lack anything?" And they answered, "Nothing" (V. 35). The disciples had everything they needed to carry out what God had called them to do. He was able to supply them with the power to do His work (MARK 6:7).

Do we trust God to supply our needs? Are we also taking personal responsibility and planning? Let's have faith that He will give us what we need to carry out His work.   *POH FANG CHIA*

You are good, Lord, and all You do is good. Help us in our endeavors to pray and to plan and to trust You.

God's will done in God's way will never lack God's supply.
HUDSON TAYLOR, FOUNDER OF CHINA INLAND MISSION

Not in Vain

Read: 1 Corinthians 15:50–58

Therefore, my dear brothers and sisters, stand firm. Let nothing move you. Always give yourselves fully to the work of the Lord, because you know that your labor in the Lord is not in vain. 1 Corinthians 15:58

A financial advisor I know describes the reality of investing money by saying, "Hope for the best and be prepared for the worst." With almost every decision we make in life there is uncertainty about the outcome. Yet there is one course we can follow where no matter what happens, we know that in the end it will not be a wasted effort.

The apostle Paul spent a year with the followers of Jesus in Corinth, a city known for its moral corruption. After he left, he urged them in a follow-up letter not to be discouraged or feel that their witness for Christ was of no value. He assured them that a day is coming when the Lord will return and even death will be swallowed up in victory (1 COR. 15:52–55).

Remaining true to Jesus may be difficult, discouraging, and even dangerous, but it is never pointless or wasted. As we walk with the Lord and witness to His presence and power, our lives are not in vain! We can be sure of that.   *DAVID MCCASLAND*

Lord, in these days of uncertainty, we hold fast to Your promise that our labor for You will accomplish Your purpose and be of great value in Your eyes.

Our life and witness for Jesus Christ are not in vain.

Thunder and Lightning

Read: Psalm 29

The voice of the LORD strikes with flashes of lightning. Psalm 29:7

Many years ago a friend and I were fishing a series of beaver ponds when it started to rain. We took cover under a nearby grove of quaking aspen, but the rain continued to fall. So we decided to call it a day and run for the truck. I had just opened the door when lightning struck the aspen grove with a thunderous fireball that stripped leaves and bark off the trees, leaving a few limbs smoldering. And then there was silence.

We were shaken and awed.

Lightning flashes and thunder rolls across our Idaho valley. I love it—despite my close call. I love the raw power. Voltage! Percussion! Shock and awe! The earth and everything in it trembles and shakes. And then there is peace.

I love lightning and thunder primarily because they are symbols of God's voice (JOB 37:4), speaking with stupendous, irresistible power through His Word. "The voice of the LORD strikes with flashes of lightning . . . The LORD gives strength to his people; the LORD blesses his people with peace" (PS. 29:7, 11). He gives strength to endure, to be patient, to be kind, to sit quietly, to get up and go, to do nothing at all.

May the God of peace be with you. *DAVID ROPER*

Calm my spirit in the storms, Lord. Grant me Your peace and the strength to walk through this day.

Faith connects our weakness to God's strength.

All Too Human

Read: Romans 7:14–25

The trouble is with me, for I am all too human. Romans 7:14 NLT

British writer Evelyn Waugh wielded his words in a way that accentuated his character flaws. Eventually the novelist converted to Christianity, yet he still struggled. One day a woman asked him, "Mr. Waugh, how can you behave as you do and still call yourself a Christian?" He replied, "Madam, I may be as bad as you say. But believe me, were it not for my religion, I would scarcely be a human being."

Waugh was waging the internal battle the apostle Paul describes: "I want to do what is right, but I can't" (ROM. 7:18 NLT). He also says, "The trouble is not with the law . . . [It] is with me, for I am all too human" (V. 14 NLT). He further explains, "In my inner being I delight in God's law; but I see another law at work in me . . . . Who will rescue me from this body that is subject to death?" (VV. 22–24). And then the exultant answer: "Thanks be to God, who delivers me through Jesus Christ our Lord!" (V. 25).

When we come in faith to Christ, admitting our wrongdoing and need of a Savior, we immediately become a new creation. But our spiritual formation remains a lifelong journey. As John the disciple observed: "Now we are children of God, and what we will be has not yet been made known. But . . . when Christ appears, we shall be like him, for we shall see him as he is" (1 JOHN 3:2).

TIM GUSTAFSON

Father, we bring our struggles to You because You know all about them, yet You love us anyway. Teach us to rely on Your Holy Spirit. Make us more like Your Son each day.

To be a Christian means to forgive the inexcusable, because God has forgiven the inexcusable in you.

C. S. LEWIS

Unseen Heroes

Read: Exodus 17:8–15

Aaron and Hur held [Moses's] hands up—one on one side, one on the other—so that his hands remained steady till sunset. Exodus 17:12

Stories in the Bible can make us stop and wonder. For instance, when Moses led God's people to the Promised Land and the Amalekites attacked, how did he know to go to the top of the hill and hold up God's staff? (EX. 17:8–15). We aren't told, but we learn that when Moses raised his hands, the Israelites would win the battle, and when he lowered them, the Amalekites would win. When Moses got tired, his brother Aaron and another man, Hur, held up Moses's arms so the Israelites could triumph.

We aren't told much about Hur, but he played a crucial role at this point in Israel's history. This reminds us that unseen heroes matter, that supporters and those who encourage leaders play a key and often overlooked role. Leaders may be the ones mentioned in the history books or lauded on social media, but the quiet, faithful witness of those who serve in other ways is not overlooked by the Lord. He sees the person who intercedes daily in prayer for friends and family. He sees the woman who puts away the chairs each Sunday in church. He sees the neighbor who reaches out with a word of encouragement.

God is using us, even if our task feels insignificant. And may we notice and thank any unseen heroes who help us.

AMY BOUCHER PYE

Dear Father, thank You for creating me and gifting me in my own unique way. Help me to serve You and others faithfully and to appreciate those You have sent to help me.

Unseen heroes are always seen by God.

Always Loved, Always Valued

Read: Romans 8:31–39

*Who shall separate us from the love of Christ? Shall trouble or
hardship or persecution or famine or nakedness or danger or sword?*
Romans 8:35

We serve a God who loves us more than our work.

Oh, it's true that God wants us to work to feed our families and to responsibly take care of the world He created. And He expects us to serve the weak, hungry, naked, thirsty, and broken people around us even as we remain alert to those who have not yet responded to the Holy Spirit's tug on their lives.

And yet we serve a God who loves us more than our work.

We must never forget this because there may come a time when our ability to "do for God" is torn from us by health or failure or unforeseen catastrophe. It is in those hours that God wants us to remember that He loves us not for what we do for Him but because of who we are: His children! Once we call on the name of Christ for salvation, nothing—"trouble or hardship or persecution or famine or nakedness or danger or sword"—will ever again separate us "from the love of God that is in Christ Jesus our Lord" (ROM. 8:35, 39).

When all we can do or all we have is taken from us, then all He wants us to do is rest in our identity in Him.

RANDY KILGORE

*Father, help us never lose sight of the unconditional love You have for us, and let
us hold on to that hope when our labor—and the fruit of our labor—are gone.*

The reason we exist is to be in fellowship with God.

Timeless Savior

Read: John 8:48–59

"Very truly I tell you," Jesus answered, "before Abraham was born, I am!"
John 8:58

Jeralean Talley died in June 2015 as the world's oldest living person—116 years of age. In 1995, the city of Jerusalem celebrated its 3,000th birthday. One hundred sixteen is old for a person, and 3,000 is old for a city, but there are trees that grow even older. A bristlecone pine in California's White Mountains has been determined to be older than 4,800 years. That precedes the patriarch Abraham by 800 years!

Jesus, when challenged by the Jewish religious leaders about His identity, also claimed to pre-date Abraham. "Very truly I tell you," He said, "before Abraham was born, I am!" (JOHN 8:58). His bold assertion shocked those who were confronting Him, and they sought to stone Him. They knew He wasn't referring to a chronological age but was actually claiming to be eternal by taking the ancient name of God, "I am" (SEE EX. 3:14). But as a member of the Trinity, He could make that claim legitimately.

In John 17:3, Jesus prayed, "This is eternal life: that they know you, the only true God, and Jesus Christ, whom you have sent." The timeless One entered into time so we could live forever. He accomplished that mission by dying in our place and rising again. Because of His sacrifice, we anticipate a future not bound by time, where we will spend eternity with Him. He is the timeless one. *BILL CROWDER*

The earth shall soon dissolve like snow, the sun forbear to shine; but God, who called me here below, will be forever mine.
JOHN NEWTON

Christ holds all things together.
COLOSSIANS 1:17

Rebuilding

Read: Nehemiah 2:11–18

Come, let us rebuild the wall of Jerusalem, and we will no longer be in disgrace. Nehemiah 2:17

When Edward Klee returned to Berlin after being away for many years, the city he remembered and loved was no longer there. It had changed dramatically, and so had he. Writing in *Hemispheres* magazine, Klee said, "Returning to a city you once loved tends to be a hit-or-miss proposition . . . . It can be a letdown." Going back to the places of our past may produce a feeling of sorrow and loss. We are not the same person we were then, nor is the place that was so significant in our lives exactly as it was.

Nehemiah had been in exile from the land of Israel for many years when he learned of the desperate plight of his people and the devastation in the city of Jerusalem. He received permission from Artaxerxes, the Persian king, to return and rebuild the walls. After a night reconnaissance to examine the situation (NEH. 2:13–15), Nehemiah told the inhabitants of the city, "You see the trouble we are in: Jerusalem lies in ruins, and its gates have been burned with fire. Come, let us rebuild the wall of Jerusalem, and we will no longer be in disgrace" (V. 17).

Nehemiah did not return to reminisce but to rebuild. It's a powerful lesson for us as we consider the damaged parts of our past that need repair. It is our faith in Christ and His power that enables us to look ahead, move forward, and rebuild.

DAVID MCCASLAND

Thank You, Lord, for the work You are doing in us and through us.

We cannot change the past, but God is changing us for the future.

The Talking Tree

Read: Colossians 1:15–20

"He himself bore our sins" in his body on the cross. 1 Peter 2:24

One of the earliest Christian poems in English literature is "The Dream of the Rood." The word *rood* comes from the Old English word *rod* or *pole* and refers to the cross on which Christ was crucified. In this ancient poem the crucifixion story is retold from the perspective of the cross. When the tree learns that it is to be used to kill the Son of God, it rejects the idea of being used in this way. But Christ enlists the help of the tree to provide redemption for all who will believe.

In the garden of Eden, a tree was the source of the forbidden fruit that our spiritual parents tasted, causing sin to enter the human race. And when the Son of God shed His blood as the ultimate sacrifice for all of humanity's sin, He was nailed to a tree on our behalf. Christ "bore our sins in his body on the cross" (1 PETER 2:24).

The cross is the turning point for all who trust Christ for salvation. And ever since the crucifixion, it has become a remarkable symbol that represents the sacrificial death of the Son of God for our deliverance from sin and death. The cross is the inexpressibly wonderful evidence of God's love for us.

DENNIS FISHER

Lord, may my heart give You praise whenever I see a cross,
for You gave Yourself for me in love.

Christ gave His life on the tree for our salvation.

Always in His Care

Read: Psalm 32:1–11

I will instruct you and teach you in the way you should go; I will counsel you with my loving eye on you. Psalm 32:8

On the day our youngest daughter was flying from Munich to Barcelona, I visited my favorite flight tracking website to follow her progress. After I entered her flight number, my computer screen showed that her flight had crossed Austria and was skirting the northern part of Italy. From there the plane would fly over the Mediterranean, south of the French Riviera toward Spain, and was scheduled to arrive on time. It seemed that the only thing I didn't know was what the flight attendants were serving for lunch!

Why did I care about my daughter's location and circumstances? Because I love her. I care about who she is, what she's doing, and where she's going in life.

In Psalm 32, David celebrated the marvel of God's forgiveness, guidance, and concern for us. Unlike a human father, God knows every detail of our lives and the deepest needs of our hearts. The Lord's promise to us is, "I will instruct you and teach you in the way you should go; I will counsel you with my loving eye on you" (V. 8).

Whatever our circumstances today, we can rely on God's presence and care because "the LORD's unfailing love surrounds the one who trusts in him" (V. 10).   *DAVID MCCASLAND*

Dear Father in heaven, thank You for watching over me in love and guiding me along Your path today.

We are never out of God's sight and His loving care.

What's the Occasion?

Read: Ecclesiastes 3:9–17

Everything God does will endure forever. Ecclesiastes 3:14

Four-year-old Asher's gleeful face peeked out from beneath his favorite hooded sweatshirt. His *alligator-head* hooded sweatshirt, complete with plush jaws that seemed to swallow his head! His mom's heart sank. She wanted the family to make a good impression as they visited a family they hadn't seen in a long time.

"Oh, Hon," she said, "that may not be appropriate for the occasion."

"Of course it is!" Asher protested brightly.

"Hmm, and what occasion might that be?" she asked. Asher replied, "You know. *Life!*" He got to wear the shirt.

That joyful boy already grasps the truth of Ecclesiastes 3:12—"There is nothing better for people than to be happy and to do good while they live." Ecclesiastes can seem depressing and is often misunderstood because it's written from a human perspective, not God's. The writer, King Solomon, asked, "What do workers gain from their toil?" (V. 9). Yet throughout the book we catch glimpses of hope. Solomon also wrote: "That each of [us] may eat and drink, and find satisfaction in all [our] toil—this is the gift of God" (V. 13).

We serve a God who gives us good things to enjoy. Everything He does "will endure forever" (V. 14). As we acknowledge Him and follow His loving commands, He infuses our lives with purpose, meaning, and joy.   *TIM GUSTAFSON*

Restore to us childlike joy that appreciates Your good gifts.

The Lord who made you wants you to make Him the center of your life.

I See You

Read: Genesis 16:1–13

I have now seen the One who sees me. Genesis 16:3

"I see you," a friend said in an online writers' group where we support and encourage each other. Having felt stressed and anxious, I experienced a sense of peace and well-being with her words. She "saw" me—my hopes, fears, struggles, and dreams—and loved me.

When I heard my friend's simple but powerful encouragement, I thought of Hagar, a slave in Abram's household. After many years of Sarai and Abram still longing for an heir, Sarai followed the custom of the culture and told her husband to conceive through Hagar. But when Hagar became pregnant, she treated Sarai with contempt. When Sarai mistreated her in return, Hagar fled far away to the desert.

The Lord saw Hagar in her pain and confusion, and He blessed her with the promise that she would be the mother of many descendants. After the encounter, Hagar called the Lord *"El Roi,"* which means "the God who sees me" (GEN. 16:13), for she knew she wasn't alone or abandoned.

As Hagar was seen—and loved—so are we. We might feel ignored or rejected by friends or family, yet we know that our Father sees not only the face we present to the world, but all of our secret feelings and fears. He speaks the words that bring us life.

AMY BOUCHER PYE

Father God, just as You saw Hagar in her distress, so You see those who are hurting, fleeing oppression, and afraid. Please send them help and encouragement.

To know that God sees us gives us comfort and confidence.

In All Circumstances

Read: 1 Thessalonians 5:16–18

Give thanks in all circumstances; for this is God's will for you in Christ Jesus. 1 Thessalonians 5:18

In our suburb we complain about the constant power outages. They can hit three times in a week and last up to twenty-four hours, plunging the neighborhood into darkness. The inconvenience is hard to bear when we cannot use basic household appliances.

Our Christian neighbor often asks, "Is this also something to thank God for?" She is referring to 1 Thessalonians 5:18: "Give thanks in all circumstances, for this is God's will for you in Christ Jesus." We always say, "Yes, of course, we thank God in all things." But the half-hearted manner in which we say it is contradicted by our grumbling every time the power goes off.

One day, however, our belief in thanking God *in all circumstances* took on new meaning. I returned from work to find our neighbor visibly shaken as she cried, "Thank Jesus the power was off. My house would have burned down, and my family and I would have perished!"

A refuse-collection truck had hit the electricity pole in front of her house and brought down the high-tension cables right over several houses. Had there been power in the cables, fatalities would have been likely.

The difficult circumstances we face can make it hard to say, "Thanks, Lord." We can be thankful to our God who sees in every situation an opportunity for us to trust Him—whether or not we see His purpose. *LAWRENCE DARMANI*

Father, we honor You with our words, but so often our actions reveal that our hearts don't trust You. Help us to see You at work in every circumstance, no matter how difficult.

By God's grace we can be thankful in all things.

Begin Where You Are

Read: Psalm 136:1–9

The heavens declare the glory of God; the skies proclaim the work of his hands. Psalm 19:1

I came across a solitary flower growing in a meadow today—a tiny purple blossom "wasting its sweetness in the desert air," to borrow from the poet Thomas Gray's wonderful line. I'm sure no one had seen this particular flower before, and perhaps no one will see it again. *Why this beauty in this place?* I thought.

Nature is never wasted. It daily displays the truth, goodness, and beauty of the One who brought it into being. Every day nature offers a new and fresh declaration of God's glory. Do I see Him through that beauty, or do I merely glance at it and shrug it off in indifference?

All nature declares the beauty of the One who made it. Our response can be worship, adoration, and thanksgiving—for the radiance of a cornflower, the splendor of a morning sunrise, the symmetry of one particular tree.

Author C. S. Lewis describes a walk in the forest on a hot summer day. He had just asked his friend how best to cultivate a heart thankful toward God. His hiking companion turned to a nearby brook, splashed his face and hands in a little waterfall, and asked, "Why not begin with this?" Lewis said he learned a great principle in that moment: "Begin where you are."

A trickling waterfall, the wind in the willows, a baby robin, the blue sky, a tiny flower. Why not begin your thankfulness with this?

DAVID ROPER

Father, may we always be reminded that You have placed beauty here because it reflects Your character. We praise You!

[God] is the beauty behind all beauty.
STEVE DEWITT

Tried and Purified

Read: Job 23:1–12

When he has tested me, I will come forth as gold. Job 23:10

During an interview, singer and songwriter Meredith Andrews spoke about being overwhelmed as she tried to balance outreach, creative work, marital issues, and motherhood. Reflecting on her distress, she said, "I felt like God was taking me through a refining season, almost through a crushing process."

Job was overwhelmed after losing his livelihood, his health, and his family. Worse still, although Job had been a daily worshiper of God, he felt that the Lord was ignoring his pleas for help. God seemed absent from the landscape of his life. Job claimed he could not see God whether he looked to the north, south, east, or west (JOB 23:2–9).

In the middle of his despair, Job had a moment of clarity. His faith flickered to life like a candle in a dark room. He said, "[God] knows the way that I take; when he has tested me, I will come forth as gold" (V. 10). Christians are tried and purified when God uses difficulty to burn away our self-reliance, pride, and earthly wisdom. If it seems as if God is silent during this process and He is not answering our cries for help, He may be giving us an opportunity to grow stronger in our faith.

Pain and problems can produce the shining, rock-solid character that comes from trusting God when life is hard.

JENNIFER BENSON SCHULDT

Dear Lord, help me to believe that You are with me, even when I can't see You working in my life. I surrender myself to Your purpose for any suffering I may endure.

Faith-testing times can be faith-strengthening times.

Does It Spark Joy?

Read: Philippians 4:4–9

Finally, brothers and sisters, whatever is true . . . noble . . . right . . . pure . . . lovely . . . admirable—if anything is excellent or praiseworthy—think about such things. Philippians 4:8

A young Japanese woman's book on decluttering and organizing has sold two million copies worldwide. The heart of Marie Kondo's message is helping people get rid of unneeded things in their homes and closets—things that weigh them down. "Hold up each item," she says, "and ask, 'Does it spark joy?'" If the answer is yes, keep it. If the answer is no, then give it away.

The apostle Paul urged the Christians in Philippi to pursue joy in their relationship with Christ. "Rejoice in the Lord always. I will say it again: Rejoice!" (PHIL. 4:4). Instead of a life cluttered with anxiety, he urged them to pray about everything and let God's peace guard their hearts and minds in Christ (VV. 6–7).

Looking at our everyday tasks and responsibilities, we see that not all of them are enjoyable. But we can ask, "How can this spark joy in God's heart and in my own?" A change in why we do things can bring a transformation in the way we feel about them.

"Finally, brothers and sisters, whatever is true . . . noble . . . right . . . pure . . . lovely . . . admirable—if anything is excellent or praiseworthy—think about such things" (V. 8).

Paul's parting words are food for thought and a recipe for joy.

DAVID MCCASLAND

Lord, show me how You want to spark joy in the tasks I face today.

A focus on the Lord is the beginning of joy.

The Good, the Bad, the Ugly

Read: 1 Samuel 20:35–42

Never will I leave you; never will I forsake you. Hebrews 13:5

A dear friend of mine sent me a text message that said, "I'm so glad we can tell each other the good, the bad, and the ugly!" We have been friends for many years, and we have learned to share our joys and our failures. We recognize we are far from perfect, so we share our struggles but we also rejoice in each other's successes.

David and Jonathan had a solid friendship too, beginning with the good days of David's victory over Goliath (1 SAM. 18:1–4). They shared their fears during the bad days of Jonathan's father's jealousy (18:6–11; 20:1–2). Finally, they suffered together during the ugly days of Saul's plans to kill David (20:42).

Good friends don't abandon us when external circumstances change. They stay with us through the good and the bad days. Good friends also may point us to God in the ugly days, when we may feel tempted to walk away from our Lord.

Real friendships are a gift from God because they exemplify the perfect Friend, who remains loyal through the good, the bad, and the ugly days. As the Lord reminds us, "Never will I leave you; never will I forsake you" (HEB. 13:5).   *KEILA OCHOA*

Dear Lord, I thank You for the good friends You have placed in my life, but above all, I thank You for Your friendship.

A friend is the first person who comes in when the whole world has gone out.

The Advocate

Read: 1 John 1:8–2:2

If anybody does sin, we have an advocate with the Father—Jesus Christ, the Righteous One. 1 John 2:1

From a Florida prison cell in June 1962, Clarence Earl Gideon wrote a note asking the United States Supreme Court to review his conviction for a crime he said he didn't commit. He added that he didn't have the means to hire a lawyer.

One year later, in the historic case of *Gideon v. Wainright*, the Supreme Court ruled that people who cannot afford the cost of their own defense must be given a public defender—an advocate—provided by the state. With this decision, and with the help of a court-appointed lawyer, Clarence Gideon was retried and acquitted.

But what if we are not innocent? According to the apostle Paul, we are all guilty. But the court of heaven provides an Advocate who, at God's expense, offers to defend and care for our soul (1 JOHN 2:2). On behalf of His Father, Jesus comes to us offering a freedom that even prison inmates have described as better than anything they've experienced on the outside. It is a freedom of heart and mind.

Whether suffering for wrongs done by us or to us, we all can be represented by Jesus. By the highest of authority He responds to every request for mercy, forgiveness, and comfort.

Jesus, our Advocate, can turn a prison of lost hope, fear, or regret into the place of His presence.   *MART DEHAAN*

Father in heaven, please help us to know what it means to have the freedom of Your love and presence. May we experience this freedom even in places that we have only seen as our confinement!

The one who died as our substitute now lives as our advocate.

Leaning on Jesus

Read: John 13:12–26

One of them, the disciple whom Jesus loved, was reclining next to him.
John 13:23

Sometimes when I put my head on my pillow at night and pray, I imagine I'm leaning on Jesus. Whenever I do this, I remember something the Word of God tells us about the apostle John. John himself writes about how he was sitting beside Jesus at the Last Supper: "One of them, the disciple whom Jesus loved, was reclining next to him" (JOHN 13:23).

John used the term "the disciple whom Jesus loved" as a way of referring to himself without mentioning his own name. He is also depicting a typical banquet setting in first-century Israel, where the table was much lower than those we use today, about knee height. Reclining without chairs on a mat or cushions was the natural position for those around the table. John was sitting so close to the Lord that when he turned to ask him a question, he was "leaning back against Jesus" (JOHN 13:25), with his head on his chest.

John's closeness to Jesus in that moment provides a helpful illustration for our lives with Him today. We may not be able to touch Jesus physically, but we can entrust the weightiest circumstances of our lives to Him. He said, "Come to me, all you who are weary and burdened, and I will give you rest" (MATT. 11:28). How blessed we are to have a Savior whom we can trust to be faithful through every circumstance of our lives! Are you "leaning" on Him today?   *JAMES BANKS*

Dear Lord Jesus, help me to lean on You today and to trust You as my source of strength and hope. I cast all my cares on You and praise You because You are faithful.

Jesus alone gives the rest we need.

I Know Everything

Read: Psalm 139:1–18

You discern my going out and my lying down; you are familiar with all my ways. Psalm 139:3

Our son and daughter-in-law had an emergency. Our grandson Cameron was suffering from pneumonia and bronchitis and needed to go to the hospital. They asked if we could pick up their five-year-old son, Nathan, from school and take him home. Marlene and I were glad to do so.

When Nathan got in the car, Marlene asked, "Are you surprised that we came to get you today?" He responded, "No!" When we asked why not, he replied, "Because I know everything!"

A five-year-old can claim to know everything, but those of us who are a bit older know better. We often have more questions than answers. We wonder about the whys, whens, and hows of life—often forgetting that though we do not know everything, we know the God who does.

Psalm 139:1 and 3 speak of our all-knowing God's all-encompassing, intimate understanding of us. David says, "You have searched me, LORD, and you know me. . . . You discern my going out and my lying down; you are familiar with all my ways." How comforting to know God loves us perfectly, is fully aware of what we will face today, and He knows how best to help us in every circumstance of life.

Our knowledge will always be limited, but knowing God is what matters most. We can trust Him.   *BILL CROWDER*

Thank You, Lord, that You know everything about me and what I need.

Knowing God is what matters most.

Look What Jesus Has Done

Read: Luke 8:1–8

See that you . . . excel in this grace of giving. 2 Corinthians 8:7

The little boy was only eight when he announced to his parents' friend Wally, "I love Jesus and want to serve God overseas someday." During the next ten years or so, Wally prayed for him as he watched him grow up. When this young man later applied with a mission agency to go to Mali, Wally told him, "It's about time! When I heard what you wanted to do, I invested some money and have been saving it for you, waiting for this exciting news." Wally has a heart for others and for getting God's good news to people.

Jesus and His disciples needed financial support as they traveled from one town and village to another, telling the good news of His kingdom (LUKE 8:1–3). A group of women who had been cured of evil spirits and diseases helped to support them "out of their own means" (V. 3). One was Mary Magdalene, who had been freed from the presence of seven demons. Another was Joanna, the wife of an official in Herod's court. Nothing is known about Susanna and "many others" (V. 3), but we know that Jesus had met their spiritual needs. Now they were helping Him and His disciples through giving their financial resources.

When we consider what Jesus has done for us, His heart for others becomes our own. Let's ask God how He wants to use us.

ANNE CETAS

How might you be a part of getting the good news of salvation to people in your neighborhood and around the world? Tell someone the story of what Jesus has done for you. Write a note of encouragement to someone. Share a gift with a missionary. Pray.

Jesus gave His all; He deserves our all.

The Death of Doubt

Read: John 11:1–16

Unless I see the nail marks in his hands and put my finger where the nails were, and put my hand into his side, I will not believe. John 20:25

We know him as Doubting Thomas (SEE JOHN 20:24–29), but the label isn't entirely fair. After all, how many of us would have believed that our executed leader had been resurrected? We might just as well call him "Courageous Thomas." After all, Thomas displayed impressive courage as Jesus moved purposefully into the events leading to His death.

At the death of Lazarus, Jesus had said, "Let us go back to Judea" (JOHN 11:7), prompting a protest from the disciples. "Rabbi," they said, "a short while ago the Jews there tried to stone you, and yet you are going back?" (V. 8). It was Thomas who said, "Let us also go, that we may die with him" (V. 16).

Thomas's intentions proved nobler than his actions. Upon Jesus's arrest, Thomas fled with the rest (MATT. 26:56), leaving Peter and John to accompany Christ to the courtyard of the high priest. Only John followed Jesus all the way to the cross.

Despite having witnessed the resurrection of Lazarus (JOHN 11:38–44), Thomas still could not bring himself to believe that the crucified Lord had conquered death. Not until Thomas the doubter—the human—saw the risen Lord, could he exclaim, "My Lord and my God!" (JOHN 20:28). Jesus's response gave assurance to the doubter and immeasurable comfort to us: "Because you have seen me, you have believed; blessed are those who have not seen and yet have believed" (V. 29).   *TIM GUSTAFSON*

Father, teach us to act on what we do know about You and Your goodness, and trust You in faith for what we don't know.

Real doubt searches for the light; unbelief is content with the darkness.

Love Revealed

Read: 1 John 4:9–16

This is how God showed his love among us: He sent his one and only Son into the world that we might live through him. 1 John 4:9

When a series of pink "I love you" signs mysteriously appeared in the town of Welland, Ontario, local reporter Maryanne Firth decided to investigate. Her sleuthing turned up nothing. Weeks later, new signs appeared featuring the name of a local park along with a date and time.

Accompanied by a crowd of curious townspeople, Firth went to the park at the appointed time. There, she met a man wearing a suit who had cleverly concealed his face. Imagine her surprise when he handed her a bouquet and proposed marriage! The mystery man was Ryan St. Denis—her boyfriend. She happily accepted.

St. Denis's expression of love toward his fiancée may seem a bit over-the-top, but God's expression of love for us is nothing short of extravagant! "This is how God showed his love among us: He sent his one and only Son into the world that we might live through him" (1 JOHN 4:9).

Jesus is not merely a token of love, like a rose passed from one person to another. He is the divine human who willingly gave up His life so that anyone who believes in Him for salvation can have an everlasting covenant relationship with God. Nothing can separate a Christian "from the love of God that is in Christ Jesus our Lord" (ROM. 8:39).   *JENNIFER BENSON SCHULDT*

Dear God, thank You for showing me, in the greatest way possible, that You love me. Help my life to demonstrate my love for You.

We know how much God loves us because He sent His Son to save us.

Little Lies and Kittens

Read: Romans 5:12–21

Just as sin ruled over all people and brought them to death, now God's wonderful grace rules instead. Romans 5:21 NLT

Mom noticed four-year-old Elias as he scurried away from the newborn kittens. She had told him not to touch them. "Did you touch the kitties, Elias?" she asked.

"No!" he said earnestly. So Mom had another question: "Were they soft?"

"Yes," he volunteered, "and the black one mewed."

With a toddler, we smile at such duplicity. But Elias's disobedience underscores our human condition. No one has to teach a four-year-old to lie. "For I was born a sinner," wrote David in his classic confession, "yes, from the moment my mother conceived me" (PS. 51:5 NLT). The apostle Paul said: "When Adam sinned, sin entered the world. Adam's sin brought death, so death spread to everyone, for everyone sinned" (ROM. 5:12 NLT). That depressing news applies equally to kings, four-year-olds, and you and me.

But there's plenty of hope! "God's law was given so that all people could see how sinful they were," wrote Paul. "But as people sinned more and more, God's wonderful grace became more abundant" (ROM. 5:20 NLT).

God is not waiting for us to blow it so He can pounce on us. He is in the business of grace, forgiveness, and restoration. We need only recognize that our sin is neither cute nor excusable and come to Him in faith and repentance.   *TIM GUSTAFSON*

Father, be merciful to me, a sinner.

There is now no condemnation for those who are in Christ Jesus.
ROMANS 8:1

The Junkyard Genius

Read: John 9:1–11

One thing I do know. I was blind but now I see! John 9:25

Noah Purifoy began his work as an "assemblage" artist with three tons of rubble salvaged from the 1965 riots in the Watts area of Los Angeles. From broken bicycle wheels and bowling balls to discarded tires and damaged TV sets—things no longer usable—he and a colleague created sculptures that conveyed a powerful message about people being treated as "throw-aways" in modern society. One journalist referred to Mr. Purifoy as "the junkyard genius."

In Jesus's time, many people considered those with diseases and physical problems as sinners being punished by God. They were shunned and ignored. But when Jesus and His disciples encountered a man born blind, the Lord said his condition was not the result of sin, but an occasion to see the power of God. "While I am in the world, I am the light of the world" (JOHN 9:5). When the blind man followed Jesus's instructions, he was able to see.

When the religious authorities questioned the man, he replied simply, "One thing I do know. I was blind but now I see!" (V. 25).

Jesus is still the greatest "junkyard genius" in our world. We are all damaged by sin, but He takes our broken lives and shapes us into His new creations.   *DAVID MCCASLAND*

Lord, I thank You today for Your amazing grace!

Jesus is the restorer of life.

Seeing to Tomorrow

Read: 2 Corinthians 5:1–9

We live by faith, not by sight. 2 Corinthians 5:7

I enjoy gazing up at a cloudless blue sky. The sky is a beautiful part of our great Creator's masterpiece, given for us to enjoy. Imagine how much pilots must love the view. They use several aeronautical terms to describe a perfect sky for flying, but my favorite is, "You can see to tomorrow."

"Seeing to tomorrow" is beyond our view. Sometimes we even struggle to see or understand what life is throwing at us today. The Bible tells us, "Why, you do not even know what will happen tomorrow. What is your life? You are a mist that appears for a little while and then vanishes" (JAMES 4:14).

But our limited visibility is not cause for despair. Just the opposite. We trust in the God who sees all of our tomorrows perfectly—and who knows what we need as we face the challenges ahead. The apostle Paul knew this. That's why Paul encourages us with hopeful words, "We live by faith, not by sight" (2 COR. 5:7).

When we trust God with our day as well as our unseen tomorrows, we don't need to worry about anything life throws at us. We walk with Him and He knows what is ahead; He is strong enough and wise enough to handle it. *BILL CROWDER*

Lord, I know I can trust You for today and tomorrow because You are kind, good, loving, wise, and powerful. Teach me not to worry.

God sees the beginning to the end.

The Lighthouse

Read: Isaiah 61:1–6

[The Lord bestows] on them a crown of beauty instead of ashes, the oil of joy instead of mourning. Isaiah 61:3

By its very existence, a ministry center in Rwanda called the "Lighthouse" symbolizes redemption. It sits on land where during the genocide in 1994 the country's president owned a grand home. This new structure, however, has been erected by Christians as a beacon of light and hope. Housed there is a Bible institute to raise up a new generation of Christian leaders, along with a hotel, restaurant, and other services for the community. Out of the ashes has come new life. Those who built the Lighthouse look to Jesus as their source of hope and redemption.

When Jesus went to the synagogue in Nazareth on the Sabbath, He read from the book of Isaiah and announced that He was the Anointed One to proclaim the Lord's favor (SEE LUKE 4:14–21). He was the One who came to bind up the brokenhearted and offer redemption and forgiveness. In Jesus we see beauty coming from the ashes (ISA. 61:3).

We find the atrocities of the Rwandan genocide, when inter-tribal fighting cost more than a half-million lives, mind-boggling and harrowing, and we hardly know what to say about them. And yet we know that the Lord can redeem the atrocities—either here on earth or in heaven. He who bestows the oil of joy instead of mourning gives us hope even in the midst of the darkest of situations. *AMY BOUCHER PYE*

Lord Jesus Christ, our hearts hurt when we hear about the pain and suffering that some endure. Have mercy, we pray.

Jesus came to bring us hope in the darkest of circumstances.

Better than a Piñata

Read: Ephesians 2:1–10

By grace you have been saved. Ephesians 2:5

There cannot be a Mexican party without a piñata—a carton or clay container filled with candies and treats. Children strike it with a stick and try to break it, hoping to enjoy its contents.

Monks used the piñatas in the sixteenth century to teach lessons to the indigenous people of Mexico. Piñatas were stars with seven points that represented the seven deadly sins. Beating the piñata showed the struggle against evil, and once the treats inside fell to the ground, people could take them home in remembrance of the rewards of keeping the faith.

But we cannot fight evil on our own. God is not waiting for our efforts so that He will show His mercy. Ephesians teaches that "by grace you have been saved through faith, . . . it is the gift of God" (2:8). We don't beat sin; Christ has done that.

Children fight for the candies from the piñata, but God's gifts come to all of us when we believe in Jesus. God "has blessed us . . . with every spiritual blessing" (1:3). We have forgiveness of sins, redemption, adoption, new life, joy, love, and much more. We don't get these spiritual blessings because we have kept the faith and are strong; we get them because we believe in Jesus. Spiritual blessings come only through grace—undeserved grace!

KEILA OCHOA

Thank You for Your mercy, Lord, which is great and free!

We have been saved by grace. Now we enjoy the many blessings that come by grace.

River Tree

Read: Jeremiah 17:5–10

They will be like a tree planted by the water. Jeremiah 17:8

This was a tree to be envied. Growing on riverfront property, it didn't have to worry about weather reports, withering temperatures, or an uncertain future. Nourished and cooled by the river, it spent its days lifting its branches to the sun, holding the earth with its roots, cleaning the air with its leaves, and offering shade to all who needed refuge from the sun.

By contrast, the prophet Jeremiah pointed to a shrub (JER. 17:6). When the rains stopped and the summer sun turned the ground to dust, the bush shriveled into itself, offering no shade or fruit to anyone.

Why would the prophet compare a flourishing tree to a withering bush? He wanted his people to recall what had happened since their miraculous rescue from the slave yards of Egypt. For forty years in a wilderness, they lived like a tree planted by a river (2:4–6). Yet in the prosperity of their promised land they had forgotten their own story; they were relying on themselves and on gods of their own making (VV. 7–8), even to the point of going back to Egypt looking for help (42:14).

So God, through Jeremiah, lovingly urged the forgetful children of Israel, and He urges us, to hope and trust in the Lord and to be like the tree—not the bush. *MART DEHAAN*

Father, in so many ways You have taught us that You alone can be trusted—even when it seems like You are nowhere to be seen. Please help us to recall today what You have already shown us along the way.

Let's remember in good times what we have learned in days of trouble.

The Viral Gospel

Read: 1 Thessalonians 1:1–10

The Lord's message rang out from you not only in Macedonia and Achaia—your faith in God has become known everywhere.
1 Thessalonians 1:8

The Viral Texts project at Northeastern University in Boston is studying how printed content in the 1800s spread through newspapers—the social media network of that day. If an article was reprinted 50 times or more, they considered that "viral" for the Industrial Age. Writing in *Smithsonian* magazine, Britt Peterson noted that a nineteenth-century news article describing which followers of Jesus were executed for their faith appeared in at least 110 different publications.

When the apostle Paul wrote to the Christians in Thessalonica, he commended them for their bold and joyful witness to Jesus. "The Lord's message rang out from you not only in Macedonia and Achaia—your faith in God has become known everywhere" (1 THESS. 1:8). The message of the gospel went viral through these people whose lives had been transformed by Jesus Christ. In spite of difficulties and persecution, they could not remain silent.

We convey the story of forgiveness and eternal life in Christ through kind hearts, helping hands, and honest words from all of us who know the Lord. The gospel transforms us and the lives of those we meet.

May the message ring out from us for all to hear today!

DAVID MCCASLAND

Lord Jesus, help us to live boldly and tell others about You today.

There's no better news than the gospel—spread the word!

Keeping Darkness at Bay

Read: Matthew 5:11–16

Let your light shine before others, that they may see your good deeds and glorify your Father in heaven. Matthew 5:16

In J. R. R. Tolkien's book *The Hobbit*, the wizard Gandalf explains why he has selected a small hobbit like Bilbo to accompany the dwarves to fight the enemy. He says, "Saruman believes it is only great power that can hold evil in check, but that is not what I have found. I found it is the small everyday deeds of ordinary folk that keep the darkness at bay. Small acts of kindness and love."

That's what Jesus teaches us as well. Warning us that we would live in dark times, He reminded us that because of Him we are "the light of the world" (MATT. 5:14) and that our good deeds would be the power against the darkness for the glory of God (V.16). And Peter, writing to believers in Christ who were facing severe persecution, told them to live so that those accusing them would "by [their] good works which they observe, glorify God" (1 PETER 2:12).

There is one force that the darkness cannot conquer—the force of loving acts of kindness done in Jesus's name. It is God's people who turn the other cheek, go the extra mile, and forgive and even love their enemies who oppose them who have the power to turn the tide against evil. So look for the privileged opportunity to perform acts of kindness today to bring the light of Christ to others.

JOE STOWELL

Lord, teach me the folly of trying to repay evil for evil. May I be so grateful to You for the loving acts of kindness that You have shown me that I gladly look to share good deeds with others as well!

Light up your world with an act of kindness.

Press On

Read: Philippians 3:12–21

I press on toward the goal to win the prize for which God has called me heavenward in Christ Jesus. Philippians 3:14

One of my favorite television programs is *The Amazing Race*. In this reality show, ten couples are sent to a foreign country where they must race, via trains, buses, cabs, bikes, and feet, from one point to another to get their instructions for the next challenge. The goal is for one couple to get to a designated finishing point before everyone else, and the prize is a million dollars.

The apostle Paul compared the Christian life to a race and admitted that he had not yet arrived at the finish line. "Brothers and sisters," he said, "I do not consider myself yet to have taken hold of it. But one thing I do: Forgetting what is behind and straining toward what is ahead. I press on toward the goal to win the prize" (PHIL. 3:13-14). Paul did not look back and allow his past failures to weigh him down with guilt, nor did he let his present successes make him complacent. He pressed on toward the goal of becoming more and more like Jesus.

We are running this race too. Despite our past failures or successes, let us keep pressing on toward the ultimate goal of becoming more like Jesus. We are not racing for an earthly prize, but for the ultimate reward of enjoying Him forever.

MARVIN WILLIAMS

Read Philippians 4:11–13. How are we able to press on toward our future hope? Read Hebrews 12:1–2. What are some practical things we must do to continue to press on and persevere?

Never call it quits in pursuing Jesus.

The Land of "What Is"

Read: Psalm 46:1–7

Brothers and sisters, we do not want you to be uninformed about those who sleep in death, so that you do not grieve like the rest of mankind, who have no hope. 1 Thessalonians 4:13

Even all these years after losing our seventeen-year-old daughter Melissa in a car accident in 2002, I sometimes find myself entering the world of "What If." It's easy, in grief, to reimagine the events of that tragic June evening and think of factors that—if rearranged—would have had Mell arriving safely home.

In reality, though, the land of "What If" is not a good place to be for any of us. It is a place of regret, second-guessing, and hopelessness. While the grief is real and the sadness endures, life is better and God is honored if we dwell in the world of "What Is."

In that world, we can find hope, encouragement, and comfort. We have the sure *hope* (1 THESS. 4:13)—the assurance—that because Melissa loved Jesus she is in a place that is "better by far" (PHIL. 1:23). We have the helpful presence of the God of all comfort (2 COR. 1:3). We have God's "ever-present help in trouble" (PS. 46:1). And we often have the encouragement of fellow believers.

We all wish to avoid the tragedies of life. But when we do face hard times, our greatest help comes from trusting God, our sure hope in the land of What Is.   *DAVE BRANON*

Father God, You know my broken heart. You know the pain of loss because You suffered through the death of Your Son. In the midst of ongoing sorrow, help me to dwell in the comfort of Your hope, encouragement, and comfort.

Our greatest hope comes from trusting God.

Wholehearted!

Read: Numbers 13:26–32; 14:20–24

Because my servant Caleb has a different spirit and follows me wholeheartedly, I will bring him into the land he went to, and his descendants will inherit it. Numbers 14:24

Caleb was a "wholehearted" person. He and Joshua were part of a twelve-man reconnaissance team that explored the Promised Land and gave a report to Moses and the people. Caleb said, "We should go up and take possession of the land, for we can certainly do it" (NUM. 13:30). But ten members of the team said they couldn't possibly succeed. In spite of God's promises, they saw only obstacles (VV. 31–33).

Ten men caused the people to lose heart and grumble against God, which led to forty years of wandering in the desert. But Caleb never quit. The Lord said, "Because my servant Caleb has a different spirit and follows me wholeheartedly, I will bring him into the land he went to, and his descendants will inherit it" (14:24). Forty-five years later God honored His promise when Caleb, at the age of 85, received the city of Hebron "because he followed the LORD, the God of Israel, wholeheartedly" (JOSH. 14:14).

Centuries later an expert in the law asked Jesus, "Which is the greatest commandment in the Law?" Jesus replied, "'Love the Lord your God with all your heart and with all your soul and with all your mind.' This is the first and greatest commandment" (MATT. 22:35–38).

Today Caleb is still inspiring us with his confidence in a God who deserves our wholehearted love, reliance, and commitment.

DAVID MCCASLAND

Lord, may we love You wholeheartedly today and follow You every day of our journey on this earth.

Commitment to Christ is a daily calling.

Complete Access

Read: Ephesians 3:7–13

Through faith in him we may approach God with freedom and confidence. Ephesians 3:12

A few years ago, a friend invited me to join him as a spectator at a pro golf tournament. Being a first-timer, I had no idea what to expect. When we arrived, I was surprised to receive gifts, information, and maps of the golf course. But what topped it all was that we gained access to a VIP tent behind the 18th green, where we had free food and a place to sit. I couldn't have gained entry to the hospitality tent on my own though. The key was my friend; it was only through him that I had complete access.

Left to ourselves, we would all be hopelessly separated from God. But Jesus, who took our penalty, offers us His life and access to God. The apostle Paul wrote, "[God's] intent was that now, through the church, the manifold wisdom of God should be made known" (EPH. 3:10). This wisdom has brought Jew and Gentile together in Christ, who has made a way for us to come to God the Father. "Through faith in [Christ] we may approach God with freedom and confidence" (V. 12).

When we put our trust in Jesus, we receive the greatest access of all—access to the God who loves us and desires relationship with us.   *BILL CROWDER*

Father! Just being able to call You "Father" is an incredible gift. Thank You for Your Son, Jesus, who has made it possible for me to come into Your presence, to know You personally, and, yes, to call You my Father.

Because of the cross of Christ, we can become friends of God.

Ring of Invisibility

Read: John 3:16–21

Everyone who does evil hates the light. John 3:20

The Greek philosopher Plato (C. 427–C. 348 BC) found an imaginative way of shining light on the dark side of the human heart. He told the story of a shepherd who innocently discovered a golden ring that had been hidden deep in the earth. One day a great earthquake opened up an ancient mountainside tomb and revealed the ring to the shepherd. By accident he also discovered that the ring had the magical ability to enable the wearer to become invisible at will. Thinking about invisibility, Plato raised this question: If people didn't have to worry about being caught and punished, would they resist doing wrong?

In John's gospel we find Jesus taking this idea in a different direction. There, Jesus, known as the Good Shepherd, speaks of hearts that stay in the cover of darkness to hide what they are doing (JOHN 3:19–20). He isn't calling attention to our desire for cover-up to condemn us, but to offer us salvation through Him (V. 17). As the Shepherd of our hearts, He brings the worst of our human nature to light to show us how much God loves us (V. 16).

God in His mercy calls us out of our darkness and invites us to follow Him in the light.   *MART DEHAAN*

Dear heavenly Father, thank You for the light of Your presence in my life. May I walk obediently in the light of Your truth in all that I do this day.

Sin's darkness retreats when Christ's light is revealed.

A Chuckle in the Darkness

Read: John 11:17–27

For God so loved the world that he gave his one and only Son, that whoever believes in him shall not perish but have eternal life. John 3:16

In a *Washington Post* article titled "Tech Titans' Latest Project: Defy Death," Ariana Cha wrote about the efforts of Peter Thiele and other tech moguls to extend human life indefinitely. They're prepared to spend billions on the project.

They are a little late. Death has already been defeated! Jesus said, "I am the resurrection and the life. The one who believes in me will live, even though they die; and whoever lives by believing in me will never die" (JOHN 11:25–26). Jesus assures us that those who put their trust in Him will never, ever, under any circumstances whatever, die.

To be clear, our bodies will die—and there is nothing anyone can do to change that. But the thinking, reasoning, remembering, loving, adventuring part of us that we call "me, myself, and I" will never, ever die.

And here's the best part: It's a gift! All you have to do is receive the salvation Jesus offers. C. S. Lewis, musing on this notion, describes it as something like "a chuckle in the darkness"—the sense that something that simple is the answer.

Some say, "It's *too* simple." Well, I say, if God loved you even before you were born and wants you to live with Him forever, why would He make it hard?   *DAVID ROPER*

Dear Jesus, I believe You died for my sins and rose from the dead. I want to accept You as my Lord and Savior and follow You. Please forgive my sins and help me, from this moment on, to live a life that is pleasing to You.

Christ has replaced the dark door of death with the shining gate of life.

All of Me

Read: Matthew 27:45–54

Offer your bodies as a living sacrifice, holy and pleasing to God—this is your true and proper worship. Romans 12:1

Young Isaac Watts found the music in his church sadly lacking, and his father challenged him to create something better. Isaac did. His hymn "When I Survey the Wondrous Cross" has been called the greatest in the English language and has been translated into many other languages.

Watts's worshipful third verse ushers us into the presence of Christ at the crucifixion.

See from His head, His hands, His feet,
Sorrow and love flow mingled down.
Did e'er such love and sorrow meet
Or thorns compose so rich a crown?

The crucifixion Watts describes so elegantly stands as history's most awful moment. We do well to pause and stand with those around the cross. The Son of God strains for breath, held by crude spikes driven through His flesh. After tortured hours, a supernatural darkness descends. Finally, mercifully, the Lord of the universe dismisses His anguished spirit. An earthquake rattles the landscape. Back in the city the thick temple curtain rips in half. Graves open, and dead bodies resurrect, walking about the city (MATT. 27:51–53). These events compel the centurion who crucified Jesus to say, "Surely he was the Son of God!" (V. 54).

"The Cross reorders all values and cancels all vanities," says the Poetry Foundation in commenting on Watts's poem. The song could only conclude: "Love so amazing, so divine demands my soul, my life, my all." *TIM GUSTAFSON*

It is our privilege to give everything we have to the One who gave us everything on the cross.

One of Us

Read: Hebrews 2:9–18

Because he himself suffered when he was tempted, he is able to help those who are being tempted. Hebrews 2:18

At the memorial service for Charles Schulz (1922–2000), creator of the beloved *Peanuts* comic strip, friend and fellow cartoonist Cathy Guisewite spoke of his humanity and compassion. "He gave everyone in the world characters who knew exactly how all of us felt, who made us feel we were never alone. And then he gave the cartoonist himself, and he made us feel that we were never alone. . . . He encouraged us. He commiserated with us. He made us feel he was exactly like us."

When we feel that no one understands or can help us, we are reminded that Jesus gave us himself, and He knows exactly who we are and what we are facing today.

Hebrews 2:9–18 presents the remarkable truth that Jesus fully shared our humanity during His life on earth (V. 14). He "taste[d] death for everyone" (V. 9), broke the power of Satan (V. 14), and freed "those who all their lives were held in slavery by their fear of death" (V. 15). Jesus was made like us, "fully human in every way, in order that he might become a merciful and faithful high priest in service to God" (V. 17). *Thank You, Lord, for sharing our humanity so that we might know Your help today and live in Your presence forever.*   DAVID MCCASLAND

What fears and concerns do you have? What should you do with those fears? (1 Peter 5:6–7). What does the Lord promise to do for you? (Heb. 13:5).

No one understands like Jesus.

Two Portraits

Read: John 16:19–24

Now is your time of grief, but I will see you again and you will rejoice, and no one will take away your joy. John 16:22

Clutching two framed photographs, the proud grandmother showed them to friends in the church foyer. The first picture was of her daughter back in her homeland of Burundi. The second was of her grandson, born recently to that daughter. But the daughter wasn't holding her newborn. She had died giving birth to him.

A friend approached and looked at the pictures. Reflexively, she reached up and held that dear grandmother's face in her hands. All she could say through her own tears was, "I know. I know."

And she did know. Two months earlier she had buried a son.

There's something special about the comfort of others who have experienced our pain. They *know.* Just before Jesus's arrest, He warned His disciples, "You will weep and mourn while the world rejoices." But in the next breath He comforted them: "You will grieve, but your grief will turn to joy" (JOHN 16:20). In mere hours, the disciples would be devastated by Jesus's arrest and crucifixion. But their crushing grief soon turned to a joy they could not have imagined when they saw Him alive again.

Isaiah prophesied of the Messiah, "Surely he took up our pain and bore our suffering" (ISA. 53:4). We have a Savior who doesn't merely know *about* our pain; He lived it. He knows. He cares. One day our grief will be turned into joy. *TIM GUSTAFSON*

Lord, thank You for going to the cross for us. We certainly know trouble in this world, but You overcame the world and took our sin and pain for us. We look forward to the day when our sorrows will be turned into joy and we see You face to face.

When we put our cares into His hands, He puts His peace into our hearts.

Of Love and Old Shoes

Read: Psalm 139:1–12

Before a word is on my tongue you, LORD, know it completely.
Psalm 139:4

Sometimes my wife and I finish each other's sentences. In over thirty years of marriage we've become increasingly familiar with the way the other thinks and speaks. We may not even have to finish a sentence at all; just a word or a glance is enough to express a thought.

There's comfort in that—like an old pair of shoes you continue to wear because they fit so well. Sometimes we even refer to each other affectionately as "my old shoe"—a compliment that might be difficult to understand if you didn't know us well! Through the years our relationship has developed a language of its own, with expressions that are the result of decades of love and trust.

It's comforting to know that God loves us with a deep familiarity. David wrote, "Before a word is on my tongue you, LORD, know it completely" (PS. 139:4). Imagine having a quiet conversation with Jesus where you're telling Him the deepest matters of your heart. Just when you're struggling to get the words out, He gives you a knowing smile and expresses exactly what you couldn't quite say. How good it is to know that we don't have to get our words just right to talk to God! He loves us and knows us well enough to understand.   *JAMES BANKS*

You know all about me, Lord, and You love me. Thank You for understanding me completely! Please help me to love You and follow You today.

God looks past our words to our hearts.

The Gift of Welcome

Read: Hebrews 13:1–2

Do not forget to show hospitality to strangers. Hebrews 13:2

The dinner where we hosted families from five nations remains a wonderful memory. Somehow the conversation didn't splinter into twos, but we all contributed to a discussion of life in London from the viewpoints of different parts of the world. At the end of the evening, my husband and I reflected that we had received more than we gave, including the warm feelings we experienced in fostering new friendships and learning about different cultures.

The writer of the book of Hebrews concluded his thoughts with some exhortations for community life, including that his readers should continue to welcome strangers. For in doing so, "some people have shown hospitality to angels without knowing it" (13:2). He may have been referring to Abraham and Sarah, who as we see in Genesis 18:1–12 welcomed three strangers, reaching out to them with generosity and treating them to a feast, as was the custom in biblical times. They didn't know that they were entertaining angels who brought them a message of blessing.

We don't ask people into our homes in the hope of gaining from them, but often we receive more than we give. May the Lord spread His love through us as we reach out with His welcome.

AMY BOUCHER PYE

Lord God, You are the source of all that we have. May we share what we receive, that You may be glorified.

When we practice hospitality, we share God's goodness and gifts.

Loving Perfectly

Read: 1 Corinthians 13:4–8

[Love] always protects, always trusts, always hopes, always perseveres.
Love never fails. 1 Corinthians 13:7–8

Her voice shook as she shared the problems she was having with her daughter. Worried about her teenager's questionable friends, this concerned mum confiscated her daughter's mobile phone and chaperoned her everywhere. Their relationship seemed only to go from bad to worse.

When I spoke with the daughter, I discovered that she loves her mum dearly but is suffocating under a smothering love. She longs to break free.

As imperfect beings, we all struggle in our relationships. Whether we are a parent or child, single or married, we grapple with expressing love the right way, saying and doing the right thing at the right time. We grow in love throughout our lifetime.

In 1 Corinthians 13 the apostle Paul outlines what perfect love looks like. His standard sounds wonderful, but putting that love into practice can be absolutely daunting. Thankfully, we have Jesus as our example. As He interacted with people with varying needs and issues, He showed us what perfect love looks like in action. As we walk with Him, keeping ourselves in His love and steeping our mind in His Word, we'll reflect more and more of His likeness. We'll still make mistakes, but God is able to redeem them and cause good to come out of every situation, for His love "always protects" and it "never fails" (VV. 7–8). *POH FANG CHIA*

Lord, our intentions are good but we fail each other in so many ways. Thank You for being our model in showing us how to live and love.

To show His love, Jesus died for us; to show our love, we live for Him.

Ruler of the Waves

Read: Job 38:1–18

[The LORD said], "This far you may come and no farther; here is where your proud waves halt." Job 38:11

King Canute was one of the most powerful men on earth in the eleventh century. In a now-famous tale, it is said that he ordered his chair to be placed on the shore as the tide was rising. "You are subject to me," he said to the sea. "I command you, therefore, not to rise on to my land, nor to wet the clothing or limbs of your master." But the tide continued to rise, drenching the king's feet.

This story is often told to draw attention to Canute's pride. Actually, it's a story about humility. "Let all the world know that the power of kings is empty," Canute says next, "save Him by whose will heaven, earth and sea obey." Canute's story makes a point: *God* is the only all-powerful One.

Job discovered the same. Compared to the One who laid Earth's foundations (JOB 38:4–7), who commands morning to appear and night to end (VV. 12–13), who stocks the storehouses of the snow and directs the stars (VV. 22, 31–33), we are small. There is only one Ruler of the waves, and it is not us (V. 11; MATT. 8:23–27).

Canute's story is good to reenact when we begin feeling too clever or proud about ourselves. Walk to the beach and tell the tide to halt or try commanding the sun to step aside. We'll soon remember who is really supreme and thank Him for ruling our lives.   *SHERIDAN VOYSEY*

You are high and above all, Lord Almighty. I bow to You as the Ruler of my life.

God is great, we are small, and that is good.

Painting a Portrait

Read: Philippians 2:1–11

In your relationships with one another, have the same mindset as Christ Jesus. Philippians 2:5

The National Portrait Gallery in London, England, houses a treasure of paintings from across the centuries, including 166 images of Winston Churchill, 94 of William Shakespeare, and 20 of George Washington. With the older portraits, we may wonder: *Is that what these individuals really looked like?*

For instance, there are eight paintings of Scottish patriot William Wallace (c. 1270–1305), but we obviously don't have photographs to compare them to. How do we know if the artists accurately represented Wallace?

Something similar might be happening with the likeness of Jesus. Without realizing it, those who believe in Him are leaving an impression of Him on others. Not with brushes and oils, but with attitudes, actions, and relationships.

Are we painting a portrait that represents the likeness of His heart? This was the concern of the apostle Paul. "In your relationships with one another, have the same mindset as Christ Jesus," he wrote (PHIL. 2:5). With a desire to accurately represent our Lord, he urged His followers to reflect the humility, self-sacrifice, and compassion of Jesus for others.

It has been said, "We are the only Jesus some people will ever see." As we "in humility value others above [ourselves]" (V. 3), we will show the world the heart and attitude of Jesus himself.

BILL CROWDER

Father, please build the heart of Christ into my heart that those around me will see Him clearly and desire to know Him too.

Christ's sacrifice of himself motivates us to sacrifice ourselves for others.

Mistakes Were Made

Read: Exodus 32:1–5, 19–26

They gave me the gold, and I threw it into the fire, and out came this calf! Exodus 32:24

"Mistakes were made," said the CEO as he discussed the illegal activity his company had been involved in. He looked regretful, yet he kept blame at arm's length and couldn't admit he had personally done anything wrong.

Some "mistakes" *are* just mistakes: driving in the wrong direction, forgetting to set a timer and burning dinner, miscalculating your checkbook balance. But then there are the deliberate deeds that go far beyond—God calls those *sin*. When God questioned Adam and Eve about why they had disobeyed Him, they quickly tried to shift the blame to another (GEN. 3:8–13). Aaron took no personal responsibility when the people built a golden calf to worship in the desert. He explained to Moses, "[The people] gave me the gold, and I threw it into the fire, and out came this calf!" (EX. 32:24).

He might as well have muttered, "Mistakes were made."

Sometimes it seems easier to blame someone else rather than admitting our own failings. Equally dangerous is to try to minimize our sin by calling it "just a mistake" instead of acknowledging its true nature.

But when we take responsibility—acknowledging our sin and confessing it—the One who "is faithful and just . . . will forgive us our sins and purify us from all unrighteousness" (1 JOHN 1:9). Our God offers His children forgiveness and restoration.

CINDY HESS KASPER

The first step to receiving God's forgiveness is to admit that we need it.

Home

Read: Ephesians 2:11–22

You are no longer foreigners and strangers, but fellow citizens with God's people. Ephesians 2:19

A young African refugee who goes by the name of Steven is a man without a country. He thinks he may have been born in Mozambique or Zimbabwe. But he never knew his father and lost his mother. She fled civil war, traveling country to country as a street vendor. Without ID and unable to prove his place of birth, Steven walked into a British police station, asking to be arrested. Jail seemed better to Steven than trying to exist on the streets without the rights and benefits of citizenship.

The plight of living without a country was on Paul's mind as he wrote his letter to the Ephesians. His non-Jewish readers knew what it was like to live as aliens and outsiders (2:12). Only since finding life and hope in Christ (1:13) had they discovered what it meant to belong to the kingdom of heaven (MATT. 5:3). In Jesus, they learned what it means to be known and cared for by the Father He came to reveal (MATT. 6:31–33).

Paul realized, however, that as the past fades from view, a short memory can cause us to forget that, while hope is the new norm, despair was the old reality.

May our God help us to live in security—to know each day the belonging that we have as members of His family is by faith in Jesus Christ and to understand the rights and benefits of having our home in Him. *MART DEHAAN*

Lord, as we remember how hopeless we were before You found us, please help us not to forget those who are still on the street.

Hope means the most to those who have lived without it.

Mayday!

Read: Psalm 86:1–13

When I am in distress, I call to you, because you answer me. Psalm 86:7

The international distress signal "Mayday" is always repeated three times in a row—"Mayday-Mayday-Mayday"—so the situation will be clearly understood as a life-threatening emergency. The word was created in 1923 by Frederick Stanley Mockford, a senior radio officer at London's Croydon Airport. That now-closed facility once had many flights to and from Le Bourget Airport in Paris. According to the National Maritime Museum, Mockford coined Mayday from the French word *m'aidez*, which means, "help me."

Throughout King David's life, he faced life-threatening situations for which there seemed to be no way out. Yet, we read in Psalm 86 that during his darkest hours, David's confidence was in the Lord. "Hear my prayer, LORD; listen to my cry for mercy. When I am in distress, I call to you, because you answer me" (VV. 6–7).

David also saw beyond the immediate danger by asking God to lead his steps: "Teach me your way, LORD, that I may rely on your faithfulness; give me an undivided heart, that I may fear your name" (V. 11). When the crisis was past, he wanted to keep walking with God.

The most difficult situations we face can become doorways to a deeper relationship with our Lord. This begins when we call on Him to help us in our trouble, and also to lead us each day in His way.   *DAVID MCCASLAND*

Lord, even as we call to You for help today, please help us to keep walking with You when this crisis is over.

God hears our cries for help and leads us in His way.

It's Not Me

Read: 1 Peter 4:7–11

Each of you should use whatever gift you have received to serve others.
1 Peter 4:10

While on vacation recently, I gave my razor a rest and grew a beard. Various responses came from friends and coworkers—and most were complimentary. One day, however, I looked at the beard and decided, "It's not me." So out came the razor.

I've been thinking about the idea of who we are and why one thing or another does not fit our personality. Primarily, it's because God has bestowed us with individual differences and preferences. It's okay that we don't all like the same hobbies, eat the same foods, or worship in the same church. We are each uniquely and "wonderfully made" (PS. 139:14). Peter noted that we are uniquely gifted in order to serve each other (1 PETER 4:10–11).

Jesus's disciples didn't check their characteristics at the door before entering His world. Peter was so impulsive that he cut off a servant's ear the night Jesus was arrested. Thomas insisted on evidence before believing Christ had risen. The Lord didn't reject them simply because they had some growing to do. He molded and shaped them for His service.

When discerning how we might best serve the Lord, it's wise to consider our talents and characteristics and to sometimes say, "It's not me." God may call us out of our comfort zone, but He does so to develop our unique gifts and personalities to serve His good purposes. We honor His creative nature when we permit Him to use us as we are. *DAVE BRANON*

Thank You, Father, for the great individuality You have built into us. Thank You for my personality and for my abilities. Guide me in using them for You.

There are no ordinary people—we were created to be unique.

Surprise Interview

Read: Acts 26:9–15

*The King will say, "I tell you the truth, when you did it to one of the
least of these my brothers and sisters, you were doing it to me!"*
Matthew 25:40 NLT

On a crowded London commuter train, an early morning rider
shoved and insulted a fellow passenger who got in his way. It
was the kind of unfortunate and mindless moment that usually
remains unresolved. But later that day, the unexpected happened. A business manager sent a quick message to his social
media friends, "Guess who just showed up for a job interview."
When his explanation appeared on the internet, people all over
the world winced and smiled. Imagine walking into a job interview only to discover that the person who greets you is the one
you had shoved and sworn at earlier that day.

Saul also ran into someone he never expected to see. While
raging against a group called the Way (ACTS 9:1–2), he was
stopped in his tracks by a blinding light. Then a voice said, "Saul,
Saul, why do you persecute me?" (V. 4). Saul asked, "Who are you,
Lord?" The One speaking to him replied, "I am Jesus, whom you
are persecuting" (26:15).

Years earlier Jesus had said that how we treat the hungry, the
thirsty, the stranger, and the prisoner reflects our relationship to
Him (MATT. 25:35–36). Who would have dreamed that when someone insults us, or when we help or hurt another, the One who
loves us takes it personally? *MART DEHAAN*

*Father, forgive us for acting as if You were not present in our moments of need,
hurt, anger, or compassion.*

When we help or hurt one another, Jesus takes it personally.

Open Arms

Read: Psalm 139:17–24

Search me, God, and know my heart; test me and know my anxious thoughts. Psalm 139:23

The day my husband, Dan, and I began our caregiving journey with our aging parents, we linked arms and felt as if we were plunging off a cliff. We didn't know that in the process of caregiving the hardest task we would face would be to allow our hearts to be searched and molded and to allow God to use this special time to make us like Him in new ways.

On days when I felt I was plunging toward earth in an out-of-control free-fall, God showed me my agendas, my reservations, my fears, my pride, and my selfishness. He used my broken places to show me His love and forgiveness.

My pastor has said, "The best day is the day you see yourself for who you are—desperate without Christ. Then see yourself as He sees you—complete in Him." This was the blessing of caregiving in my life. As I saw who God had created me to be, I turned and ran weeping into His arms. I cried out with the psalmist: "Search me, God, and know my heart" (PS. 139:23).

This is my prayer for you—that as you see yourself in the midst of your own circumstances, you will turn and run into the open, loving, and forgiving arms of God.   *SHELLY BEACH*

Gracious Father, I recognize today my desperate need of Your love, wisdom, and grace. Search me and know me. Pour out Your grace and mercy in my life to bring healing to my heart.

When worry walks in, strength runs out. But strength returns when we run to God.

A Good Inheritance

Read: 2 Timothy 1:1–5

I am reminded of your sincere faith, which first lived in your grandmother Lois and in your mother Eunice. 2 Timothy 1:5

Grandpa and Grandma Harris didn't have a lot of money, yet they managed to make each Christmas memorable for my cousins and me. There was always plenty of food, fun, and love. And from an early age we learned that it was Christ who made this celebration possible.

We want to leave the same legacy to our children. When we got together last December to share Christmas with family, we realized this wonderful tradition had started with Grandpa and Grandma. They couldn't leave us a monetary inheritance, but they were careful to plant the seeds of love, respect, and faith so that we—their children's children—might imitate their example.

In the Bible we read about grandma Lois and mom Eunice, who shared with Timothy genuine faith (2 TIM. 1:5). Their influence prepared this man to share the good news with many others.

We can prepare a spiritual inheritance for those whose lives we influence by living in close communion with God. In practical ways, we make His love a reality to others when we give them our undivided attention, show interest in what they think and do, and share life with them. We might even invite them to share in our celebrations! When our lives reflect the reality of God's love, we leave a lasting legacy for others.   *KEILA OCHOA*

Father, may I leave a good spiritual inheritance to my family as You use me to show Your everlasting love.

If someone has left you a godly inheritance, invest it in others.

Spilling Through My Fingers

Read: Isaiah 40:9–17

Who has measured the waters in the hollow of his hand . . . ?
Isaiah 40:12

After I clumsily knocked over my glass on the restaurant counter, the spilled beverage began to cascade over the edge and onto the floor. Out of sheer embarrassment, I tried to catch the waterfall with cupped hands. My efforts were largely unsuccessful; most of my beverage rushed through my fingers. In the end, my upturned palms held little more than a meager tablespoon each, while my feet stood in puddles.

My life feels similar on many days. I find myself scrambling to solve problems, oversee details, and control circumstances. No matter how hard I try, my feeble hands are incapable of managing all the pieces and parts. Something invariably slips through my fingers and pools on the floor at my feet, leaving me feeling overwhelmed. No amount of contorting my hands or squeezing my fingers more tightly together makes me able to handle it all.

Yet God can. Isaiah tells us that God can measure the globe's waters—all the oceans and rivers and rain—in the hollow of His hands (40:12). Only His hands are large enough to hold them all. We needn't try to hold more than the tablespoon He's designed our hands to carry. When we feel overwhelmed, we can entrust our cares and concerns into His capable hands.

KIRSTEN HOLMBERG

Help me, Lord, to stop trying to hold everything in my hands, but instead to trust my needs and concerns into Your perfect care.

We can trust God to handle the things that overwhelm us.

After You

Read: Genesis 13:1–18

Is not the whole land before you? Let's part company. If you go to the left, I'll go to the right; if you go to the right, I'll go to the left. Genesis 13:9

In some cultures a younger person is expected to permit his elder to enter a room first. In others, the most important or highest ranking individual enters first. No matter what our traditions, there are times when we find it difficult to allow someone to choose first on important matters, especially when that privilege rightfully belongs to us.

Abram (later called Abraham) and his nephew Lot had so many flocks, herds, and tents that the land could not support both of them as they traveled together. To avoid conflict, Abram suggested they part company and generously gave Lot first choice of the land. His nephew took the fertile Jordan Valley, leaving Abram with the less desirable land.

Abram did not insist on his rights as the elder in this situation but trusted his future to God. "So Abram said to Lot, 'Let's not have any quarreling between you and me. . . . Is not the whole land before you? Let's part company. If you go to the left, I'll go to the right; if you go to the right, I'll go to the left'" (GEN. 13:8–9). Lot's choice eventually led to dire consequences for his entire family (SEE GEN. 19).

Today, as we face choices of many kinds, we can trust our Father to guide us in His way. He has promised to care for us. He will always give us what we need.   *DAVID MCCASLAND*

Father, Your unfailing love and faithfulness guide us in every choice we make.
May our lives speak well of You and honor You today.

God always gives His best to those who leave the choice with Him.
JIM ELLIOT

Something's Wrong

Read: Psalm 34:11–18

The Lord is close to the brokenhearted and saves those who are crushed in spirit. Psalm 34:18

The morning after our son, Allen, was born, the doctor sat down in a chair near the foot of my bed and said, "Something's wrong." Our son, so perfect on the outside, had a life-threatening birth defect and needed to be flown to a hospital 700 miles away for immediate surgery.

When the doctor tells you something is wrong with your child, your life changes. Fear of what lies ahead can crush your spirit and you stumble along, desperate for a God who will strengthen you so you can support your child. *Would a loving God allow this?* you wonder. *Does He care about my child? Is He there?* These and other thoughts shook my faith that morning.

Then my husband, Hiram, arrived and heard the news. After the doctor left, Hiram said, "Jolene, let's pray." I nodded and he took my hand. "Thank You, Father, for giving Allen to us. He's Yours, God, not ours. You loved him before we knew him, and he belongs to You. Be with him when we can't. Amen."

Hiram has always been a man of few words. He struggles to speak his thoughts and often doesn't try, knowing that I have enough words to fill any silence. But on a day when my heart was broken, my spirit crushed, and my faith gone, God gave Hiram strength to speak the words I couldn't say. And clinging to my husband's hand, in deep silence and through many tears, I sensed that God was very near. *JOLENE PHILO*

The best kind of friend is a praying friend.

A Small Fire

Read: James 3:3–12

*The tongue is a small part of the body, but it makes great boasts.
Consider what a great forest is set on fire by a small spark. James 3:5*

It was a Sunday night in September and most people were sleeping when a small fire broke out in Thomas Farriner's bakery on Pudding Lane. Soon the flames spread from house to house and London was engulfed in the Great Fire of 1666. Over 70,000 people were left homeless by the blaze that leveled four-fifths of the city. So much destruction from such a small fire!

The Bible warns us of another small but destructive fire. James was concerned about lives and relationships, not buildings, when he wrote, "The tongue is a small part of the body, but it makes great boasts. Consider what a great forest is set on fire by a small spark" (JAMES 3:5).

But our words can also be *constructive*. Proverbs 16:24 reminds us, "Gracious words are a honeycomb, sweet to the soul and healing to the bones." The apostle Paul says, "Let your conversation be always full of grace, seasoned with salt, so that you may know how to answer everyone" (COL. 4:6). As salt flavors our food, grace flavors our words for building up others.

Through the help of the Holy Spirit our words can encourage people who are hurting, who want to grow in their faith, or who need to come to the Savior. Our words can put out fires instead of starting them.   *BILL CROWDER*

Lord, I can always use help with the way I talk. For this day, help me to speak words of hope and encouragement to build up others.

What will our words be like today?

Running and Rest

Read: Mark 6:30–46

[Jesus] said to them, "Come with me by yourselves to a quiet place and get some rest." Mark 6:31

The headline caught my eye: "Rest Days Important for Runners." In Tommy Manning's article, the former member of the U.S. Mountain Running Team emphasized a principle that dedicated athletes sometimes ignore—the body needs time to rest and rebuild after exercise. "Physiologically, the adaptations that occur as a result of training only happen during rest," Manning wrote. "This means rest is as important as workouts."

The same is true in our walk of faith and service. Regular times of rest are essential to avoid burnout and discouragement. Jesus sought spiritual balance during His life on Earth, even in the face of great demands. When His disciples returned from a strenuous time of teaching and healing others, "He said to them, 'Come with me by yourselves to a quiet place and get some rest'" (MARK 6:31). But a large crowd followed them, so Jesus taught them and fed them with only five loaves and two fish (VV. 32–44). When everyone was gone, Jesus "went up on a mountainside to pray" (V. 46).

If our lives are defined by work, then what we do becomes less and less effective. Jesus invites us to regularly join Him in a quiet place to pray and get some rest.   *DAVID MCCASLAND*

Lord Jesus, thank You for Your example of prayer alone with Your Father. Give us wisdom and determination to make rest a priority as we follow You.

In our life of faith and service, rest is as important as work.

Refreshing Spring Rains

Read: Hosea 6:1–4

He will come to us like the . . . spring rains that water the earth.
Hosea 6:3

Needing a break, I went for a walk in the nearby park. As I headed down the path, a burst of green caught my attention. Out of the mud appeared shoots of life that in a few weeks would be cheerful daffodils, heralding spring and the warmth to come. We had made it through another winter!

As we read through the book of Hosea, it can feel in parts like an unrelenting winter. For the Lord gave this prophet the unenviable task of marrying an unfaithful woman as a picture of the Creator's love for His people Israel (1:2–3). Hosea's wife, Gomer, broke their wedding vows, but Hosea welcomed her back, yearning that she would love him devotedly (3:1–3). So too the Lord desires that we love Him with a strength and commitment that won't evaporate like the morning mist.

How do we relate to God? Do we seek Him mainly in times of trouble, searching for answers in our distress but ignoring Him during our seasons of celebration? Are we like the Israelites, easily swayed by the idols of our age, including such things as busyness, success, and influence?

Today, may we recommit ourselves to the Lord, who loves us as surely as the flowers bud in the spring.   *AMY BOUCHER PYE*

Lord Jesus, You gave Yourself that we might be free. Help us to love You wholeheartedly.

Though we may be unfaithful to God, He will never turn from us.

What Are You Known For?

Read: Hebrews 11:23–28

[Moses] regarded disgrace for the sake of Christ as of greater value than the treasures of Egypt, because he was looking ahead to his reward.
Hebrews 11:26

A memorial stone stands in the grounds of a former Japanese prison camp in China where a man died in 1945. It reads, "Eric Liddell was born in Tianjin of Scottish parents in 1902. His career reached its peak with his gold medal victory in the 400 metres event at the 1924 Olympic Games. He returned to China to work in Tianjin as a teacher. . . . His whole life was spent encouraging young people to make their best contributions to the betterment of mankind."

In the eyes of many, Eric's greatest achievement was on the sports field. But he is also remembered for his contribution to the youth of Tianjin in China, the country where he was born and that he loved. He lived and served by faith.

What will we be remembered for? Our academic achievements, job position, or financial success may get us recognized by others. But it is the quiet work we do in the lives of people that will live long after we are gone.

Moses is remembered in the faith chapter of the Bible, Hebrews 11, as someone who chose to align himself with the people of God instead of enjoying the treasures of Egypt (V. 26). He led and served God's people by faith.   *C. P. HIA*

Ask God to show you how you can make a difference in the lives of others.
For what would you like to be remembered?

Faithfulness to God is true success.

Cradled in Comfort

Read: Isaiah 66:12–16

As a mother comforts her child, so will I comfort you. Isaiah 66:13

My friend entrusted me with the privilege of holding her precious, four-day-old daughter. Not long after I took the baby into my arms, she started to fuss. I hugged her closer, my cheek pressed against her head, and began to sway and hum in a gentle rhythm to soothe her. Despite these earnest attempts, and my decade and a half of parenting experience, I couldn't pacify her. She became increasingly upset until I placed her back into the crook of her mother's eager arm. Peace washed over her almost instantaneously; her cries subsided and her newborn frame relaxed into the safety she already trusted. My friend knew precisely how to hold and pat her daughter to alleviate her distress.

God extends comfort to His children like a mother: tender, trustworthy, and diligent in her efforts to calm her child. When we are weary or upset, He carries us affectionately in His arms. As our Father and Creator, He knows us intimately. He "will keep in perfect peace all who trust in [him], all whose thoughts are fixed on [him]" (ISA. 26:3 NLT).

When the troubles of this world weigh heavy on our hearts, we can find comfort in the knowledge that He protects and fights for us, His children, as a loving parent.   *KIRSTEN HOLMBERG*

Lord, help me to look to You for my comfort in times of distress.

God's comfort soothes us perfectly.

His Wonderful Face

Read: 1 Chronicles 16:8–27

Look to the LORD and his strength; seek his face always.
1 Chronicles 16:11

My four-year-old son is full of questions, and chatters constantly. I love talking with him, but he's developed an unfortunate habit of talking to me even when his back is turned. I often find myself saying, "I can't hear you—please look at me when you're talking."

Sometimes I think God wants to say the same thing to us—not because He can't hear us, but because we can tend to talk to Him without really "looking" at Him. We pray, but we remain caught up in our own questions and focused on ourselves, forgetting the character of the One we're praying to. Like my son, we ask questions without paying attention to the person we're talking to.

Many of our concerns are best addressed by reminding ourselves of who God is and what He has done. By simply refocusing, we find comfort in what we know of His character: that He is loving, forgiving, sovereign, graceful.

The psalmist believed we ought to seek God's face continually (PS. 105:4). When David appointed leaders for worship and prayer, he encouraged the people to praise God's character and tell stories of His past faithfulness (1 CHRON. 16:8–27).

When we turn our eyes toward the beautiful face of God, we can find strength and comfort that sustain us even in the midst of unanswered questions.   *AMY PETERSON*

Lord, let the light of Your face shine upon us.

Seeking the face of God can strengthen our faith.

Not the One

Read: 1 Chronicles 17:1–4, 16–25

Do as you promised, so that it will be established and that your name will be great forever. 1 Chronicles 17:23–24

David had drawn up the plans. He designed the furniture. He collected the materials. He made all the arrangements (SEE 1 CHRON. 28:11–19). But the first temple built in Jerusalem is known as Solomon's Temple, not David's.

For God had said, "You are not the one" (1 CHRON. 17:4). God had chosen David's son Solomon to build the temple. David's response to this denial was exemplary. He focused on what God would do, instead of what he himself could not do (VV. 16–25). He maintained a thankful spirit. He did everything he could and rallied capable men to assist Solomon in building the temple (SEE 1 CHRON. 22).

Bible commentator J. G. McConville wrote: "Often we may have to accept that the work which we would dearly like to perform in terms of Christian service is not that for which we are best equipped, and not that to which God has in fact called us. It may be, like David's, a preparatory work, leading to something more obviously grand."

David sought God's glory, not his own. He faithfully did all he could for God's temple, laying a solid foundation for the one who would come after him to complete the work. May we, likewise, accept the tasks God has chosen for us to do and serve Him with a thankful heart! Our loving God is doing something "more obviously grand."

POH FANG CHIA

Father, we want our hopes and dreams and our hearts to align with Yours. Teach us to praise You when we are tempted to doubt Your goodness.

God may conceal the purpose of His ways, but His ways are not without purpose.

East Meets West

Read: Romans 14:1–12

Who are you to judge someone else's servant? Romans 14:4

When students from Southeast Asia met a teacher from North America, the visiting instructor learned a lesson. After giving his class their first multiple-choice test, he was surprised to find many questions left unanswered. While handing back the corrected papers, he suggested that, next time, instead of leaving answers blank they should take a guess. Surprised, one of the students raised their hand and asked, "What if I accidentally get the answer right? I would be implying that I knew the answer when I didn't." The student and teacher had a different perspective and practice.

In the days of the New Testament, Jewish and Gentile converts were coming to Christ with perspectives as different as East and West. Before long they were disagreeing over matters as diverse as worship days and what a Christ-follower is free to eat or drink. The apostle Paul urged them to remember an important fact: None of us is in a position to know or judge the heart of another.

For the sake of harmony with fellow believers, God urges us to realize that we are all accountable to our Lord, to act according to His Word and our conscience. However, He alone is in a position to judge the attitudes of our heart (ROM. 14:4–7).

MART DEHAAN

Father in heaven, please have mercy on us for presuming to judge the heart of those who see so many things differently than we do.

Be slow to judge others but quick to judge yourself.

Image Management

Read: Isaiah 43:1–9

You are precious and honored in my sight, and . . . I love you.
Isaiah 43:4

To celebrate Winston Churchill's eightieth birthday, the British parliament commissioned artist Graham Sutherland to paint a portrait of the celebrated statesman. "How are you going to paint me?" Churchill reportedly asked the artist: "As a cherub, or the Bulldog?" Churchill liked these two popular perceptions of him. Sutherland, however, said he would paint what he saw.

Churchill was not happy with the results. Sutherland's portrait had Churchill slumped in a chair wearing his trademark scowl—true to reality, but hardly flattering. After its official unveiling, Churchill hid the painting in his cellar. It was later secretly destroyed.

Like Churchill, most of us have an image of ourselves we want others to have of us also—whether of success, godliness, beauty, or strength. We can go to great lengths to conceal our "ugly" sides. Perhaps deep down we fear we won't be loved if the real us is known.

When the Israelites were taken captive by Babylon, they were seen at their worst. Because of their sins, God allowed their enemies to conquer them. But He told them not to fear. He knew them by name, and He was with them in every humiliating trial (ISA. 43:1–2). They were secure in His hands (V. 13) and "precious" to Him (V. 4). Despite their ugliness, God loved them.

We will find ourselves less motivated to seek the approval of others when such a truth truly sinks in. God knows the real us and still loves us immeasurably (EPH. 3:18).   *SHERIDAN VOYSEY*

God's deep love means we can be real with others.

Bearing Good Fruit

Read: Psalm 1:1–3

That person is like a tree planted by streams of water, which yields its fruit in season. Psalm 1:3

The view from my airplane window was striking: a narrow ribbon of ripening wheat fields and orchards wending between two barren mountains. Running through the valley was a river—life-giving water, without which there would be no fruit.

Just as a bountiful harvest depends on a source of clean water, the quality of the "fruit" in my life—my words, actions, and attitude—depends on my spiritual nourishment. The psalmist describes this in Psalm 1: The person "whose delight is in the law of the LORD . . . is like a tree planted by streams of water, which yields its fruit in season" (VV. 1–3). And Paul writes in Galatians 5 that those who walk in step with the Spirit are marked by "love, joy, peace, forbearance, kindness, goodness, faithfulness, gentleness, and self-control" (VV. 22–23).

Sometimes my perspective on my circumstances turns sour, or my actions and words become persistently unkind. There is no good fruit, and I realize I haven't spent time being quiet before the words of my God. But when the rhythm of my days is rooted in reliance on Him, I bear good fruit. Patience and gentleness characterize my interactions with others; it's easier to choose gratitude over complaint.

The God who has revealed himself to us is our source of strength, wisdom, joy, understanding, and peace (PS. 119:28, 98, 111, 144, 165). As we steep our souls in the words that point us to Him, the work of God's Spirit will be evident in our lives.

PETER CHIN

God's Spirit lives in His people, in order to work through them.

Trial by Fire

Read: James 1:1–12

Blessed is the one who perseveres under trial because, having stood the test, that person will receive the crown of life. James 1:12

Last winter while visiting a natural history museum in Colorado, I learned some remarkable facts about the aspen tree. An entire grove of slender, white-trunked aspens can grow from a single seed and share the same root system. These root systems can exist for thousands of years whether or not they produce trees. They sleep underground, waiting for fire, flood, or avalanche to clear a space for them in the shady forest. After a natural disaster has cleared the land, aspen roots can sense the sun at last. The roots send up saplings, which become trees.

For aspens, new growth is made possible by the devastation of a natural disaster. James writes that our growth in faith is also made possible by difficulties. "Consider it pure joy," he writes, "whenever you face trials of many kinds, because you know that the testing of your faith produces perseverance. Let perseverance finish its work so that you may be mature and complete, not lacking anything" (JAMES 1:2–4).

It's difficult to be joyful during trials, but we can take hope from the fact that God will use difficult circumstances to help us reach maturity. Like aspen trees, faith can grow in times of trial when difficulty clears space in our hearts for the light of God to touch us.   *AMY PETERSON*

Thank You, God, for being with us in our trials, and for helping us to grow through difficult circumstances.

Trials and tests can draw us closer to Christ.

Life and Death

Read: Genesis 50:22–26

I am about to die. But God will surely come to your aid. Genesis 50:24

I will never forget sitting at the bedside of my friend's brother when he died; the scene was one of the ordinary visited by the extraordinary. Three of us were talking quietly when we realized that Richard's breathing was becoming more labored. We gathered around him, watching, waiting, and praying. When he took his last breath, it felt like a holy moment; the presence of God enveloped us in the midst of our tears over a wonderful man dying in his forties.

Many of the heroes of our faith experienced God's faithfulness when they died. For instance, Jacob announced he would soon be "gathered to [his] people" (GEN. 49:29–33). Jacob's son Joseph also announced his impending death: "I am about to die," he said to his brothers while instructing them how to hold firm in their faith. He seems to be at peace, yet eager that his brothers trust the Lord (50:24).

None of us knows when or how we will breathe our last breath, but we can ask God to help us trust that He will be with us. We can believe the promise that Jesus will prepare a place for us in His Father's house (JOHN 14:2–3). *AMY BOUCHER PYE*

Lord God, Your dwelling place will be with Your people, and You will be our God, wiping away our tears and banishing death. May it be so!

The Lord will never abandon us, especially at the time of our death.

The Greatest Invitation

Read: Isaiah 55:1–7

*Come, all you who are thirsty, come to the waters; and you who have
no money, come, buy and eat! Isaiah 55:1*

During a recent week, I received several invitations in the mail.
Those inviting me to attend "free" seminars on retirement,
real estate, and life insurance were immediately thrown away.
But the invitation to a gathering honoring a longtime friend
caused me to reply immediately, "Yes! I accept." Invitation +
Desire = Acceptance.

Isaiah 55:1 is one of the great invitations in the Bible. The
Lord said to His people who were in difficult circumstances,
"Come, all you who are thirsty, come to the waters; and you who
have no money, come, buy and eat! Come, buy wine and milk
without money and without cost." This is God's remarkable offer
of inner nourishment, deep spiritual satisfaction, and everlasting life (VV. 2–3).

Jesus's invitation is repeated in the last chapter of the Bible:
"The Spirit and the bride say, 'Come!' And let the one who hears
say, 'Come!' Let the one who is thirsty come; and let the one who
wishes take the free gift of the water of life" (REV. 22:17).

We often think of eternal life as beginning when we die. In
reality, it begins when we receive Jesus Christ as our Savior and
Lord.

God's invitation to find eternal life in Him is the greatest invitation of all! Invitation + Desire = Acceptance.

DAVID MCCASLAND

*Lord Jesus, thank You for Your promise of mercy, pardon, and eternal life. I
acknowledge my failures and receive Jesus as my Savior today.*

**When we accept Jesus's invitation to follow Him, our whole
life changes direction.**

When Yes Means No

Read: Romans 8:22–28

I call on the LORD in my distress, and he answers me. Psalm 120:1

I thanked God for the privilege of serving as my mom's live-in caregiver during her battle against leukemia. When medicines began to hurt more than help, she decided to stop treatment. "I don't want to suffer anymore," she said. "I want to enjoy my last days with family. God knows I'm ready to go home."

I pleaded with our loving heavenly Father—the Great Physician—confident He could work miracles. But to say yes to my mom's prayers, He would have to say no to mine. Sobbing, I surrendered, "Your will be done, Lord."

Soon after, Jesus welcomed my mama into a pain-free eternity.

In this fallen world, we'll experience suffering until Jesus returns (ROM. 8:22–25). Our sinful nature, limited vision, and fear of pain can distort our ability to pray. Thankfully, "the Spirit intercedes for God's people in accordance with the will of God" (V. 27). He reminds us that in all things God works for the good of those who love Him (V. 28), even when His yes to someone else means a heartbreaking no for us.

When we accept our small part in His greater purpose, we can echo my mom's watchword: "God is good, and that's all there is to it. Whatever He decides, I'm at peace." With confidence in the Lord's goodness, we can trust Him to answer every prayer according to His will and for His glory.   *XOCHITL DIXON*

God's answers are wiser than our prayers.

Behind the Scenes

Read: Daniel 10:1–14

Your words were heard, and I have come in response to them.
Daniel 10:12

My daughter sent a text message to a friend, in hopes of having a question answered quickly. Her phone's messaging service showed that the recipient had read the message, so she waited anxiously for a reply. Mere moments passed, yet she grew frustrated, groaning her annoyance at the delay. Irritation eroded into worry; she wondered whether the lack of response meant there was a problem between them. Eventually a reply came and my daughter was relieved to see their relationship was fine. Her friend had simply been sorting out the details needed to answer the question.

The Old Testament prophet Daniel also anxiously awaited a reply. After receiving a frightening vision of great war, Daniel fasted and sought God through humble prayer (10:3, 12). For three weeks, he received no reply (VV. 2, 13). Finally, an angel arrived and assured Daniel his prayers had been heard "since the first day." In the meantime, the angel had been battling on behalf of those prayers. Though Daniel didn't know it at first, God was at work during each of the twenty-one days that elapsed between his first prayer and the angel's coming.

The confidence that God hears our prayers can cause us to become anxious when His reply doesn't come when we want it to. We are prone to wonder whether He cares. Yet Daniel's experience reminds us that God is at work on behalf of those He loves even when it isn't obvious to us.   *KIRSTEN HOLMBERG*

Lord, help me to trust Your care for me even when I can't see it.

God is always at work on behalf of His people.

A Heart of Compassion

Read: Colossians 3:12–17

Clothe yourselves with compassion, kindness, humility, gentleness and patience. Colossians 3:12

Seven of us were attending a musical production at a crowded amusement park. Wanting to sit together, we tried to squeeze into one row. But as we did, a woman rushed between us. My wife mentioned to her that we wanted to stay together, but the woman quickly said, "Too bad," as she and her two companions pushed on into the row.

As three of us sat one row behind the other four, my wife, Sue, noticed that the woman had an adult with her who appeared to have special needs. She had been trying to keep her little group together so she could take care of her friend. Suddenly, our irritation faded. Sue said, "Imagine how tough things are for her in a crowded place like this." Yes, perhaps the woman did respond rudely. But we could respond with compassion rather than anger.

Wherever we go, we will encounter people who need compassion. Perhaps these words from the apostle Paul can help us view everyone around us in a different light—as people who need the gentle touch of grace. "As God's chosen people, holy and dearly loved, clothe yourselves with compassion, kindness, humility, gentleness and patience" (COL. 3:12). He also suggests that we "bear with each other and forgive one another" (V. 13).

As we show compassion, we will be pointing others to the One who poured out His heart of grace and compassion on us.

DAVE BRANON

Your compassions never fail, Father. May we mirror Your heart by showing compassion to others.

Compassion is understanding the troubles of others.

His Word the Last Word

Read: Psalm 63:1–11

On my bed I remember you; I think of you through the watches of the night. Because you are my help, I sing in the shadow of your wings.
Psalm 63:6–7

Dawson Trotman, a dynamic Christian leader of the mid-twentieth century and founder of The Navigators, emphasized the importance of the Bible in the life of every Christian. Trotman ended each day with a practice he called "His Word the last word." Before going to sleep he meditated on a memorized Bible verse or passage, then prayed about its place and influence in his life. He wanted the last words he thought about each day to be God's words.

The psalmist David wrote, "On my bed I remember you; I think of you through the watches of the night. Because you are my help, I sing in the shadow of your wings" (PS. 63:6–7). Whether we are in great difficulty or enjoying a time of peace, our last thought at night can ease our minds with the rest and comfort God gives. It may also set the tone for our first thought the next morning.

A friend and his wife conclude each day by reading aloud a Bible passage and daily devotional with their four children. They welcome questions and thoughts from each child and talk about what it means to follow Jesus at home and school. They call it their version of "His Word the last word" for each day.

What better way to end our day! *DAVID MCCASLAND*

Thank You Father, for Your Word in our hearts and our minds—our last thought at night as we rest securely in You.

The Spirit of God renews our minds when we meditate on the Word of God.

Kossi's Courage

Read: 2 Kings 23:12–14, 21–25

You shall have no other gods before me. . . . You shall not bow down to them or worship them. Exodus 20:3, 5

As he awaited his baptism in Togo's Mono River, Kossi stooped to pick up a worn wooden carving. His family had worshiped the object for generations. Now they watched as he tossed the grotesque figure into a fire prepared for the occasion. No longer would their choicest chickens be sacrificed to this god.

In the West, most Christians think of idols as metaphors for what they put in place of God. In Togo, West Africa, idols represent literal gods that must be appeased with sacrifice. Idol burning and baptism make a courageous statement about a new believer's allegiance to the one true God.

As an eight-year-old, King Josiah came to power in an idol-worshiping, sex-obsessed culture. His father and grandfather had been two of the worst kings in all of Judah's sordid history. Then the high priest discovered the book of the law. When the young king heard its words, he took them to heart (2 KINGS 22:8–13). Josiah destroyed the pagan altars, burned the vile items dedicated to the goddess Asherah, and stopped the ritual prostitution (CH. 23). In place of these practices, he celebrated the Passover (23:21–23).

Whenever we look for answers apart from God—consciously or subconsciously—we pursue a false god. It would be wise to ask ourselves: What idols, literal or figurative, do we need to throw on the fire?   *TIM GUSTAFSON*

Lord, forgive us for those things we turn to that show our hearts are not focused on You. Show us what we need to give up, and replace it with the presence of Your Holy Spirit.

Dear children, keep yourselves from idols.
1 JOHN 5:21

What Lasts Forever?

Read: Psalm 102:25–28

You remain the same, and your years will never end. Psalm 102:27

My friend, who had gone through many difficulties recently, wrote, "As I reflect on the past four semesters of student life, so many things have changed. . . . It is scary, really scary. Nothing stays forever."

Indeed, many things can happen in two years—a career change, newfound friendship, illness, death. Good or bad, a life-altering experience may be lurking just around the corner, waiting to pounce! We simply don't know. What great comfort, then, to know that our loving heavenly Father does not change.

The psalmist says, "You remain the same, and your years will never end" (PS. 102:27). The implication of this truth is immense. It means that God is *forever* loving, just, and wise. As Bible teacher Arthur W. Pink so wonderfully states: "Whatever the attributes of God were before the universe was called into existence, they are precisely the same now, and will remain so forever."

In the New Testament, James writes, "Every good and perfect gift is from above, coming down from the Father of the heavenly lights, who does not change like shifting shadows" (JAMES 1:17). In our changing circumstances, we can be assured that our good God will always be consistent to His character. He is the source of everything good, and everything He does is good.

It may seem that nothing lasts forever, but our God will remain consistently good to those who are His own.

POH FANG CHIA

Lord, You are the One who never changes, and You are so good to us. Calm our hearts today with the grace and peace that come only from You.

The One who holds the universe together will not let go of you.

Godliman Street

Read: 1 Samuel 9:1–10

Look, in this town there is a man of God. 1 Samuel 9:6

My wife, Carolyn, and I were walking in London and came across a road named Godliman Street. We were told that a man once lived there whose life was so saintly that his street became known as "that godly man's street." This reminded me of an Old Testament story.

Saul's father sent his son and a servant to look for some donkeys that had wandered away. The young men searched for many days but couldn't find the animals.

Saul was ready to give up and go home, but his servant pointed toward Ramah, the prophet Samuel's village, and replied, "Look, in this town there is a man of God; he is highly respected, and everything he says comes true. Let's go there now. Perhaps he will tell us what way to take" (1 SAM. 9:6).

Throughout his years and into old age, Samuel had sought friendship and fellowship with God, and his words were weighty with truth. People knew him to be a prophet of the Lord. So Saul and his servant "set out for the town where the man of God was" (V. 10).

Oh, that our lives would so reflect Jesus that we would leave a mark on our neighborhoods, and that the memory of our godliness would linger on!   *DAVID ROPER*

I'm not sure, Lord, how my neighbors would describe me. But I want to be close to You and to be a light in my corner of the world.

The most powerful testimony is a godly life.

A Shepherd for Life

Read: Genesis 48:8–16

God . . . has been my shepherd all my life to this day. Genesis 48:15

When my son changed grades in school he cried, "I want my teacher for life!" We had to help him realize that changing teachers is a part of life. We may wonder: Is there any relationship that can last a lifetime?

Jacob, the patriarch, found out there is one. After living through many dramatic changes and losing loved ones along the way, he realized there had been a constant presence in his life. He prayed, "May the God . . . who has been my shepherd all my life to this day . . . bless these boys" (GEN. 48:15–16).

Jacob had been a shepherd, so he compared his relationship to God as that of a shepherd and his sheep. From the time a sheep is born through its growth to old age the shepherd cares for it day and night. He guides it during the day and protects it during the night. David, also a shepherd, had the same conviction, but he highlighted the eternal dimension to it when he said, "I will dwell in the house of the LORD forever" (PS. 23:6).

Changing teachers is a part of life. But how good it is to know that we can have a relationship for life. The Shepherd has promised to be with us every day of our earthly existence (MATT. 28:20). And when life here ends, we will be closer to Him than ever.

KEILA OCHOA

Father, I thank You for being the Shepherd of my life. I praise Your faithfulness.

God never abandons us.

Sweet Scent

Read: 2 Corinthians 2:14–16

Thanks be to God, who . . . uses us to spread the aroma of the knowledge of him everywhere. 2 Corinthians 2:14

Author Rita Snowden tells a delightful story about visiting a small village in Dover, England. Sitting outside a café one afternoon enjoying a cup of tea, she became aware of a beautiful scent. Rita asked a waiter where it was coming from, and was told it was the people she could see passing by. Most of the villagers were employed at a nearby perfume factory. As they walked home, they carried the fragrance that permeated their clothes out into the street.

What a beautiful image of the Christian life! As the apostle Paul says, we are the aroma of Christ, spreading His fragrance everywhere (2 COR. 2:15). Paul uses the image of a king returning from battle, his soldiers and captives in tow, wafting the smell of celebratory incense in the air, declaring the king's greatness (V. 14).

We spread the aroma of Christ in two ways. First, through our words: telling others about the One who is beautiful. Second, through our lives: doing deeds of Christlike sacrifice (EPH. 5:1–2). While not everyone will appreciate the divine fragrance we share, it will bring life to many.

Rita Snowden caught a scent and was driven to seek its source. As we follow Jesus we too become permeated with His fragrance, and we carry His aroma into the streets through our words and deeds.   SHERIDAN VOYSEY

Lord Jesus, make us carriers and communicators of Your beauty to the people in our homes, offices, and neighborhoods.

We are the aroma of Christ to others.

Our Best Friend

Read: Hebrews 10:19–23

Yet to all who did receive him, to those who believed in his name, he gave the right to become children of God. John 1:12

When I was twelve years old our family moved to a town in the desert. After gym classes in the hot air at my new school, we rushed for the drinking fountain. Being skinny and young for my grade, I sometimes got pushed out of the way while waiting in line. One day my friend Jose, who was big and strong for his age, saw this happening. He stepped in and stuck out a strong arm to clear my way. "Hey!" he exclaimed, "You let Banks get a drink first!" I never had trouble at the drinking fountain again.

Jesus understood what it was like to face the ultimate unkindness of others. The Bible tells us, "He was despised and rejected by mankind" (ISA. 53:3). But Jesus was not just a victim of suffering, He also became our advocate. By giving His life, Jesus opened a "new and living way" for us to enter into a relationship with God (HEB. 10:20). He did for us what we could never do for ourselves, offering us the free gift of salvation when we repent of our sins and trust in Him.

Jesus is the best friend we could ever have. He said, "Whoever comes to me I will never drive away" (JOHN 6:37). Others may hold us at arm's length or even push us away, but God has opened His arms to us through the cross. How strong is our Savior!

JAMES BANKS

Love's redeeming work is done, fought the fight, the battle won. Death in vain forbids him rise; Christ has opened paradise.
CHARLES WESLEY

God's free gift to us cost Him dearly.

Why Forgive?

Read: Luke 23:32–34

Jesus said, "Father, forgive them, for they do not know what they are doing." And they divided up his clothes by casting lots. Luke 23:34

When a friend betrayed me, I knew I would need to forgive her, but I wasn't sure that I could. Her words pierced deeply inside me, and I felt stunned with pain and anger. Although we talked about it and I told her I forgave her, for a long time whenever I'd see her I felt tinges of hurt, so I knew I still clung to some resentment. One day, however, God answered my prayers and gave me the ability to let go completely. I was finally free.

Forgiveness lies at the heart of the Christian faith, with our Savior extending forgiveness even when He was dying on the cross. Jesus loved those who had nailed Him there, uttering a prayer asking His Father to forgive them. He didn't hang on to bitterness or anger, but showed grace and love to those who had wronged Him.

This is a fitting time to consider before the Lord any people we might need to forgive as we follow Jesus's example in extending His love to those who hurt us. When we ask God through His Spirit to help us forgive, He will come to our aid—even if we take what we think is a long time to forgive. When we do, we are freed from the prison of unforgiveness.   *AMY BOUCHER PYE*

Lord Jesus Christ, through Your grace and power as You dwell in me, help me to forgive, that Your love will set me free.

Even on the cross, Jesus forgave those who hurt Him.

At Home with Jesus

Read: John 14:1–4

I go and prepare a place for you. John 14:3

"There's no place like home." The phrase reflects a deeply rooted yearning within us to have a place to rest, be, and belong. Jesus addressed this desire for rootedness when, after He and His friends had their last supper together, He spoke about His impending death and resurrection. He promised that although He would go away, He would come back for them. And He would prepare a room for them. A dwelling-place. A home.

He made this place for them—and us—through fulfilling the requirements of God's law when He died on the cross as the sinless man. He assured His disciples that if He went to the trouble of creating this home, that of course He would come back for them and not leave them alone. They didn't need to fear or be worried about their lives, whether on earth or in heaven.

We can take comfort and assurance from Jesus's words, for we believe and trust that He makes a home for us; that He makes His home within us (SEE JOHN 14:23); and that He has gone ahead of us to prepare our heavenly home. Whatever sort of physical place we live in, we belong with Jesus, upheld by His love and surrounded in His peace. With Him, there's no place like home.

AMY BOUCHER PYE

Lord Jesus Christ, if and when we feel homeless, remind us that You are our home. May we share this sense of belonging with those we meet.

Jesus prepares a place for us to live forever.

Enjoy the View

Read: Psalm 148:1–6

Praise him, sun and moon; praise him, all you shining stars.
Psalm 148:3

Sunsets. People tend to stop what they are doing to watch them . . . snap pictures of them . . . enjoy the beautiful view.

My wife and I watched the sun setting over the Gulf of Mexico recently. A crowd of people surrounded us, mostly strangers who had gathered at the beach to watch this nightly phenomenon. At the moment the sun fully slipped below the horizon, the crowd broke out with applause.

Why do people respond like that? The book of Psalms offers a clue. The psalmist wrote of God ordering the sun to praise its Creator (PS. 148:3). And wherever the rays of the sun shine across the earth, people are moved to praise along with them.

The beauty that comes to us through nature speaks to our souls like few things do. It not only has the capacity to stop us in our tracks and captivate our attention, it also has the power to turn our focus to the Maker of beauty itself.

The wonder of God's vast creation can cause us to pause and remember what's truly important. Ultimately, it reminds us that there is a Creator behind the stunning entrance and exit of the day, One who so loved the world He made that He entered it in order to redeem and restore it.   *JEFF OLSON*

I enjoy the world You have created with its variety and color. You and what You
have made are awesome, Lord!

Join God in taking delight in all that He has made.

A Journey of Belief

Read: John 20:24–31

These are written that you may believe that Jesus is the Messiah, the Son of God, and that by believing you may have life in his name. John 20:31

Since its first publication in 1880, Lew Wallace's novel *Ben-Hur: A Tale of the Christ* has never been out of print. It has been called the most influential Christian book of the nineteenth century, and it continues to draw readers today as it weaves the true story of Jesus with that of a fictional young Jewish nobleman named Judah Ben-Hur.

Amy Lifson, writing in *Humanities* magazine, said that the writing of the book transformed the life of the author. "As Ben-Hur guided readers through the scenes of the Passion, so did he lead the way for Lew Wallace to believe in Jesus Christ." Wallace said, "I have seen the Nazarene. . . . I saw him perform works which no mere man could perform."

The Gospels' record of the life of Jesus allows us to walk alongside Him, witness His miracles, hear His words, and see His triumphal entry into Jerusalem on what we call Palm Sunday. At the conclusion of John's gospel, he wrote, "Jesus performed many other signs in the presence of his disciples, which are not recorded in this book. But these are written that you may believe that Jesus is the Messiah, the Son of God, and that by believing you may have life in his name" (JOHN 20:30–31).

Just as Lew Wallace's research, reading of the Bible, and writing led him to believe in Jesus, so God's Word draws us to a transformation of mind and heart by which we have eternal life in and through Him.   *DAVID MCCASLAND*

Lord, may the record of Your life be written on our minds and hearts so that we may have ever-increasing faith in You.

Many books can inform, but only the Bible can transform.

Letting Go

Read: Genesis 12:1–9

The Lord had said to Abram, "Go . . . to the land I will show you."
Genesis 12:1

For our wedding anniversary, my husband borrowed a tandem bike so we could enjoy a romantic adventure together. As we began to pedal on our way, I quickly realized that as the rider on the back my vision of the road ahead was eclipsed by my husband's broad shoulders. Also, my handlebars were fixed; they didn't affect the steering of our bike. Only the front handlebars determined our direction; mine served merely as support for my upper body. I had the choice to either be frustrated by my lack of control or to embrace the journey and trust Mike would guide us safely on our route.

When God asked Abram to leave his homeland and family, He didn't offer much information concerning the destination. No geographic coordinates. No description of the new land or its natural resources. Not even an indication of how long it would take to get there. God simply gave the instruction to "go" to the land He would show him. Abram's obedience to God's instruction, despite lacking the details most humans crave, is credited to him as faith (HEB. 11:8).

If we find ourselves grappling with uncertainty or a lack of control in our lives, let's seek to adopt Abram's example of following and trusting God. The Lord will steer us well.

KIRSTEN HOLMBERG

Help me, Lord, to trust You with the uncertainty in my life.

God can be trusted to guide us.

The Gift of Giving

Read: Luke 3:7–14

Each of you should give what you have decided in your heart to give, not reluctantly or under compulsion. 2 Corinthians 9:7

A pastor breathed life into the phrase "He'd give you the shirt off his back" when he gave this unsettling challenge to his church: "What would happen if we took the coats off our backs and gave them to the needy?" Then he took his own coat and laid it at the front of the church. Dozens of others followed his example. This was during the winter, so the trip home was less comfortable that day. But for dozens of people in need, the season warmed up just a bit.

When John the Baptist roamed the Judean wilderness, he had a stern warning for the crowd that came to hear him. "You brood of vipers!" he said. "Produce fruit in keeping with repentance" (LUKE 3:7–8). Startled, they asked him, "What should we do then?" He responded with this advice: "Anyone who has two shirts should share with the one who has none, and anyone who has food should do the same" (VV. 10–11). True repentance produces a generous heart.

Because "God loves a person who gives cheerfully" (NLT), giving should never be guilt-based or pressured (2 COR. 9:7). But when we give freely and generously, we find that it truly is more blessed to give than to receive. *TIM GUSTAFSON*

Lord, thank You for the many ways You bless us. Forgive us for so often taking Your goodness for granted. Show us what we have that we might use to bless someone else today.

Whoever refreshes others will be refreshed.
PROVERBS 11:25

Let Down Your Hair

Read: John 12:1–8

Mary took about a pint of pure nard, an expensive perfume; she poured it on Jesus' feet and wiped his feet with her hair. John 12:3

Shortly before Jesus was crucified, a woman named Mary poured a bottle of expensive perfume on His feet. Then, in what may have been an even more daring act, she wiped His feet with her hair (JOHN 12:3). Not only did Mary sacrifice what may have been her life's savings, she also sacrificed her reputation. In first-century Middle Eastern culture, respectable women never let down their hair in public. But true worship is not concerned about what others think of us (2 SAM. 6:21–22). To worship Jesus, Mary was willing to be thought of as immodest, perhaps even immoral.

Some of us may feel pressured to be perfect when we go to church so that people will think well of us. Metaphorically speaking, we work hard to make sure we have every hair in place. But a healthy church is a place where we can let down our hair and not hide our flaws behind a façade of perfection. In church, we should be able to reveal our weaknesses to find strength rather than conceal our faults to appear strong.

Worship doesn't involve behaving as if nothing is wrong; it's making sure everything is right—right with God and with one another. When our greatest fear is letting down our hair, perhaps our greatest sin is keeping it up. *JULIE ACKERMAN LINK*

Search me, God, and know my heart. . . . See if there is any offensive way in me and lead me in the way everlasting.
PSALM 139:23–24

Our worship is right when we are right with God.

Forsaken for Our Sake

Read: Matthew 26:36–46

God has said, "Never will I leave you; never will I forsake you."
Hebrews 13:5

Does having a friend nearby make pain more bearable? Researchers at the University of Virginia conducted a fascinating study to answer that question. They wanted to see how the brain reacted to the prospect of pain, and whether it behaved differently if a person faced the threat of pain alone, holding a stranger's hand, or holding the hand of a close friend.

Researchers ran the test on dozens of pairs, and found consistent results. When a person was alone or holding a stranger's hand while anticipating a shock, the regions of the brain that process danger lit up. But when holding the hand of a trusted person, the brain relaxed. The comfort of a friend's presence made the pain seem more bearable.

Jesus needed comfort as He prayed in the Garden of Gethsemane. He knew what He was about to face: betrayal, arrest, and death. He asked His closest friends to stay and pray with Him, telling them that His soul was "overwhelmed with sorrow" (MATT. 26:38). But Peter, James, and John kept falling asleep.

Jesus faced the agony of the garden without the comfort of a hand to hold. But because He bore that pain, we can be confident that God will never leave or forsake us (HEB. 13:5). Jesus suffered so that we will never have to experience separation from the love of God (ROM. 8:39). His companionship makes anything we endure more bearable.

AMY PETERSON

Jesus, thank You for bearing the pain and isolation of the Garden of Gethsemane and the cross for us. Thank You for giving us a way to live in communion with the Father.

Because of God's love, we are never truly alone.

Remember the Cross

Read: Mark 15:19–20, 33–39

Surely this man was the Son of God! Mark 15:39

In the church I attend, a large cross stands at the front of the sanctuary. It represents the original cross where Jesus died—the place where our sin intersected with His holiness. There God allowed His perfect Son to die for the sake of every wrong thing we have ever done, said, or thought. On the cross, Jesus finished the work that was required to save us from the death we deserve (ROM. 6:23).

The sight of a cross causes me to consider what Jesus endured for us. Before being crucified, He was flogged and spit on. The soldiers hit Him in the head with sticks and got down on their knees in mock worship. They tried to make Him carry His own cross to the place where He would die, but He was too weak from the brutal flogging. At Golgotha, they hammered nails through His flesh to keep Him on the cross when they turned it upright. Those wounds bore the weight of His body as He hung there. Six hours later, Jesus took His final breath (MARK 15:37). A centurion who witnessed Jesus's death declared, "Surely this man was the Son of God!" (V. 39).

The next time you see the symbol of the cross, consider what it means to you. God's Son suffered and died there and then rose again to make eternal life possible. *JENNIFER BENSON SCHULDT*

Dear Jesus, I can't begin to thank You enough for taking care of my sin when You died on the cross. I acknowledge Your sacrifice, and I believe in the power of Your resurrection.

The cross of Christ reveals our sin at its worst and God's love at its best.

The Price of Love

Read: Isaiah 53:9–12

He poured out his life unto death. Isaiah 53:12

Our daughter burst into tears as we waved goodbye to my parents. After visiting us in England, they were starting their long journey back to their home in the US. "I don't want them to go," she said. As I comforted her, my husband remarked, "I'm afraid that's the price of love."

We might feel the pain of being separated from loved ones, but Jesus felt the ultimate separation when He paid the price of love on the cross. He, who was both human and God, fulfilled Isaiah's prophecy 700 years after Isaiah gave it when He "bore the sin of many" (ISA. 53:12). In this chapter we see rich pointers to Jesus being the suffering Servant, such as when He was "pierced for our transgressions" (V. 5), which happened when He was nailed to the cross and when one of the soldiers pierced His side (JOHN 19:34), and that "by his wounds we are healed" (ISA. 53:5).

Because of love, Jesus came to earth and was born a baby. Because of love, He received the abuse of the teachers of the law, the crowds, and the soldiers. Because of love, He suffered and died to be the perfect sacrifice, standing in our place before the Father. We live because of love.   *AMY BOUCHER PYE*

Lord Jesus Christ, the Lamb of God who takes away our sins, have mercy on us, and help us to extend mercy and love to others. Show us how we might share Your love with others today.

Jesus was the perfect sacrifice who died to give us life.

He Understands and Cares

Read: Isaiah 53:1–8

Surely he took up our pain and bore our suffering. Isaiah 53:4

When asked if he thought that ignorance and apathy were problems in modern society, a man joked, "I don't know and I don't care."

I suppose many discouraged people feel that way about the world today and the people in it. But when it comes to the perplexities and concerns of our lives, Jesus fully understands, and He deeply cares. Isaiah 53, an Old Testament prophecy of the crucifixion of Jesus, gives us a glimpse of what He went through for us. "He was oppressed and afflicted . . . led like a lamb to the slaughter" (V. 7). "For the transgression of my people he was punished" (V. 8). "It was the LORD's will to crush him and cause him to suffer, and though the LORD makes his life an offering for sin, he will see his offspring and prolong his days, and the will of the LORD will prosper in his hand" (V. 10).

On the cross Jesus willingly bore our sin and guilt. No one ever suffered more than our Lord did for us. He knew what it would cost to save us from our sins and, in love, He willingly paid it (VV. 4–6).

Because of Jesus's resurrection from the dead, He is alive and present with us today. Whatever situation we face, Jesus understands and cares. And He will carry us through.

DAVID MCCASLAND

Lord, we give thanks for Your knowledge of our circumstances and Your care for us. Today we want to walk with You and honor You in all we do.

He is not here; He has risen!
LUKE 24:6

Always Listening

Read: Nehemiah 2:1–9

The LORD is near to all who call on him, to all who call on him in truth.
Psalm 145:18

Dad was a man of few words. He had hearing damage due to years of military duty and wore hearing aids. One afternoon when Mom and I were talking a little longer than he thought necessary, he responded playfully, "Whenever I want peace and quiet, all I have to do is this." Lifting both hands in a single motion, he turned off both hearing aids, folded his hands behind his head and closed his eyes in a serene smile.

We laughed. As far as he was concerned, the conversation was over!

My father's actions that day remind me how different God is from us. He always wants to hear His children. This is underscored by one of the shortest prayers in the Bible. One day Nehemiah, a servant to King Artaxerxes of Persia, was visibly sad in the king's presence. Fearful when the king asked him why, Nehemiah confessed it was because Jerusalem, the conquered city of his ancestors, lay in ruins. Nehemiah recounts, "The king said to me, 'What is it you want?' *Then I prayed to the God of heaven*, and I answered the king..." (NEH. 2:4–5, ITALICS ADDED).

Nehemiah's prayer lasted only a moment, but God heard it. It set in motion God's merciful response to the many prayers Nehemiah had already offered for Jerusalem. In that moment, Artaxerxes granted Nehemiah's request to rebuild the city.

Isn't it comforting to know that God cares enough to listen to all of our prayers—from the shortest to the longest?   *JAMES BANKS*

Thank You, loving Father, for blessing me with the beautiful privilege and
opportunity of prayer.

Our God is big enough to hear the smallest voice.

The Shrinking Piano

Read: Philippians 1:1–11

He who began a good work in you will carry it on to completion until the day of Christ Jesus. Philippians 1:6

For three consecutive years, my son participated in a piano recital. The last year he played, I watched him mount the steps and set up his music. He played two songs and then sat down next to me and whispered, "Mom, this year the piano was smaller." I said, "No, it's the same piano you played last year. You're bigger! You've grown."

Spiritual growth, like physical growth, often happens slowly over time. It is an ongoing process that involves becoming more like Jesus, and it happens as we are transformed through the renewing of our minds (ROM. 12:2).

When the Holy Spirit is at work in us, we may become aware of sin in our lives. Wanting to honor God, we make an effort to change. Sometimes we experience success, but at other times, we try and fail. If it seems like nothing changes, we get discouraged. We may equate failure with a lack of progress, when it's often proof that we are in the middle of the process.

Spiritual growth involves the Holy Spirit, our willingness to change, and time. At certain points in our lives, we may look back and see that we have grown spiritually. May God give us the faith to continue to believe that "He who began a good work in [us] will carry it on to completion until the day of Christ Jesus" (PHIL. 1:6).

JENNIFER BENSON SCHULDT

Dear God, give me a desire to grow spiritually. I want to honor You with my life and experience the joy of the Spirit's work inside of me.

Spiritual growth is a process.

The Small Things

Read: Psalm 116:1–9

Every good and perfect gift is from above. James 1:17

My friend Gloria called with excitement in her voice. She had not been able to leave her home except for doctors' appointments. So I understood why she was so happy to tell me, "My son just attached new speakers to my computer, so now I can go to my church!" Now she could hear the live broadcast of her church's worship service. She raved about God's goodness and the "best gift my son could have given me!"

Gloria teaches me about having a thankful heart. Despite her many limitations, she's thankful for the smallest of things—sunsets, helpful family and neighbors, quiet moments with God, the ability to remain in her own apartment. She's had a lifetime of seeing God provide for her, and she talks about Him to anyone who visits or calls.

We don't know what difficulties the author of Psalm 116 was encountering. Some Bible commentaries say it was probably sickness because he said, "the cords of death entangled me" (V. 3). But he gave thanks to the Lord for being gracious and full of compassion when he was "brought low" (VV. 5–6).

When we're low, it can be hard to look up. Yet if we do, we see that God is the giver of all good gifts in our life—great and small—and we learn to give Him thanks.　　　*ANNE CETAS*

What shall I render to the LORD for all his benefits to me? . . . I will offer to you the sacrifice of thanksgiving.
PS. 116:12, 17 ESV

Praise to God comes naturally when you count your blessings.

Don't Give Up

Read: Galatians 6:1–10

Let us not become weary in doing good, for at the proper time we will reap a harvest if we do not give up. Galatians 6:9

Bob Foster, my mentor and friend for more than fifty years, never gave up on me. His unchanging friendship and encouragement, even during my darkest times, helped carry me through.

We often find ourselves determined to reach out and help someone we know who is in great need. But when we fail to see improvement right away, our resolve can weaken and we may eventually give up. We discover that what we hoped would be an immediate change has become an ongoing process.

The apostle Paul urges us to be patient in helping one another through the stumbles and struggles of life. When he writes, "Carry each other's burdens" and so "fulfill the law of Christ" (GAL. 6:2), he is comparing our task to the work, time, and waiting it takes for a farmer to see a harvest.

How long should we keep praying and reaching out to those we love? "Let us not become weary in doing good, for at the proper time we will reap a harvest if we do not give up" (V. 9). How many times should we reach out? "As we have opportunity, let us do good to all people, especially to those who belong to the family of believers" (V. 10).

The Lord encourages us today to trust Him, to remain faithful to others, to keep on praying, and to not give up!

DAVID MCCASLAND

Father in heaven, we ask for hope and perseverance to continue reaching out to others.

In prayer we call on God "who is able to do immeasurably more than all we ask or imagine."
EPHESIANS 3:20

Someone to Touch

Read: Luke 5:12–16

Jesus reached out his hand and touched the man. Luke 5:13

Commuters on a Canadian Metro train witnessed a heart-moving conclusion to a tense moment. They watched as a 70-year old woman gently reached out and offered her hand to a young man whose loud voice and disturbing words were scaring other passengers. The lady's kindness calmed the man who sank to the floor of the train with tears in his eyes. He said, "Thanks, Grandma," stood up, and walked away. The woman later admitted to being afraid. But she said, "I'm a mother and he needed someone to touch." While better judgment might have given her reason to keep her distance, she took a risk of love.

Jesus understands such compassion. He didn't side with the fears of unnerved onlookers when a desperate man, full of leprosy, showed up begging to be healed. Neither was He helpless as other religious leaders were—men who could only have condemned the man for bringing his leprosy into the village (LEV. 13:45–46). Instead, Jesus reached out to someone who probably hadn't been touched by anyone for years, and healed him.

Thankfully, for that man and for us, Jesus came to offer what no law could ever offer—the touch of His hand and heart.

MART DEHAAN

Father in heaven, please help us to see ourselves and one another in that desperate man—and in the merciful eyes of Your Son who reached out and touched him.

No one is too troubled or unclean to be touched by Jesus.

Learning the Language

Read: Acts 17:22–32

As I walked around and looked carefully at your objects of worship, I even found an altar with this inscription: TO AN UNKNOWN GOD. Acts 17:23

I stood before the gathering at a small Jamaican church and said in my best local dialect, "Wah Gwan, Jamaica?" The reaction was better than I expected, as smiles and applause greeted me.

In reality, all I had said was the standard greeting, "What's going on?" in Patois [pa-twa], but to their ears I was saying, "I care enough to speak your language." Of course I did not yet know enough Patois to continue, but a door had been opened.

When the apostle Paul stood before the people of Athens, he let them know that he knew their culture. He told them that he had noticed their altar to "an unknown god," and he quoted one of their poets. Of course, not everyone believed Paul's message about Jesus's resurrection, but some said, "We want to hear you again on this subject" (ACTS 17:32).

As we interact with others about Jesus and the salvation He offers, the lessons of Scripture show us to invest ourselves in others—to learn their language, as it were—as a way to open the door to telling them the good news (see also 1 Cor. 9:20–23).

As we find out "Wah Gwan?" in others' lives, it will be easier to share what God has done in ours.   *DAVE BRANON*

Show us, Lord, what is important to others. Help us to think of their interests first, and allow opportunities to speak about the love of Jesus.

**Before you tell others about Christ, let them see
how much you care.**

An Alternative to Anger

Read: Proverbs 20:1–15

It is to one's honor to avoid strife. Proverbs 20:3

One morning in Perth, Australia, Fionn Mulholland discovered his car was missing. That's when he realized he had mistakenly parked in a restricted zone and his car had been towed away. After considering the situation—even the $600 towing and parking fine—Mulholland was frustrated, but he decided not to be angry with the person he would work with to retrieve his car. Instead of venting his feelings, Mulholland wrote a humorous poem about the situation and read it to the worker he met at the tow yard. The worker liked the poem, and a possible ugly confrontation never took place.

The book of Proverbs teaches, "It is to one's honor to avoid strife" (20:3). Strife is that friction that either simmers under the surface or explodes in the open between people who disagree about something.

God has given us the resources to live peacefully with other people. His *Word* assures us that it's possible to feel anger without letting it boil over into rage (EPH. 4:26). His *Spirit* enables us to override the sparks of fury that prompt us to do and say things to strike out at people who upset us. And God has given us His *example* to follow when we feel provoked (1 PETER 2:23). He is compassionate, gracious, and slow to anger, abounding in love and faithfulness (PS. 86:15).   *JENNIFER BENSON SCHULDT*

Dear God, please help me to manage my anger in a way that does not lead me into sin. Give me self-control through the power of Your Holy Spirit.

Be slow to anger.

When Morning Comes

Read: Hebrews 11:1–8

Now faith is confidence in what we hope for and assurance about what we do not see. Hebrews 11:1

It was very late when we stopped for the night at a country inn outside of Munich. We were delighted to see that our cozy room had a balcony, although an oppressive fog made it impossible to see into the darkness. But when the sun rose a few hours later, the haze began to fade. Then we could see what had been grimly shrouded the night before—a completely idyllic scene—peaceful and lush green meadow, sheep grazing with tiny tinkling bells about their necks, and big white clouds in the sky that looked exactly like more sheep—*huge*, fluffy sheep!

Sometimes life can get clouded over by a heavy fog of despair. Our situation may look so dark that we begin to lose hope. But just as the sun burns away a fog, our faith in God can burn away the haze of doubt. Hebrews 11 defines faith as "confidence in what we hope for and assurance about what we do not see" (V. 1). The passage goes on to remind us of the faith of Noah, who was "warned about things not yet seen," yet obeyed God (V. 7). And Abraham who went where God directed—even though he didn't know where that would be (V. 8).

Though we have not seen Him and cannot always feel His presence, God is always present and will help us through our darkest nights. *CINDY HESS KASPER*

Father, thank You for Your promise to walk with us through all of life. In moments of doubt, help us to have the confidence You are in control and we can trust You.

Faith is the radar that sees through the fog.
CORRIE TEN BOOM

Forever Loved

Read: Psalm 4:1–8

Know that the Lord has set apart his faithful servant for himself.
Psalm 4:3

It's almost impossible for us to get through a day without being snubbed, ignored, or put down in some way. Sometimes we even do it to ourselves.

David's enemies were talking smack—bullying, threatening, pummeling him with insults. His sense of self-worth and well-being had plummeted (PS. 4:1-2). He asked for relief "from my distress."

Then David remembered, "Know that the Lord has set apart his faithful servant for himself" (V. 3). Various English versions try to capture the full essence of David's bold statement by translating "faithful servant" as "godly." The Hebrew word here, *hesed*, literally refers to God's covenant love and might well be rendered "those whom God will love forever and ever and ever."

Here's what we too must remember: We are loved *forever*, set apart in a special way, as dear to God as His own Son. He has called us to be His children for all eternity.

Instead of despairing, we can remind ourselves of the love we freely receive from our Father. We are His dearly beloved children. The end is not despair but peace and joy (VV. 7-8). He never gives up on us, and He never ever stops loving us.

DAVID ROPER

Father in heaven, the words of others can wound us deeply. Your words to us heal and comfort, and You assure us that we are loved forever.

The true measure of God's love is that He loves without measure.
BERNARD OF CLAIRVAUX

Questions for God

Read: Judges 6:11–16, 24

Go with the strength you have. . . . I will be with you.
Judges 6:14, 16 NLT

What would you do if the Lord showed up in the middle of your workday with a message? This happened to Gideon, one of the ancient Israelites. "The angel of the LORD appeared to him and said, 'Mighty hero, the LORD is with you!'" Gideon could have responded with a wordless nod and gulp, but instead he said, "If the LORD is with us, why has all this happened to us?" (JUDG. 6:12–13 NLT). Gideon wanted to know why it seemed as if God had abandoned His people.

God didn't answer that question. After Gideon had endured seven years of enemy attacks, starvation, and hiding in caves, God didn't explain why He never intervened. God could have revealed Israel's past sin as the reason, but instead He gave Gideon hope for the future. God said, "Go with the strength you have . . . . I will be with you. And you will destroy the Midianites" (VV. 14, 16 NLT).

Do you ever wonder why God has allowed suffering in your life? Instead of answering that specific question, God may satisfy you with His nearness today and remind you that you can rely on His strength when you feel weak. When Gideon finally believed that God was with him and would help him, he built an altar and called it "The LORD Is Peace" (V. 24).

There is peace in knowing that whatever we do and wherever we go, we go with God who promised never to leave or forsake His followers. *JENNIFER BENSON SCHULDT*

What could be better than getting answers to our why questions? Trusting a good and powerful God.

Just a Touch

Read: Matthew 8:1–4

Jesus reached out his hand and touched the man. Matthew 8:3

Kiley leaped at the chance to go to a remote area of East Africa to assist a medical mission, yet she felt uneasy. She didn't have any medical experience. Still, she could provide basic care.

While there, she met a woman with a horrible but treatable disease. The woman's distorted leg repulsed her, but Kiley knew she had to do something. As she cleaned and bandaged the leg, her patient began crying. Concerned, Kiley asked if she was hurting her. "No," she replied. "It's the first time anyone has touched me in nine years."

Leprosy is another disease that can render its victims repulsive to others, and ancient Jewish culture had strict guidelines to prevent its spread: "They must live alone," the law declared. "They must live outside the camp" (LEV. 13:46).

That's why it's so remarkable that a leper approached Jesus to say, "Lord, if you are willing, you can make me clean" (MATT. 8:2). "Jesus reached out his hand and touched the man. 'I am willing,' he said. 'Be clean!'" (V. 3).

In touching a lonely woman's diseased leg, Kiley began to show the fearless, bridge-building love of Jesus. A single touch made a difference.   *TIM GUSTAFSON*

Lord, we want to show the fearless love You showed when
You walked this earth.

What difference might we make if we overcome our fears and trust God to use us?

Alone in Space

Read: Genesis 28:10–17

Surely the LORD is in this place, and I was not aware of it. Genesis 28:16

A pollo 15 astronaut Al Worden knew what it felt like to be on the far side of the moon. For three days back in 1971, he flew alone in his command module, *Endeavor,* while two crewmates worked thousands of miles below on the surface of the moon. His only companions were the stars overhead that he remembers as being so thick they seemed to wrap him in a sheet of light.

As the sun went down on the Old Testament character Jacob's first night away from home, he too was profoundly alone, but for a different reason. He was on the run from his older brother—who wanted to kill him for stealing the family blessing normally given to the firstborn son. Yet on falling asleep, Jacob had a dream of a staircase joining heaven and earth. As he watched angels ascending and descending, he heard the voice of God promising to be with him and to bless the whole earth through his children. When Jacob woke he said, "Surely the LORD is in this place, and I was not aware of it" (GEN. 28:16).

Jacob had isolated himself because of his deceit. Yet as real as his failures, and as dark as the night, he was in the presence of the One whose plans are always better and more far-reaching than our own. Heaven is closer than we think, and the "God of Jacob" is with us.   *MART DEHAAN*

Father, thank You for using the story of Jacob to show us that the glory of Your unseen presence and goodness is far greater than we could imagine.

God is nearer than we think.

Five-Minute Rule

Read: Psalm 102:1–17

He will respond to the prayer of the destitute; he will not despise their plea. Psalm 102:17

I read about a five-minute rule that a mother had for her children. They had to be ready for school and gather together five minutes before it was time to leave each day.

They would gather around Mom, and she would pray for each one by name, asking for the Lord's blessing on their day. Then she'd give them a kiss and off they'd run. Even neighborhood kids would be included in the prayer circle if they happened to stop by. One of the children said many years later that she learned from this experience how crucial prayer is to her day.

The writer of Psalm 102 knew the importance of prayer. This psalm is labeled, "A prayer of an afflicted person who has grown weak and pours out a lament before the LORD." He cried out, "Hear my prayer, LORD; . . . when I call, answer me quickly" (V V. 1–2). God looks down "from his sanctuary on high, from heaven he [views] the earth" (V. 19).

God cares for you and wants to hear from you. Whether you follow the five-minute rule asking for blessings on the day, or need to spend more time crying out to Him in deep distress, talk to the Lord each day. Your example may have a big impact on your family or someone close to you.   *ANNE CETAS*

Teach me to be aware of Your presence, Lord, and to talk to You freely and often.

Prayer is an acknowledgment of our need for God.

The Ministry of Memory

Read: Jeremiah 29:4–14

"For I know the plans I have for you," declares the LORD, "plans to prosper you and not to harm you, plans to give you hope and a future."
Jeremiah 29:11

Our experiences of loss and disappointment may leave us feeling angry, guilty, and confused. Whether our choices have closed some doors that will never reopen or, through no fault of our own, tragedy has invaded our lives, the result is often what Oswald Chambers called "the unfathomable sadness of 'the might have been.'" We may try to suppress the painful memory, but discover we can't.

Chambers reminds us that the Lord is still active in our lives. "Never be afraid when God brings back the past," he said. "Let memory have its way. It is a minister of God with its rebuke and chastisement and sorrow. God will turn the 'might have been' into a wonderful [place of growth] for the future."

In Old Testament days when God sent the people of Israel into exile in Babylon, He told them to serve Him in that foreign land and grow in faith until He brought them back to their home. "'For I know the plans I have for you,' declares the LORD, 'plans to prosper you and not to harm you, plans to give you hope and a future'" (JER. 29:11).

God urged them not to ignore or be trapped by events of the past but instead to focus on Him and look ahead. The Lord's forgiveness can transform the memory of our sorrow into confidence in His everlasting love.   *DAVID MCCASLAND*

*Father, thank You for Your plans for us, and for the future that awaits us
in Your love.*

**God can use our deepest disappointments to
nurture our faith in Him.**

Should I Forgive?

Read: Matthew 18:23–35

Forgive as the Lord forgave you. Colossians 3:13

I arrived early at my church to help set up for an event. A woman stood crying at the opposite end of the sanctuary. She'd been cruel and gossiped about me in the past, so I quickly drowned out her sobs with a vacuum cleaner. Why should I care about someone who didn't like me?

When the Holy Spirit reminded me how much God had forgiven me, I crossed the room. The woman shared that her baby had been in the hospital for months. We cried, embraced, and prayed for her daughter. After working through our differences, we're now good friends.

In Matthew 18, Jesus compares the kingdom of heaven to a king who decided to settle his accounts. A servant who owed a staggering amount of money pleaded for mercy. Soon after the king canceled his debt, that servant tracked down and condemned a man who owed him far less than what he'd owed the king. When word got back to the king, the wicked servant was imprisoned because of his own unforgiving spirit (VV. 23–34).

Choosing to forgive doesn't condone sin, excuse the wrongs done to us, or minimize our hurts. Offering forgiveness simply frees us to enjoy God's undeserved gift of mercy, as we invite Him to accomplish beautiful works of peace-restoring grace in our lives and our relationships. *XOCHITL DIXON*

Lord, help us give our grievances to You so that You may turn them into something good. Make us ready to forgive completely and earnestly. Give us Your spirit of unity.

Forgiving others expresses our trust in God's right to judge according to His perfection and goodness.

Praise in the Dark

Read: Matthew 26:17–30

Through Jesus, therefore, let us continually offer to God a sacrifice of praise—the fruit of lips that openly profess his name. Hebrews 13:15

Even though my friend Mickey was losing his eyesight, he told me, "I'm going to keep praising God every day, because He's done so much for me."

Jesus gave Mickey, and us, the ultimate reason for such never-ending praise. The twenty-sixth chapter of Matthew tells us about how Jesus shared the Passover meal with His disciples the night before He went to the cross. Verse 30 shows us how they concluded the meal: "When they had sung a hymn, they went out to the Mount of Olives."

It wasn't just any hymn they sang that night—it was a hymn of praise. For millennia, Jews have sung a group of Psalms called "The Hallel" at Passover (*hallel* is the Hebrew word for "praise"). The last of these prayers and songs of praise, found in Psalms 113–118, honors the God who has become our salvation (118:21). It refers to a rejected stone that became a cornerstone (V. 22) and one who comes in the name of the Lord (V. 26). They may very well have sung, "The LORD has done it this very day; let us rejoice today and be glad" (V. 24).

As Jesus sang with His disciples on this Passover night, He was giving us the ultimate reason to lift our eyes above our immediate circumstances. He was leading us in praise of the never-ending love and faithfulness of our God. *JAMES BANKS*

You are always worthy of praise, Lord, even when I don't feel like praising You! Help me to learn to praise You more and more.

Praising God helps us recall His goodness that never ends.

The Burden of Waiting

Read: Psalm 90

Teach us to number our days, that we may gain a heart of wisdom.
Psalm 90:12

Over the last few years, two members of my family have faced life-threatening diagnoses. For me, the hardest part of supporting them through their treatments has been the constant uncertainty. I am always desperate for a definitive word from a doctor, but things are rarely that straightforward. Instead of being given clarity, we are often asked to wait.

It's hard to bear the burden of uncertainty, always wondering what the next test will reveal. Will we have weeks, months, years, or decades before death separates us? But regardless of disease and diagnosis, each of us will die one day—things like cancer just bring our mortality to the forefront instead of letting it hide in the recesses of our minds.

Faced with sobering reminders of our mortality, I find myself praying words that Moses once prayed. Psalm 90 tells us that though our lives are like grass that withers and fades (VV. 5–6), we have an eternal home with God (V. 1). Like Moses, we can ask God to teach us to number our days so we can make wise decisions (V. 12), and to make our brief lives fruitful by making what we do for Him count (V. 17). Ultimately, the psalm reminds us that our hope is not in a doctor's diagnosis, but in a God who is "from everlasting to everlasting."   *AMY PETERSON*

How can we best spend the time we've been given?

We can face the reality of our own mortality because we trust in God.

Too Good Not to Share

Read: John 1:6–14

[John] came as a witness to testify concerning that light, so that through him all might believe. John 1:7

During court proceedings, witnesses are more than onlookers or spectators. They are active participants who help determine the outcome of a case. The same is true of our witness for Christ. We are to be active participants in a matter of absolute importance—the truth of Jesus's death and resurrection.

When John the Baptist came to tell people about Jesus, the light of the world, he did so by declaring his knowledge of Jesus. And John the disciple, who recorded the events, testified of his experience with Jesus: "We have seen his glory, the glory of the one and only Son, who came from the Father, full of grace and truth" (JOHN 1:14). The apostle Paul would elaborate on this idea as he told young Timothy, "The things you have heard me say in the presence of many witnesses entrust to reliable people who will also be qualified to teach others" (2 TIM. 2:2).

All Christians have been summoned before the courtroom of the world. The Bible says we are not mere spectators but active participants. We testify to the truth about Jesus's death and resurrection. John the Baptist was the voice of one calling in the desert. Our voices can be heard in our workplace, neighborhood, church, and among our family and friends. We can be active witnesses, telling them about the reality of Jesus in our lives.

LAWRENCE DARMANI

Do our actions enable us to witness for Jesus? In what creative ways might we witness today?

The gospel is too good not to share.

Unlighted Paths

Read: Joshua 1:1–9

The LORD your God will be with you wherever you go. Joshua 1:9

As we ventured home from a family vacation, the road took us through some desolate parts of central Oregon. For nearly two hours after dusk we drove through deep canyons and across desert plateaus. Fewer than twenty sets of headlights punctuated the darkness. Eventually the moon rose on the horizon, visible to us when the road crested hills but eclipsed when we traveled through the lowlands. My daughter remarked on its light, calling it a reminder of God's presence. I asked whether she needed to see it to know He was there. She replied, "No, but it sure helps."

After Moses's death, Joshua inherited leadership of the Israelites and was charged to take God's chosen people into the Promised Land. Despite his divine commission, Joshua must have felt challenged by the daunting nature of his task. God graciously offered Joshua assurance to be with him on the journey ahead (JOSH. 1:9).

The road of life often travels through uncharted territory. We voyage through seasons when the path ahead isn't clearly visible. God's plan may not always be apparent to us, but He has promised to be with us "always, to the very end of the age" (MATT. 28:20). What greater assurance could we hope for, no matter what uncertainty or challenge we might face? Even when the path is unlit, the Light is with us.   *KIRSTEN HOLMBERG*

Lord, thank You for being near me even when I cannot see You. Please comfort me with Your presence.

God is with us even when we can't see Him.

Singing with Violet

Read: Philippians 1:21–26

I desire to depart and be with Christ, which is better by far; but it is more necessary for you that I remain in the body. Philippians 1:23–24

An elderly woman named Violet sat on her bed in a Jamaican infirmary and smiled as some teenagers stopped to visit with her. The hot, sticky, midday air came into her little group home unabated, but she didn't complain. Instead, she began wracking her mind for a song to sing. Then a huge smile appeared and she sang, "I am running, skipping, jumping, praising the Lord!" As she sang, she swung her arms back and forth as if she were running. Tears came to those around her, for Violet had no legs. She was singing because, she said, "Jesus loves me—and in heaven I will have legs to run with."

Violet's joy and hopeful anticipation of heaven give new vibrancy to Paul's words in Philippians 1 when he referred to life-and-death issues. "If I am to go on living in the body, this will mean fruitful labor for me," he said. "I am torn between the two: I desire to depart and be with Christ, which is better by far" (VV. 22–23).

Each of us faces tough times that may cause us to long for the promise of heavenly relief. But as Violet showed us joy despite her current circumstances, we too can keep "running, skipping, praising the Lord"—both for the abundant life He gives us here and for the ultimate joy that awaits us.   *DAVE BRANON*

Lord, when times are tough, help me to find joy. Help us to live in the tough times of this world with happiness while looking ahead to something "better by far."

When God gives us a new beginning, we find a joy that's never ending.

The Advocate

Read: John 16:7–15

When he, the Spirit of truth, comes, he will guide you into all the truth.
John 16:13

As I boarded the airplane to study in a city a thousand miles from home, I felt nervous and alone. But during the flight, I remembered how Jesus promised His disciples the comforting presence of the Holy Spirit.

Jesus's friends must have felt bewildered when He told them, "It is for your good that I am going away" (JOHN 16:7). How could they who witnessed His miracles and learned from His teaching be better off without Him? But Jesus told them that if He left, then the Advocate—the Holy Spirit—would come.

Jesus, nearing His last hours on earth, shared with His disciples (in John 14–17, today known as the "Farewell Discourse") to help them understand His death and ascension. Central in this conversation was the coming Holy Spirit, an advocate who would be with them (14:16-17), teaching (15:15), testifying (V. 26), and guiding them (16:13).

We who have accepted God's offer of new life have been given this gift of His Spirit living within us. From Him we receive so much: He convicts us of our sins and helps us to repent. He brings us comfort when we ache, strength to bear hardships, wisdom to understand God's teaching, hope and faith to believe, love to share.

We can rejoice that Jesus sent us the Advocate.

AMY BOUCHER PYE

Heavenly Father, You sent Your Son to save us and Your Spirit to comfort and convict us. May we bring You glory as we thank You for Your goodness and love.

The Holy Spirit fills Jesus's followers.

Camping Psalms

Read: Psalm 8:1–9

LORD, our Lord, how majestic is your name in all the earth! Psalm 8:1

When my husband and I go for nature walks, we bring our cameras and take close-ups of the plants at our feet, which are like microcosms of the world. What amazing variety and beauty we see, even in the fungi that spring up overnight and dot the woods with splashes of bright orange, red, and yellow!

The snapshots of life that surround us inspire me to lift my eyes to the Maker who created not only mushrooms but also the stars in the heavens. He designed a world of infinite scope and variety. And He made you and me and placed us in the very middle of this beauty to enjoy and to rule over it (GEN. 1:27–28; PS. 8:6–8).

My thoughts turn to one of our family's "camping psalms"— psalms we read as we sit around the fire. "LORD, our Lord, how majestic is your name in all the earth! You have set your glory in the heavens. . . . When I consider your heavens, the work of your fingers, the moon and the stars, which you have set in place, what is mankind that you are mindful of them, human beings that you care for them?" (PS. 8:1–4).

How amazing that the great God who created the world in all its splendor cares for you and me! *ALYSON KIEDA*

O Lord, our majestic Maker, our hearts turn toward praise when we see snapshots of Your beautiful world. Thank You for creating us! Help us to rule Your world with wisdom.

A God wise enough to create me and the world I live in is wise enough to watch out for me.
PHILIP YANCEY

Scattering Seeds

Read: Matthew 13:1–9

The seed falling on good soil . . . produces a crop, yielding a hundred, sixty or thirty times what was sown. Matthew 13:23

I received a wonderful email from a woman who wrote, "Your mom was my first-grade teacher at Putnam City in 1958. She was a great teacher and very kind, but strict! She made us learn the 23rd Psalm and say it in front of the class, and I was horrified. But it was the only contact I had with the Bible until 1997 when I became a Christian. And the memories of Mrs. McCasland came flooding back as I re-read it."

Jesus told a large crowd a parable about the farmer who sowed his seed that fell on different types of ground—a hard path, rocky ground, clumps of thorns, and good soil (MATT. 13:1-9). While some seeds never grew, "the seed falling on good soil refers to someone who hears the word and understands it" and "produces a crop yielding a hundred, sixty or thirty times what was sown" (V. 23).

During the twenty years my mother taught first grade in public schools, along with reading, writing, and arithmetic she scattered seeds of kindness and the message of God's love.

Her former student's email concluded, "I have had other influences in my Christian walk later in life, of course. But my heart always returns to [Psalm 23] and [your mom's] gentle nature."

A seed of God's love sown today may produce a remarkable harvest. *DAVID MCCASLAND*

Lord, today I want my life to sow good seeds in those around me. Help me to give out what You have put into me.

We sow the seed—God produces the harvest.

Forever Flowers

Read: Isaiah 40:1–8

The grass withers and the flowers fall, but the word of our God endures forever. Isaiah 40:8

As a toddler, my son Xavier enjoyed giving me flowers. I appreciated every freshly picked weed or store-bought blossom he purchased with his dad. I treasured each gift until it wilted and had to be thrown away.

One day, Xavier gave me a beautiful bouquet of artificial flowers. He grinned as he arranged the silk white calla lily, yellow sunflower, and purple hydrangea in a glass vase. "Look, Mommy," he said. "They'll last forever. That's how much I love you."

Since then, my boy has grown into a young man. Those silk petals have frayed. The colors have faded. Still, the Forever Flowers remind me of his adoration. And there is something else it brings to mind—one thing that truly stands forever—the limitless and lasting love of God, as revealed in His infallible and enduring Word (ISA. 40:8).

As the Israelites faced continual trials, Isaiah comforted them with confidence in God's enduring words (40:1). He proclaimed that God paid the debt caused by the Israelites' sin (V. 2), securing their hope in the coming Messiah (VV. 3–5). They trusted the prophet because his focus remained on God rather than their circumstances.

In a world filled with uncertainties and affliction, the opinions of man and even our own feelings are ever-shifting and as limited as our mortality (VV. 6–7). Still, we can trust God's unchanging love and character as revealed through His constant and eternally true Word.   *XOCHITL DIXON*

God affirms His love through His dependable and unchanging Word, which endures now and forevermore.

Being a True Friend

Read: Genesis 14:17–24

Melchizedek king of Salem brought out bread and wine. Genesis 14:18

Poet Samuel Foss wrote, "Let me live by the side of the road and be a friend to man" ("The House by the Side of the Road"). That's what I want to be—a friend of people. I want to stand by the way, waiting for weary travelers. To look for those who have been battered and wronged by others, who carry the burden of a wounded and disillusioned heart. To nourish and refresh them with an encouraging word and send them on their way. I may not be able to "fix" them or their problems, but I can leave them with a blessing.

Melchizedek, both the king of Salem and a priest, blessed Abram when he was returning weary from battle (GEN. 14). A "blessing" is more than a polite response to a sneeze. We bless others when we bring them to the One who is the source of blessing. Melchizedek blessed Abram, saying, "Blessed be Abram by God Most High, Creator of heaven and earth" (V. 19).

We can bless others by praying with them; we can take them with us to the throne of grace to find help in time of need (HEB. 4:16). We may not be able to change their circumstances, but we can show them God. That's what a true friend does.

DAVID ROPER

Jesus, teach us to be a friend of people as You are with us. Give us eyes to see others and their needs and to take the time to listen. Help us to take them to You, the source of life.

A big part of loving is listening.

Living with Lions

Read: Daniel 6:19–28

He is the living God and He endures forever. Daniel 6:26

When I visited a museum in Chicago, I saw one of the original Striding Lions of Babylon. It was a large, mural-type image of a winged lion with a ferocious expression. Symbolizing Ishtar, the Babylonian goddess of love and war, the lion was an example of 120 similar lions that would have lined a Babylonian pathway during the years of 604–562 BC.

Historians say that after the Babylonians defeated Jerusalem, the Hebrew captives would have seen these lions during their time in Nebuchadnezzar's kingdom. Historians also say it's likely that some of the Israelites would have believed Ishtar had defeated the God of Israel.

Daniel, one of the Hebrew captives, did not share the doubts that might have troubled some of his fellow Israelites. His view of God and his commitment to God stayed steady. He prayed three times a day—with his windows open—even when he knew it would mean entering a den of lions. After God rescued Daniel from the hungry animals, King Darius said, "[Daniel's God] is the living God and he endures forever . . . . He rescues and he saves" (DAN. 6:26–27). Daniel's faithfulness allowed him to influence Babylonian leaders.

Staying faithful to God despite pressure and discouragement can inspire other people to give Him glory.

JENNIFER BENSON SCHULDT

Dear God, give me the strength to continue to trust in You when I am discouraged. Help me to experience Your never-ending love and stay close to Your side.

Faithfulness to God inspires others.

Clothed by God

Read: Zechariah 3

See, I have taken away your sin, and I will put fine garments on you.
Zechariah 3:4

When my kids were toddlers, they would play outside in our sodden English garden and quickly become covered in mud and dirt. For their good and the good of my floor, I'd remove their clothes at the door and wrap them in towels before sticking them in the bath. They'd soon move from dirty to clean with the addition of soap, water, and hugs.

In a vision given to Zechariah, we see Joshua, a high priest, covered in rags that represent sin and wrongdoing (ZECH. 3:3). But the Lord makes him clean, removing his filthy clothes and covering him in rich garments (3:5). The new turban and robe signify that the Lord has taken his sins from him.

We too can receive God's cleansing as we become free of our wrongdoing through the saving work of Jesus. As a result of His death on the cross, we can have the mud and sins that cling to us washed away as we receive the robes of God's sons and daughters. No longer are we defined by what we've done wrong (whether lying, gossiping, stealing, coveting, or other), but we can claim the names God gives to those He loves—restored, renewed, cleansed, free.

Ask God to remove any filthy rags you're wearing so you too can put on the wardrobe He has reserved for you.

AMY BOUCHER PYE

Lord Jesus, through Your saving death on the cross we can find acceptance and love. May we receive this gift for Your glory.

Who can wash away my sin? Jesus!

Prepare the Child

Read: Psalm 78:1–8

We will tell the next generation the praiseworthy deeds of the LORD, his power, and the wonders he has done. Psalm 78:4

A phrase on many parenting websites says, "Prepare the child for the road, not the road for the child." Instead of trying to remove all obstacles and pave the way for the children in our life, we should instead equip them to deal with the difficulties they encounter on the road ahead.

The psalmist wrote, "We will tell the next generation the praiseworthy deeds of the LORD, his power, and the wonders he has done. He decreed statutes . . . , which he commanded our ancestors to teach their children, so the next generation would know them . . . and they in turn would tell their children" (PS. 78:4–6). The goal is that "they would put their trust in God and would not forget his deeds but would keep his commands" (V. 7).

Think of the powerful spiritual impact others had on us through what they said and how they lived. Their conversation and demonstration captured our attention and kindled a fire in us to follow Jesus just as they did.

It's a wonderful privilege and responsibility to share God's Word and His plan for our lives with the next generation and the generations to come. No matter what lies ahead on their road through life, we want them to be prepared and equipped to face it in the strength of the Lord.   *DAVID MCCASLAND*

Father in heaven, we seek Your wisdom and guidance to prepare the children we know and love to walk with You in faith.

Through conversation and demonstration, help prepare children to follow the Lord on the road ahead.

Finding the Way Out

Read: 1 Corinthians 10:1–13

God is faithful; he will not let you be tempted beyond what you can bear. But when you are tempted, he will also provide a way out so that you can endure it. 1 Corinthians 10:13

There's a street with an intriguing name in the city of Santa Barbara, California. It's called "Salsipuedes," which means "leave if you can." When the street was first named, the area bordered on a marsh that sometimes flooded, and the Spanish-speaking city planners dubbed the location with a not-so-subtle warning to stay away.

God's Word cautions us to stay away from the "wrong road" of sin and temptation: "Avoid it, do not travel on it; turn from it and go on your way" (PROV. 4:15). But Scripture doesn't just say "leave if you can." It offers assurance and tells us where to turn: "God is faithful; he will not let you be tempted beyond what you can bear. But when you are tempted, he will also provide a way out so that you can endure it" (1 COR. 10:13).

The promise that God will not allow us to be tempted above our ability to withstand is an encouraging reminder. When we turn to God in the moments when temptation comes, we know He is more than willing to help us stay away.

The Bible affirms that Jesus is able "to empathize with our weaknesses." But He was "tempted in every way, just as we are—yet he did not sin" (HEB. 4:15). Jesus knows the way out of every temptation. He will show us as we run to Him!   *JAMES BANKS*

Thank You, Lord, for Your promise to be faithful to me and provide a way out whenever I face temptation. I praise You that You are willing to give me all the strength I need!

God promises to help us when we are tempted.

Seeing God

Read: Exodus 34:1–9

The LORD is slow to anger, abounding in love and forgiving sin and rebellion. Yet he does not leave the guilty unpunished. Numbers 14:18

Caricature artists set up their easels in public places and draw pictures of people who are willing to pay a modest price for a humorous image of themselves. Their drawings amuse us because they exaggerate one or more of our physical features in a way that is recognizable but funny.

Caricatures of God, on the other hand, are not funny. Exaggerating one of His attributes presents a distorted view that people easily dismiss. Like a caricature, a distorted view of God is not taken seriously. Those who see God portrayed only as an angry and demanding judge are easily lured away by someone who emphasizes mercy. Those who see God as a kindhearted grandfather will reject that image when they need justice. Those who see God as an intellectual idea rather than a living, loving being eventually find other ideas more appealing. Those who see God as a best friend often leave Him behind when they find human friends who are more to their liking.

God declares himself to be merciful and gracious, but also just in punishing the guilty (EX. 34:6–7).

As we put our faith into action, we need to avoid portraying God as having only our favorite attributes. We must worship all of God, not just what we like. *JULIE ACKERMAN LINK*

Father, Son, and Holy Spirit, I worship You. You are holy, just, kind, and loving.
You are God alone.

God is God alone.

Blink and Think of God

Read: Deuteronomy 32:1–12

He shielded him and cared for him; he guarded him as the apple of his eye. Deuteronomy 32:10

"God is like an eyelid," my friend Ryley said, and I blinked in surprise. What could she mean by that?

"Tell me more," I replied. Together, we had been studying surprising pictures of God in the Bible, things like God as a laboring mother (ISA. 42:14) or as a beekeeper (7:18), but this one was new to me. Ryley pointed me to Deuteronomy 32, where Moses praises the way God takes care of His people. Verse 10 says that God shields and protects His people, guarding them "as the apple of his eye."

But the word we translate *apple*, Ryley told me, literally means pupil. And what encircles and guards the pupil? The eyelid, of course! God is like the eyelid, which instinctively protects the tender eye. The eyelid guards the eye from danger, and by blinking helps remove dirt or dust. It keeps sweat out of the eye. It lubricates the eyeball, keeping it healthy. It closes, allowing rest.

As I considered the picture of God as an eyelid, I couldn't help but thank God for the many metaphors He's given us to help us understand His love for us. When we close our eyes at night and open them in the morning, we can think of God, and praise Him for His tender protection and care for us.   *AMY PETERSON*

Thank You, God, for using surprising metaphors to help us understand You better. Thanks for guarding us just as the eyelid guards the eye.

When you blink, remember to thank God for His protection.

Defending God

Read: Luke 9:51–56

A gentle answer turns away wrath, but a harsh word stirs up anger.
Proverbs 15:1

The anti-God bumper stickers covering the car seized the attention of a university professor. As a former atheist himself, the professor thought perhaps the owner wanted to make believers angry. "The anger helps the atheist to justify his atheism," he explained. Then he warned, "All too often, the atheist gets exactly what he is looking for."

In recalling his own journey to faith, this professor noted the concern of a Christian friend who invited him to consider the truth of Christ. His friend's "sense of urgency was conveyed without a trace of anger." He never forgot the genuine respect and grace he received that day.

Believers in Jesus often take offense when others reject Him. But how does *He* feel about that rejection? Jesus constantly faced threats and hatred, yet He never took doubt about His deity personally. Once, when a village refused Him hospitality, James and John wanted instant retaliation. "Lord," they asked, "do you want us to call fire down from heaven to destroy them?" (LUKE 9:54). Jesus didn't want that, and He "turned and rebuked them" (V. 55). After all, "God did not send his Son into the world to condemn the world, but to save the world through him" (JOHN 3:17).

It may surprise us to consider that God doesn't need us to defend Him. He wants us to *represent* Him! That takes time, work, restraint, and love.   *TIM GUSTAFSON*

Lord, when we are confronted with hate, help us not to be haters but to respond as Your Son did: "Father, forgive them, for they do not know what they are doing" (Luke 23:34).

The best way to defend Jesus is to live like Him.

Lookalikes

Read: 2 Corinthians 3:17–4:2

We all . . . are being transformed into his image with ever-increasing glory, which comes from the Lord, who is the Spirit. 2 Corinthians 3:18

They say we all have one: *Doppelgangers*, some call them. Lookalikes. People unrelated to us who look very much like us.

Mine happens to be a star in the music field. When I attended one of his concerts, I got a lot of double takes from fellow fans during intermission. But alas, I am no James Taylor when it comes to singing and strumming a guitar. We just happen to look alike.

Who do you look like? As you ponder that question, reflect on 2 Corinthians 3:18, where Paul tells us that we "are being transformed into [the Lord's] image." As we seek to honor Jesus with our lives, one of our goals is to take on His image. Of course, this doesn't mean we have to grow a beard and wear sandals—it means that the Holy Spirit helps us demonstrate Christlike characteristics in how we live. For example, in attitude (humility), in character (loving), and in compassion (coming alongside the down and out), we are to look like Jesus and imitate Him.

As we "contemplate the Lord's glory," by fixing our eyes on Jesus, we can grow more and more like Him. What an amazing thing it would be if people could observe us and say, "I see Jesus in you"! *DAVE BRANON*

Lord, help us to gaze on You, to study You, to know You. Transform us into Your image by what we say, how we love others, and how we worship You. May others see Jesus in us.

Love is the family resemblance the world should see in followers of Christ.

The Remedy for Jealousy

Read: 1 Samuel 18:5–15

So from that time on Saul kept a jealous eye on David.
1 Samuel 18:9 NLT

I gladly agreed to babysit my grandkids while their parents went out for the evening. After hugs, I asked the boys what they did over the weekend. (Both had separate adventures.) Bridger, age three, recounted breathlessly how he got to stay overnight with his aunt and uncle—and he had ice cream and rode a carousel and watched a movie! Next it was five-year-old Samuel's turn. When asked what he did, he said, "Camping." "Did you have fun?" I asked. "Not so much," he answered forlornly.

Samuel experienced the age-old feeling of jealousy. He forgot how much fun he had camping with his dad when he heard his brother excitedly tell about his weekend.

All of us can fall prey to jealousy. King Saul gave in to the green-eyed monster of jealousy when the praise David received exceeded his: "Saul has killed his thousands, and David his ten thousands!" (1 SAM. 18:7 NLT). Saul was outraged and "from that time on . . . kept a jealous eye on David" (V. 9 NLT). He was so incensed he tried to kill David!

The comparison game is foolish and self-destructive. Someone will always have something we don't or enjoy experiences different from ours. But God has already given us many blessings, including both life on this earth and the promise of eternal life to all who believe. Depending on His help and focusing on Him in thankfulness can help us to overcome jealousy.   *ALYSON KIEDA*

Lord, You have given us life and the promise of life eternal if we trust in You as our Savior. For that—and so many other blessings—we give You praise!

The remedy for jealousy is thankfulness to God.

Navigating Rough Waters

Read: 1 Chronicles 28:9–20

*Do not be afraid or discouraged, for the LORD God, my God, is with you.
He will not fail you or forsake you. 1 Chronicles 28:20*

I was enjoying the start of my first whitewater rafting experience—until I heard the roar of the rapids up ahead. My emotions were flooded with feelings of uncertainty, fear, and insecurity at the same time. Riding through the whitewater was a first-rate, white-knuckle experience! And then, suddenly, it was over. The guide in the back of the raft had navigated us through. I was safe—at least until the next set of rapids.

Transitions in our lives can be like whitewater experiences. The inevitable leaps from one season of life to the next—college to career, changing jobs, living with parents to living alone or with a spouse, career to retirement, youth to old age—are all marked by uncertainty and insecurity.

In one of the most significant transitions recorded in Old Testament history, Solomon assumed the throne from his father David. I'm sure he was filled with uncertainty about the future. His father's advice? "Be strong and courageous, and do the work. . . . For the LORD God, my God, is with you" (1 CHRON. 28:20).

We'll have our fair share of tough transitions in life. But with God in our raft we're not alone. Keeping our eyes on the One who is navigating the rapids brings joy and security. He's taken lots of others through before. *JOE STOWELL*

God guides us through the rapids of change.

Dysfunctional

Read: Romans 3:10–26

For all have sinned and fall short of the glory of God. Romans 3:23

The word *dysfunctional* is often used to describe individuals, families, relationships, organizations, and even governments. While *functional* means it's in proper working order, *dysfunctional* is the opposite—it's broken, not working properly, unable to do what it was designed to do.

In his letter to the Romans, the apostle Paul begins by describing a spiritually dysfunctional humanity (1:18–32). We are all part of that rebellious company: "All have turned away, they have together become worthless; there is no one who does good, not even one. . . . For all have sinned and fall short of the glory of God" (3:12, 23).

The good news is that "all are justified freely by [God's] grace through the redemption that came by Christ Jesus . . . to be received by faith" (VV. 24–25). When we invite Christ into our lives and accept God's offer of forgiveness and new life, we are on the path to becoming the person He created us to be. We don't immediately become perfect, but we no longer have to remain broken and dysfunctional.

Through the Holy Spirit we receive daily strength to honor God in what we say and do and to "put off [our] old self . . . to be made new in the attitude of [our] minds; and to put on the new self, created to be like God in true righteousness and holiness" (EPH. 4:22–24).   *DAVID MCCASLAND*

Lord, in our dysfunctional lives we turn to You for restoration and strength. Thank You for Your amazing grace and love!

Drawing close to Christ helps us to live as He designed us.

Not One Sparrow

Read: Matthew 10:28–33

Precious in the sight of the LORD is the death of his faithful servants.
Psalm 116:15

My mother, so dignified and proper her entire life, now lay in a hospice bed, held captive by debilitating age. Struggling for breath, her declining condition contradicted the gorgeous spring day that danced invitingly on the other side of the windowpane.

All the emotional preparation in the world cannot sufficiently brace us for the stark reality of goodbye. *Death is such an indignity!* I thought.

I diverted my gaze to the birdfeeder outside the window. A grosbeak flitted close to help itself to some seed. Instantly a familiar phrase popped into my mind: "Not a single sparrow can fall to the ground without your Father knowing it" (MATT. 10:29 NLT). Jesus had said that to His disciples as He gave them marching orders for a mission to Judea, but the principle applies to all of us. "You are worth more than many sparrows," He told them (V. 31).

My mom stirred and opened her eyes. Reaching back to her childhood, she used a Dutch term of endearment for her own mother and declared, "Muti's dead!"

"Yes," my wife agreed. "She's with Jesus now." Uncertain, Mom continued. "And Joyce and Jim?" she questioned of her sister and brother. "Yes, they're with Jesus too," said my wife. "But we'll be with them soon!"

"It's hard to wait," Mom said quietly.   *TIM GUSTAFSON*

Heavenly Father, this life can be so hard and painful. But You! . . . You are right there with us, loving us, keeping us, holding us! And You promise never to leave us or forsake us.

Death is the last shadow before heaven's dawn.

Let Honor Meet Honor

Read: Matthew 6:1–6

Be careful not to practice your righteousness in front of others to be seen by them. If you do, you will have no reward from your Father in heaven. Matthew 6:1

I've always been impressed by the solemn, magnificent simplicity of the Changing of the Guard at the Tomb of the Unknowns at Arlington National Cemetery. The carefully choreographed event is a moving tribute to soldiers whose names—and sacrifice—are "known but to God." Equally moving are the private moments of steady pacing when the crowds are gone: back and forth, hour after hour, day by day, in even the worst weather.

In September 2003, Hurricane Isabel was bearing down on Washington, DC, and the guards were told they could seek shelter during the worst of the storm. Surprising almost no one, the guards refused! They unselfishly stood their post to honor their fallen comrades even in the face of a hurricane.

Underlying Jesus's teaching in Matthew 6:1–6, I believe, is His desire for us to live with an unrelenting, selfless devotion to Him. The Bible calls us to good deeds and holy living, but these are to be acts of worship and obedience (VV. 4–6), not orchestrated acts for self-glorification (V. 2). The apostle Paul endorses this whole-life faithfulness when he pleads with us to make our bodies "a living sacrifice" (ROM. 12:1).

May our private and public moments speak of our devotion and wholehearted commitment to You, Lord.   *RANDY KILGORE*

Grant me the strength this day, O Lord, to persevere, to return honor to Your name where I am serving. My desire is to give myself in selfless devotion because of Your love for me.

The more we serve Christ, the less we will serve self.

Expect and Extend Mercy

Read: Luke 18:9–14

God, have mercy on me, a sinner. Luke 18:13

When I complained that a friend's choices were leading her deeper into sin and how her actions affected me, the woman I prayed with weekly placed her hand over mine. "Let's pray for all of us."

I frowned. "All of us?"

"Yes," she said. "Aren't you the one who always says Jesus sets our standard of holiness, so we shouldn't compare our sins to the sins of others?"

"That truth hurts a little," I said, "but you're right. My judgmental attitude and spiritual pride are no better or worse than her sins."

"And by talking about your friend, we're gossiping. So—"

"We're sinning." I lowered my head. "Please, pray for us."

In Luke 18, Jesus shared a parable about two men approaching the temple to pray in very different ways (VV. 9–14). Like the Pharisee, we can become trapped in a circle of comparing ourselves to other people. We can boast about ourselves (VV. 11–12) and live as though we have the right to judge and the responsibility or the power to change others.

But when we look to Jesus as our example of holy living and encounter His goodness firsthand, like the tax collector, our desperate need for God's grace is magnified (V. 13). As we experience the Lord's loving compassion and forgiveness personally, we'll be forever changed and empowered to expect and extend mercy, not condemnation, to others.   *XOCHITL DIXON*

Lord, please keep us from falling into the trap of comparing ourselves to others. Mold us and make us more like You.

When we realize the depth of our need for mercy, we can more readily offer mercy to others.

The Beauty of Brokenness

Read: Psalm 51

My sacrifice, O God, is a broken spirit. Psalm 51:17

Kintsugi is a centuries-old Japanese art of mending broken pottery. Gold dust mixed with resin is used to reattach broken pieces or fill in cracks, resulting in a striking bond. Instead of trying to hide the repair, the art makes something beautiful out of brokenness.

The Bible tells us that God also values our brokenness, when we are genuinely sorry for a sin we have committed. After David engaged in adultery with Bathsheba and plotted the death of her husband, the prophet Nathan confronted him, and he repented. David's prayer afterwards gives us insight into what God desires when we have sinned: "You do not delight in sacrifice, or I would bring it; you do not take pleasure in burnt offerings. My sacrifice, O God, is a broken spirit; a broken and contrite heart you, God, will not despise" (PS. 51:16–17).

When our heart is broken over a sin, God mends it with the priceless forgiveness generously offered by our Savior at the cross. He receives us with love when we humble ourselves before Him, and closeness is restored.

How merciful is God! Given His desire for a humble heart and the breathtaking beauty of His kindness, may another scriptural prayer be ours today: "Search me, God, and know my heart; test me and know my anxious thoughts. See if there is any offensive way in me, and lead me in the way everlasting" (PS. 139:23–24).

JAMES BANKS

Loving Father, I want to bring You joy by having a humble and repentant heart today.

Godly sorrow leads to joy.

Everything We Need

Read: 2 Peter 1:1–11

His divine power has given us everything we need for a godly life through our knowledge of him who called us by his own glory and goodness. 2 Peter 1:3

I often feel completely inadequate for the tasks I face. Whether it's teaching Sunday school, advising a friend, or writing articles for this publication, the challenge often seems to be larger than my ability. Like Peter, I have a lot to learn.

The New Testament reveals Peter's shortcomings as he tried to follow the Lord. While walking on water to Jesus, Peter began to sink (MATT. 14:25–31). When Jesus was arrested, Peter swore he didn't know Him (MARK 14:66–72). But Peter's encounter with the risen Christ and the power of the Holy Spirit changed his life.

Peter came to understand that God's "divine power has given us everything we need for a godly life through our knowledge of him who called us by his own glory and goodness" (2 PETER 1:3). An amazing statement from a man who had many flaws!

"[God] has given us his very great and precious promises, so that through them you may participate in the divine nature, having escaped the corruption in the world caused by evil desires" (V. 4).

Our relationship with the Lord Jesus Christ is the source of the wisdom, patience, and power we need to honor God, help others, and meet the challenges of today. Through Him, we can overcome our hesitations and feelings of inadequacy.

In every situation, He has given us everything we need to serve and honor Him. *DAVID MCCASLAND*

Thank You, Father, for giving me everything I need to serve You and encourage others today. May I honor You in all I do.

God promises to provide everything we need to honor Him with our lives.

Table Rock

Read: Luke 6:46–49

Why do you call me "Lord, Lord," and do not do what I say? Luke 6:46

A large, illuminated cross stands erect on Table Rock, a rocky plateau overlooking my hometown. Several homes were built on neighboring land, but recently the owners have been forced to move out due to safety concerns. Despite their close proximity to the firm bedrock of Table Rock, these homes aren't secure. They have been shifting atop their foundations—nearly three inches every day—causing risk of major water pipes breaking, which would accelerate the sliding.

Jesus compares those who hear and obey His words to those who build their homes on rock (LUKE 6:47–48). These homes survive the storms. By contrast, He says homes built without a firm foundation—like people who don't heed His instruction—cannot weather the torrents.

On many occasions, I've been tempted to ignore my conscience when I knew God asked more of me than I had given, thinking my response had been "close enough." Yet the homes in the shifting foothills nearby have depicted for me that being "close" is nowhere near enough when it comes to obeying Him. To be like those who built their homes on a firm foundation and withstand the storms of life that so often assail us, we must heed the words of our Lord completely.   *KIRSTEN HOLMBERG*

Help me, Lord, to obey You fully and with my whole heart. Thank You for being my firm foundation.

God's Word is the only sure foundation for life.

Someone to Trust

Read: John 13:33–35

Many proclaim themselves loyal, but who can find one worthy of trust?
Proverbs 20:6 NRSV

"I just can't trust anyone," my friend said through tears. "Every time I do, they hurt me." Her story angered me—an ex-boyfriend, whom she really thought she could trust, had started spreading rumors about her as soon as they broke up. Struggling to trust again after a pain-filled childhood, this betrayal seemed just one more confirmation that people could not be trusted.

I struggled to find words that would comfort. One thing I *could not* say was that she was wrong about how hard it is to find someone to fully trust, that most people are completely kind and trustworthy. Her story was painfully familiar, reminding me of moments of unexpected betrayal in my own life. In fact, Scripture is very candid about human nature. In Proverbs 20:6, the author voices the same lament as my friend, forever memorializing the pain of betrayal.

What I *could* say is that the cruelty of others is only part of the story. Although wounds from others are real and painful, Jesus has made genuine love possible. In John 13:35, Jesus told His disciples that the world would know they were His followers because of their love. Although some people may still hurt us, because of Jesus there will also always be those who, freely sharing His love, will unconditionally support and care for us. Resting in His unfailing love, may we find healing, community, and the courage to love others as He did.   *MONICA BRANDS*

Jesus has made true love possible.

Perfect Peace

Read: John 14:25–31

Peace I leave with you; my peace I give you. John 14:27

A friend shared with me that for years she searched for peace and contentment. She and her husband built up a successful business, so she was able to buy a big house, fancy clothes, and expensive jewelry. But these possessions didn't satisfy her inner longings for peace, nor did her friendships with influential people. Then one day, when she was feeling low and desperate, a friend told her about the good news of Jesus. There she found the Prince of Peace, and her understanding of true peace and contentment was forever changed.

Jesus spoke words of such peace to His friends after their last supper together (JOHN 14), when He prepared them for the events that would soon follow: His death, resurrection, and the coming of the Holy Spirit. Describing a peace—unlike anything the world can give—He wanted them to learn how to find a sense of well-being even in the midst of hardship.

Later, when the resurrected Jesus appeared to the frightened disciples after His death, He greeted them, saying, "Peace be with you!" (JOHN 20:19). Now He could give them, and us, a new understanding of resting in what He has done for us. As we do, we can find the awareness of a confidence far deeper than our ever-changing feelings.   *AMY BOUCHER PYE*

Heavenly Father, You will keep in perfect peace those whose minds are fixed on You. Help us to trust in You forever, for You are our Rock eternal.

Jesus came to usher peace into our lives and our world.

What Do We Want?

Read: Romans 8:1–11

He who raised Christ from the dead will also give life to your mortal bodies because of his Spirit who lives in you. Romans 8:11

"I went from the horse-and-buggy to a man walking on the moon," said the elderly man to his granddaughter, who shared this story with me recently. But then he mused, "I never thought it would be so short."

Life *is* short, and many of us turn to Jesus because we want to live forever. That's not bad, but we don't comprehend what eternal life really is. We tend to crave the wrong things. We long for something better, and we think it's just ahead. *If only I were out of school. If only I had that job. If only I were married. If only I could retire. If only . . .* And then one day we catch an echo of our grandfather's voice as we wonder where the time has flown.

The truth is, we possess eternal life *now.* The apostle Paul wrote, "The law of the Spirit who gives life has set you free from the law of sin and death" (ROM. 8:2). Then he said, "Those who live in accordance with the Spirit have their minds set on what the Spirit desires" (V. 5). In other words, our desires change when we come to Christ. This naturally gives us what we most desire. "The mind governed by the Spirit is life and peace" (V. 6).

It's one of life's great lies that we need to be somewhere else, doing something else, with someone else before we start truly living. When we find our life in Jesus, we exchange regret over life's brevity for the full enjoyment of life with Him, both now and forever. *TIM GUSTAFSON*

Lord, You said You came to give us life to the fullest, but so often we have our own agenda and the wrong goals in mind. Please forgive us, and help us desire what You want.

To live forever we must let Jesus live in us now.

Fifteen-Minute Challenge

Read: Psalm 119:33–40

Turn my heart toward your statutes. Psalm 119:36

Dr. Charles W. Eliot, longtime president of Harvard University, believed that ordinary people who read consistently from the world's great literature for even a few minutes a day could gain a valuable education. In 1910, he compiled selections from books of history, science, philosophy, and fine art into fifty volumes called The Harvard Classics. Each set of books included Dr. Eliot's Reading Guide titled "Fifteen Minutes A Day," containing recommended selections of eight to ten pages for each day of the year.

What if we spent fifteen minutes a day reading God's Word? We could say with the psalmist, "Turn my heart toward your statutes and not toward selfish gain. Turn my eyes away from worthless things; preserve my life according to your word" (PS. 119:36–37).

Fifteen minutes a day adds up to ninety-one hours a year. But for whatever amount of time we decide to read the Bible each day, consistency is the secret and the key ingredient is not perfection but persistence. If we miss a day or a week, we can start reading again. As the Holy Spirit teaches us, God's Word moves from our minds to our hearts, then to our hands and feet—taking us beyond education to transformation.

"Teach me, LORD, the way of your decrees, that I may follow it to the end" (V. 33).   *DAVID MCCASLAND*

I turn to You, the Author, to teach me as I read Your Word today. I want to hear from You, to know You, and to grow closer to You.

The Bible is the only Book whose Author is always present when it is read.

God Calling

Read: Genesis 3:1–10

This is how God showed his love . . . He sent his one and only Son into the world. 1 John 4:9

One morning my daughter gave her eleven-month-old son her cell phone for a moment to entertain him. Less than a minute later my phone rang, and as I picked it up I heard his little voice. He had somehow hit the "speed dial" to my number, and what followed was a "conversation" I will long remember. My grandson can only say a few words, but he knows my voice and responds to it. So I talked to him and told him how much I love him.

The joy I felt at the sound of my grandson's voice was a reminder to me of God's deep desire for a relationship with us. From the very beginning, the Bible shows God actively pursuing us. After Adam and Eve sinned by disobeying God and then hid from Him in the garden, "the LORD God called" to Adam (GEN. 3:9).

God continued to pursue humanity through Jesus. Because God desires a relationship with us, He sent Jesus to earth to pay the penalty for our sin by His death on the cross. "This is how God showed his love . . . . He sent his Son as a sacrifice to clear away our sins and the damage they've done to our relationship with God" (1 JOHN 4:9–10 MSG).

How good it is to know that God loves us and wants us to respond to His love through Jesus. Even when we don't quite know what to say, our Father longs to hear from us!

JAMES BANKS

Heavenly Father, thank You for loving me and pursuing a relationship with me. Help me to be a joy to You by drawing near to You.

God's love for us is revealed through Jesus.

Rings and Grace

Read: Hebrews 8:6–13

[I] will remember their sins no more. Hebrews 8:12

When I look at my hands, I am reminded that I lost my wedding and engagement rings. I was multitasking as I packed for a trip, and I still have no idea where they ended up.

I dreaded telling my husband about my careless mistake—worried how the news would affect him. But he responded with more compassion and care for me than concern over the rings. However, there are times when I still want to do something to earn his grace! He, on the contrary, doesn't hold this episode against me.

So many times we remember our sins and feel we must do something to earn God's forgiveness. But God has said it is by grace, not by works, that we are saved (EPH. 2:8–9). Speaking of a new covenant, God promised Israel, "I will forgive their wickedness and will remember their sins no more" (JER. 31:34). We have a God who forgives and no longer calls to mind the wrongs we have done.

We may still feel sad about our past, but we need to trust His promise and believe His grace and forgiveness is real through faith in Jesus Christ. This news should lead us to thankfulness and the assurance faith brings. When God forgives, He forgets.

KEILA OCHOA

Dear Lord, thank You for Your grace and Your offer of salvation and forgiveness through Christ. Thank You for this free gift that is not based on anything I can do.

Grace and forgiveness are unearned gifts.

A Reason to Sing

Read: 2 Chronicles 20:14–22

Sing praises to God, sing praises; sing praises to our King, sing praises.
Psalm 47:6

Singing changes the brain! Some studies show that when we sing, our bodies release hormones that relieve anxiety and stress. Other research indicates that when a group of people sings together, their heartbeats actually synchronize with each other.

The apostle Paul's writing encourages the church to speak to one another with psalms, hymns, and spiritual songs (EPH. 5:19). And the Bible repeats, "Sing praise" more than fifty times.

In 2 Chronicles 20, we read a story of God's people demonstrating their trust in God by singing as they marched into battle. Enemies were heading toward the people of Judah. Alarmed, King Jehoshaphat called everyone together. He led the community in intense prayer. They didn't eat or drink, but only prayed, "We don't know what to do, but our eyes are on you" (V. 12). The next day, they set out. They weren't led by their fiercest warriors, but by their choir. They believed God's promise that they would be delivered without having to fight at all (V. 17).

While they sang and walked toward the conflict, their enemies fought each other! By the time God's people reached the battlefield, the fighting had ended. God saved His people as they marched by faith toward the unknown, singing His praises.

God encourages us to praise Him for good reasons. Whether or not we are marching into battle, praising God has power to change our thoughts, our hearts, and our lives.   *AMY PETERSON*

God, we praise Your everlasting love and faithfulness! You protect and guide us, and we trust You with our lives.

Hearts in tune with God sing His praises.

Finding Waldo

Read: Acts 8:26–40

The [Ethiopian] asked Philip, "Tell me, please, who is the prophet talking about, himself or someone else?" Acts 8:34

Waldo is the cartoonish star of "Where's Waldo," a now-classic best-selling children's book series. Waldo hides himself in the crowded scenes on each page, inviting children to find where he's hiding. Parents around the world love the moments of sweet discovery when their children's faces signal they've found Waldo. They also enjoy the occasions when they're invited to help find him.

Shortly after Stephen, a deacon in the early church, was stoned to death for proclaiming Christ (SEE ACTS 7), widespread persecution broke out against Christians, causing many to flee Jerusalem. Another deacon, Philip, followed these fleeing Christians into Samaria, where he proclaimed Christ and it was well received (8:6). While there, the Holy Spirit sent Philip on a special mission to "the desert road." It must have seemed a strange request given the fruit his preaching was producing in Samaria itself. Imagine Philip's joy, then, when he met and helped the Ethiopian court official find Jesus in the pages of Isaiah (VV. 26–40).

We, too, are often given the chance to help others "find Jesus" throughout the Scriptures so they may know Him more fully. Like a parent witnessing the joy of discovery in their child's eyes and like Philip helping the Ethiopian find Jesus, it can be exhilarating for us to witness the moment of discovery in those around us. As we go through our days, may we be prepared to share Christ as the Spirit leads us, whether they are people we know well or those we meet even just once.   *RANDY KILGORE*

The biggest work a Christian can do is to find his friend and introduce him to Jesus Christ.

Postures of the Heart

Read: 2 Chronicles 6:7–9, 12–15

[Solomon] knelt in front of the entire community of Israel and lifted his hands toward heaven [and] he prayed. 2 Chronicles 6:13–14 NLT

When my husband plays the harmonica for our church praise team, I have noticed that he sometimes closes his eyes when he plays a song. He says this helps him focus and block out distractions so he can play his best—just his harmonica, the music, and him—all praising God.

Some people wonder if our eyes must be closed when we pray. Since we can pray at any time in any place, however, it might prove difficult to always close our eyes—especially if we are taking a walk, pulling weeds, or driving a vehicle!

There are also no rules on what position our body must be in when we talk to God. When King Solomon prayed to dedicate the temple he had built, he knelt down and "spread out his hands toward heaven" (2 CHRON. 6:13-14). Kneeling (EPH. 3:14), standing (LUKE 18:10-13), and even lying face down (MATT. 26:39) are all mentioned in the Bible as positions for prayer.

Whether we kneel or stand before God, whether we lift our hands heavenward or close our eyes so we can better focus on God—it is not the posture of our body, but of our heart that is important. Everything we do "flows from [our heart]" (PROV. 4:23). When we pray, may our hearts always be bowed in adoration, gratitude, and humility to our loving God, for we know that His eyes are "open and [His] ears attentive to the prayers" of His people (2 CHRON. 6:40).   *CINDY HESS KASPER*

Lord, direct my focus always toward You and teach me to follow You in obedience and love.

The highest form of prayer comes from the depths of a humble heart.

Nothing Is Useless

Read: 1 Corinthians 15:42–58

Nothing you do for the Lord is ever useless. 1 Corinthians 15:58 NLT

In my third year battling discouragement and depression caused by limited mobility and chronic pain, I confided to a friend, "My body's falling apart. I feel like I have nothing of value to offer God or anyone else."

Her hand rested on mine. "Would you say it doesn't make a difference when I greet you with a smile or listen to you? Would you tell me it's worthless when I pray for you or offer a kind word?"

I settled into my recliner. "Of course not."

She frowned. "Then why are you telling yourself those lies? You do all those things for me and for others."

I thanked God for reminding me that nothing we do for Him is useless.

In 1 Corinthians 15, Paul assures us that our bodies may be weak now but they will be "raised in power" (V. 43). Because God promises we'll be resurrected through Christ, we can trust Him to use every offering, every small effort done for Him, to make a difference in His kingdom (V. 58).

Even when we're physically limited, a smile, a word of encouragement, a prayer, or a display of faith during our trial can be used to minister to the diverse and interdependent body of Christ. When we serve the Lord, no job or act of love is too menial to matter. *XOCHITL DIXON*

Jesus, thank You for valuing us and using us to build up others.

Do what you can with what you have and leave the results to God.

Consider the Clouds

Read: Job 37:1–16

Do you know how the clouds hang poised? Job 37:16

One day many years ago my boys and I were lying on our backs in the yard watching the clouds drift by. "Dad," one asked, "why do clouds float?" "Well, son," I began, intending to give him the benefit of my vast knowledge, but then I lapsed into silence. "I don't know," I admitted, "but I'll find out for you."

The answer, I discovered, is that condensed moisture, descending by gravity, meets warmer temperatures rising from the land. That moisture then changes into vapor and ascends back into the air. That's a natural explanation for the phenomenon.

But natural explanations are not final answers. Clouds float because God in His wisdom has ordered the natural laws in such a way that they reveal the "wonders of him who has perfect knowledge" (JOB 37:16). Clouds then can be thought of as a symbol—an outward and visible sign of God's goodness and grace in creation.

So someday when you're taking some time to see what images you can imagine in the clouds, remember this: The One who made all things beautiful makes the clouds float through the air. He does so to call us to wonder and adoration. The heavens—even the cumulus, stratus, and cirrus clouds—declare the glory of God.

DAVID ROPER

We are amazed at You, wonderful Creator, as we look at Your world. You deserve all the praise our hearts can give and so much more!

Creation is filled with signs that point to the Creator.

Rhythms of Grace

Read: Matthew 11:25–30

Take my yoke upon you and learn from me, for I am gentle and humble in heart, and you will find rest for your souls. Matthew 11:29

A friend and his wife, now in their early nineties and married for sixty-six years, wrote their family history for their children, grandchildren, and generations to come. The final chapter, "A Letter from Mom and Dad," contains important life-lessons they've learned. One caused me to pause and take inventory of my own life: "If you find that Christianity exhausts you, draining you of your energy, then you are practicing religion rather than enjoying a relationship with Jesus Christ. Your walk with the Lord will not make you weary; it will invigorate you, restore your strength, and energize your life" (MATT. 11:28–29).

Eugene Peterson's paraphrase of Jesus's invitation in this passage begins, "Are you tired? Worn out? Burned out on religion? . . . Walk with me and work with me. . . . Learn the unforced rhythms of grace" (MSG).

When I think that serving God is all up to me, I've begun working *for* Him instead of walking *with* Him. There is a vital difference. If I'm not walking with Christ, my spirit becomes dry and brittle. People are annoyances, not fellow humans created in God's image. Nothing seems right.

When I sense that I'm practicing religion instead of enjoying a relationship with Jesus, it's time to lay the burden down and walk with Him in His "unforced rhythms of grace."

DAVID MCCASLAND

Lord Jesus, I come to You today to exchange my frenzied work for Your pathway of grace.

Jesus wants us to walk with Him.

The Bond of Peace

Read: Ephesians 4:1–6

Make every effort to keep the unity of the Spirit through the bond of peace. Ephesians 4:3

After I confronted my friend by email over a matter on which we had differed, she didn't respond. Had I overstepped? I didn't want to worsen the situation by pestering her, but neither did I want to leave things unresolved before she went on a trip overseas. As she popped into my mind throughout the following days, I prayed for her, unsure of the way forward. Then one morning I went for a walk in our local park and saw her, pain etched on her face as she glimpsed me. "Thank You, Lord, that I can talk to her," I breathed as I approached her with a welcoming smile. We talked openly and were able to resolve matters.

Sometimes when hurt or silence intrudes on our relationships, mending them seems out of our control. But as the apostle Paul says in his letter to the church at Ephesus, we are called to work for peace and unity through God's Spirit, donning the garments of gentleness, humility, and patience as we seek God's healing in our relationships. The Lord yearns for us to be united, and through His Spirit He can bring His people together—even unexpectedly when we go walking in the park.   *AMY BOUCHER PYE*

Have you experienced an unexpected encounter that revealed God working in a situation? How might you work toward peace and unity today?

God desires unity among believers.

Made Alive

Read: Ephesians 2:1–10

You were dead in your transgressions and sins. Ephesians 2:1

As a young man, my dad was traveling with a group of friends to an out-of-town sporting event when the tires of their car slipped on the rain-soaked roads. They had an accident—a bad accident. One of his friends was paralyzed and another was killed. My dad was declared dead and taken to the morgue. His shocked and grief-stricken parents came to identify him. But my dad revived from what turned out to be a deep coma. Their mourning turned to joy.

In Ephesians 2, the apostle Paul reminds us that apart from Christ we are "dead in [our] transgressions and sins" (V. 1). But because of His great love for us, "God, who is rich in mercy, made us alive with Christ even when we were dead in transgressions" (VV. 4–5). Through Christ we have been brought from death to life.

So in every sense, we all owe our life to the Father in heaven. Through His great love, He has made it possible for those of us who were dead in sin to have life and purpose through His Son.

BILL CROWDER

Thank You, Father, for love that conquers sin, life that conquers death, and grace that has conquered my heart. May my life be a sweet aroma of praise to You.

We owed a debt we could not pay, but Jesus paid the debt He did not owe.

Time Together

Read: Psalm 147:1–11

The LORD delights in those who fear him, who put their hope in his unfailing love. Psalm 147:11

On the two-hour drive home from a family member's wedding, my mom asked me for the third time what was new in my job. I once again repeated some of the details as if telling her for the first time, while wondering what might *possibly* make my words more memorable. My mom has Alzheimer's, a disease that progressively destroys the memory, can adversely affect behavior, and eventually leads to the loss of speech—and more.

I grieve because of my mom's disease but am thankful she is still here and we can spend time together—and even converse. It thrills me that whenever I go to see her she lights up with joy and exclaims, "Alyson, what a pleasant surprise!" We enjoy each other's company; and even in the silences when words escape her, we commune together.

This perhaps is a small picture of our relationship with God. Scripture tells us, "The LORD delights in those who fear him, who put their hope in his unfailing love" (PS. 147:11). God calls those who believe in Jesus as their Savior His children (JOHN 1:12). And although we may make the same requests over and over again or lack for words, He is patient with us because He has a loving relationship with us. He is happy when we converse with Him in prayer—even when the words escape us. *ALYSON KIEDA*

Dear Lord, it thrills us that You want to have a relationship with us! Thank You for the opportunity to learn of You through the Bible and to talk with You in prayer.

God delights to hear from us!

A Perfect Father

Read: Proverbs 20:3–7

The righteous lead blameless lives; blessed are their children after them. Proverbs 20:7

My father once admitted to me, "When you were growing up, I was gone a lot."

I don't remember that. Besides working his full-time job, he was gone some evenings to direct choir practice at church, and he occasionally traveled for a week or two with a men's quartet. But for all the significant (and many small) moments of my life—he was there.

For instance, when I was eight, I had a tiny part in an afternoon play at school. All the mothers came, but only one dad— mine. In many little ways, he has always let my sisters and me know that we are important to him and that he loves us. And seeing him tenderly caring for my mom in the last few years of her life taught me exactly what unselfish love looks like. Dad isn't perfect, but he's always been a dad who gives me a good glimpse of my heavenly Father. And ideally, that's what a Christian dad should do.

At times earthly fathers disappoint or hurt their children. But our Father in heaven is "compassionate and gracious, slow to anger, abounding in love" (PS. 103:8). When a dad who loves the Lord corrects, comforts, instructs, and provides for the needs of his children, he models for them our perfect Father in heaven.

CINDY HESS KASPER

Heavenly Father, thank You for Your faithfulness that I can always count on. Please help me to live today in a way that leaves behind a legacy of faithfulness and love.

A life lived for Christ is the best inheritance we can leave our children.

Driven by God

Read: 1 Kings 8:54–63

May he turn our hearts to him, to walk in obedience to him.
1 Kings 8:58

A few months ago I received an email inviting me to join a community of "driven people." I decided to look up the word *driven*, and I learned that a driven person is someone highly motivated to succeed and who will work hard to achieve his goals.

Is it good to be a driven person? There is a test that never fails: "Do it all for the glory of God" (1 COR. 10:31). Many times we do things for self-glory. After the flood in Noah's day, a group of people decided to build a tower in order to "make a name" for themselves (GEN. 11:4). They wanted to be famous and avoid being scattered all over the world. Because they were not doing it for God's glory, though, they were erroneously driven.

In contrast, when King Solomon dedicated the ark of the covenant and the newly constructed temple, he said, "I have built the temple for the Name of the LORD" (1 KINGS 8:20). Then he prayed, "May he turn our hearts to him, to walk in obedience to him and keep the commands" (V. 58).

When our greatest desire is to bring glory to God and walk in obedience, we become driven people who seek to love and serve Jesus in the power of the Spirit. Let our prayer echo Solomon's. May our "hearts be fully committed to the LORD our God, to live by his decrees and obey his commands" (V. 61).   *KEILA OCHOA*

Father, give me the desire to obey You and do everything for Your glory.

Do everything for the glory of God.

Reason to Smile

Read: 1 Thessalonians 5:9–28

Therefore encourage one another and build each other up, just as in fact you are doing. 1 Thessalonians 5:11

In the workplace, words of encouragement matter. How employees talk to one another has a bearing on customer satisfaction, company profits, and coworker appreciation. Studies show that members of the most effective work groups give one another six times more affirmation than disapproval, disagreement, or sarcasm. Least productive teams tend to use almost three negative comments for every helpful word.

Paul learned by experience about the value of words in shaping relationships and outcomes. Before meeting Christ on the road to Damascus, his words and actions terrorized followers of Jesus. But by the time he wrote his letter to the Thessalonians, he had become a great encourager because of God's work in his heart. Now by his own example he urged his readers to cheer one another on. While being careful to avoid flattery, he showed how to affirm others and reflect the Spirit of Christ.

In the process, Paul reminded his readers where encouragement comes from. He saw that entrusting ourselves to God, who loved us enough to die for us, gives us reason to comfort, forgive, inspire, and lovingly challenge one another (1 THESS. 5:10–11).

Paul shows us that encouraging one another is a way of helping one another get a taste of the patience and goodness of God.

MART DEHAAN

Father in heaven, please help us to give others a small taste of the mercy and kindness You are forever offering us.

What could be better than working to bring out the best in one another?

Sharing a Cup of Comfort

Read: 2 Corinthians 1:3–11

Our hope for you is firm, because we know that just as you share in our sufferings, so also you share in our comfort. 2 Corinthians 1:7

A friend mailed me some of her homemade pottery. Upon opening the box, I discovered the precious items had been damaged during their journey. One of the cups had shattered into a few large pieces, a jumble of shards, and clumps of clay dust. After my husband glued the broken mess back together, I displayed the beautifully blemished cup on a shelf.

Like that pieced-together pottery, I have scars that prove I can still stand strong after the difficult times God's brought me through. That cup of comfort reminds me that sharing how the Lord has worked in and through my life can help others during their times of suffering.

The apostle Paul praises God because He is the "Father of compassion and the God of all comfort" (2 COR. 1:3). The Lord uses our trials and sufferings to make us more like Him. His comfort in our troubles equips us to encourage others as we share what He did for us during our time of need (V. 4).

As we reflect on Christ's suffering, we can be inspired to persevere in the midst of our own pain, trusting that God uses our experiences to strengthen us and others toward patient endurance (VV. 5–7). Like Paul, we can be comforted in knowing that the Lord redeems our trials for His glory. We can share His cups of comfort and bring reassuring hope to the hurting.

XOCHITL DIXON

Lord, thank You for using us to provide comfort, encouragement, and hope to others who are suffering. We praise You for all You've done, are doing, and will continue to do to comfort us through our own afflictions.

God comforts others as we share how He comforted us.

Silence

Read: Habakkuk 1:1–4; 2:20

How long, LORD, must I call for help, but you do not listen? Habakkuk 1:2

Skittish chickens scattered as relief trucks clattered past the weathered huts of the village. Barefoot children stared. Traffic on this rain-ravaged "road" was rare.

Suddenly, a walled mansion loomed into view of the convoy. It was the mayor's house—although he didn't live in it. His people lacked basic necessities, while he lounged in luxury in a distant city.

Such unfairness angers us. It angered God's prophet too. When Habakkuk saw rampant oppression he asked, "How long, LORD, must I call for help, but you do not listen?" (HAB. 1:2). But God *had* noticed, and He said, "Woe to him who piles up stolen goods . . . who builds his house by unjust gain!" (2:6, 9). Judgment was coming!

We welcome God's judgment of others, but there's a pivot point in Habakkuk that gives us pause: "The LORD is in his holy temple; let all the earth be silent before him" (2:20). *All* the earth. The oppressed along with oppressors. Sometimes the appropriate response to God's seeming silence is . . . silence!

Why silence? Because we easily overlook our own spiritual poverty. Silence allows us to recognize our sinfulness in the presence of a holy God.

Habakkuk learned to trust God, and we can too. We don't know all His ways, but we do know that He is good. Nothing is beyond His control and timing. *TIM GUSTAFSON*

Lord, when trouble comes we can pray like Habakkuk, "We have heard of your fame; we stand in awe of your deeds. Repeat them in our day; in our time make them known" (Hab. 3:2).

The righteous care about justice for the poor, but the wicked have no such concern.
PROVERBS 29:7

Playing in Concert

Read: Romans 12:3–8

So in Christ we, though, many, form one body, and each member belongs to all the others. We have different gifts, according to the grace given to each of us. Romans 12:5–6

During our granddaughter's school band concert, I was impressed by how well this group of 11- and 12-year-olds played together. If each of them had wanted to be a solo performer, they could not have achieved individually what the band did collectively. The woodwinds, brass, and percussion sections all played their parts and the result was beautiful music!

To the followers of Jesus in Rome, Paul wrote, "In Christ we, though many, form one body, and each member belongs to all the others. We have different gifts, according to the grace given to each of us" (ROM. 12:5–6). Among the gifts Paul mentioned are prophecy, service, teaching, encouragement, giving, leadership, and mercy (VV. 7–8). Each gift is to be exercised freely for the good of all (1 COR. 12:7).

One definition of *in concert* is "agreement in design or plan; combined action; harmony or accord." That's the Lord's plan for us as His children through faith in Jesus Christ. "Be devoted to one another in love. Honor one another above yourselves" (V. 10). The goal is cooperation, not competition.

In a sense, we are "on stage" before a watching and listening world every day. There are no soloists in God's concert band, but every instrument is essential. The music is best when we each play our part in unity with others. DAVID MCCASLAND

Lord, You are the Conductor of our lives. We want to play Your song of love and grace in concert with Your children today.

There are no soloists in God's orchestra.

Here to Serve

Read: John 13:3–17

[Jesus] poured water into a basin and began to wash his disciples' feet.
John 13:5

It was time for our church to commission a new group of leaders. To symbolize their roles as servant-leaders, the church elders participated in a memorable foot-washing ceremony. Each of the leaders—including the pastor—washed each other's feet as the congregation observed them.

What they did that day was modeled for us by Jesus Christ, as recorded in John 13. In that incident, which happened at what is called the Last Supper, Jesus "got up from the meal, . . . poured water into a basin and began to wash his disciples' feet" (JOHN 13:4–5). Later, as Jesus was explaining to His disciples why He had done this, He said, "No servant is greater than his master, nor is a messenger greater than the one who sent him" (V. 16). He also said, "I am among you as one who serves" (LUKE 22:27).

If it is not below Jesus's dignity to do such a lowly task, it is not below any of us to serve others. What an amazing example He set for all of us. Indeed, He "did not come to be served, but to serve" (MARK 10:45). He showed us what it means to be a leader and a servant. That's Jesus, the One who serves. *DAVE BRANON*

Dear Lord, help me serve others. Guide me to set aside my personal interests and desires to provide help to those who need it.

No deed is small when done for Christ.

Soaking Up God's Word

Read: Deuteronomy 6:1–9

These commandments that I give to you today are to be on your hearts. Impress them on your children. Deuteronomy 6:6–7

When our son Xavier was a toddler, we took a family trip to the Monterey Bay Aquarium. As we entered the building, I pointed to a large sculpture suspended from the ceiling. "Look. A humpback whale."

Xavier's eyes widened. "Enormous," he said.

My husband turned to me. "How does he know that word?"

"He must have heard us say it." I shrugged, amazed that our toddler had soaked up vocabulary we'd never intentionally taught him.

In Deuteronomy 6, God encouraged His people to be intentional about teaching younger generations to know and obey the Scriptures. As the Israelites increased their knowledge of God, they and their children would be more likely to grow in reverence of Him and to enjoy the rewards that come through knowing Him intimately, loving Him completely, and following Him obediently (VV. 2–5).

By intentionally saturating our hearts and our minds with Scripture (V. 6), we will be better prepared to share God's love and truth with children during our everyday activities (V. 7). Leading by example, we can equip and encourage young people to recognize and respect the authority and relevance of God's unchanging truth (VV. 8–9).

As God's words flow naturally from our hearts and out of our mouths, we can leave a strong legacy of faith to be passed down from generation to generation (4:9). *XOCHITL DIXON*

The words we take in determine the words we speak, live by, and pass on to those around us.

Very Good!

Read: Genesis 1:24–31

Then God looked over all he had made, and he saw that it was very good! Genesis 1:31 NLT

Some days seem to have a theme running through them. Recently I had one of those days. Our pastor began his sermon on Genesis 1 with two minutes of breathtaking, time-lapse photography of blossoming flowers. Then, at home, a scroll through social media revealed numerous posts of flowers. Later on a walk in the woods, the wildflowers of spring surrounded us—trilliums, marsh marigolds, and wild iris.

God created flowers and every other variety of vegetation (and dry ground to grow in), on the third day of creation. And twice on that day, God pronounced it "good" (GEN. 1:10, 12). On only one other day of creation—the sixth—did God make that double pronouncement of "good" (VV. 25, 31). In fact, on this day when He created humans and His masterpiece was complete, He looked over all He had made and "saw that it was very good!" (NLT).

In the creation story, we see a Creator God who delighted in His creation—and seemed to take joy in the very act of creating. Why else design a world with such colorful and amazing variety? And He saved the best for last when He "created mankind in his own image" (V. 27). As His image-bearers we are blessed and inspired by His beautiful handiwork.   *ALYSON KIEDA*

Dear Creator God, thank You for creating the world in all its beauty for our enjoyment—and Yours. Thank You too for making us in Your image so that we would be inspired to create.

All creation bears God's autograph.

Five-Finger Prayers

Read: James 5:13–18

Pray for each other. James 5:16

Prayer is a conversation with God, not a formula. Yet sometimes we might need to use a "method" to freshen up our prayer time. We can pray the Psalms or other Scriptures (such as The Lord's Prayer), or use the ACTS method (Adoration, Confession, Thanksgiving, and Supplication). I recently came across this "Five-Finger Prayer" to use as a guide when praying for others:

- **When you fold your hands, the thumb is nearest you.** So begin by praying for those closest to you—your loved ones (PHIL. 1:3–5).

- **The index finger is the pointer.** Pray for those who teach—Bible teachers and preachers, and those who teach children (1 THESS. 5:25).

- **The next finger is the tallest.** It reminds you to pray for those in authority over you—national and local leaders, and your supervisor at work (1 TIM. 2:1–2).

- **The fourth finger is usually the weakest.** Pray for those who are in trouble or who are suffering (JAMES 5:13–16).

- **Then comes your little finger.** It reminds you of your smallness in relation to God's greatness. Ask Him to supply your needs (PHIL. 4:6, 19).

Whatever method you use, just talk with your Father. He wants to hear what's on your heart. *ANNE CETAS*

Father, give me the wisdom to know how to pray for others.

It's not the words we pray that matter; it's the condition of our heart.

Unfinished Works

Read: Romans 7:14–25

Who will rescue me from this body that is subject to death? Thanks be to God, who delivers me through Jesus Christ our Lord! Romans 7:24–25

At his death, the great artist Michelangelo left many unfinished projects. But four of his sculptures were never meant to be completed. The *Bearded Slave*, the *Atlas Slave*, the *Awakening Slave*, and the *Young Slave*, though they appear unfinished, are just as Michelangelo intended them to be. The artist wanted to show what it might feel like to be forever enslaved.

Rather than sculpting figures in chains, Michelangelo made figures stuck in the very marble out of which they are carved. Bodies emerge from the stone, but not completely. Muscles flex, but the figures are never able to free themselves.

My empathy with the slave sculptures is immediate. Their plight is not unlike my struggle with sin. I am unable to free myself: like the sculptures I am stuck, "a prisoner of the law of sin at work within me" (ROM 7:23). No matter how hard I try, I cannot change myself. But thanks be to God, you and I will not remain unfinished works. We won't be complete until heaven, but in the meantime as we welcome the transforming work of the Holy Spirit, He changes us. God promises to finish the good work He has begun in us (PHIL. 1:6).   *AMY PETERSON*

God, thank You that You make us new creatures through the work of Your Son Jesus Christ, freeing us from our slavery to sin.

He is the potter; we are the clay.

Faith in Action

Read: James 2:14–26

Show me your faith without deeds, and I will show you my faith by my deeds. James 2:18

As a friend drove to the grocery store, she noticed a woman walking along the side of the road and felt she should turn the car around and offer her a ride. When she did, she was saddened to hear that the woman didn't have money for the bus so was walking home many miles in the hot and humid weather. Not only was she making the long journey home, but she had also walked several hours that morning to arrive at work by 4 a.m.

By offering a ride, my friend put into practice in a modern setting James's instruction for Christians to live out their faith with their deeds: "Faith by itself, if it is not accompanied by action, is dead" (V. 17). He was concerned that the church take care of the widows and the orphans (JAMES 1:27), and he also wanted them to rely not on empty words but to act on their faith with deeds of love.

We are saved by faith, not works, but we live out our faith by loving others and caring for their needs. May we, like my friend who offered the ride, keep our eyes open for those who might need our help as we walk together in this journey of life.

AMY BOUCHER PYE

Lord Jesus Christ, You did the ultimate deed by dying on the cross for me. May I never forget the sacrifice that gives me life.

We live out our faith through our good deeds.

Time to Flourish

Read: Luke 13:1–9

"Sir," the man replied, "leave it alone for one more year, and I'll dig around it and fertilize it." Luke 13:8

Last spring I decided to cut down the rose bush by our back door. In the three years we'd lived in our home, it hadn't produced many flowers, and its ugly, fruitless branches were now creeping in all directions.

But life got busy, and my gardening plan got delayed. It was just as well—only a few weeks later that rose bush burst into bloom like I'd never seen before. Hundreds of big white flowers, rich in perfume, hung over the back door, flowed into our yard, and showered the ground with beautiful petals.

My rose bush's revival reminded me of Jesus's parable of the fig tree in Luke 13:6–9. In Israel, it was customary to give fig trees three years to produce fruit. If they didn't, they were cut down so the soil could be better used. In Jesus's story, a gardener asks his boss to give one particular tree a fourth year to produce. In context (VV. 1–5), the parable implies this: The Israelites hadn't lived as they should, and God could justly judge them. But God is patient and had given extra time for them to turn to Him, be forgiven, and bloom.

God wants all people to flourish and has given extra time so that they can. Whether we are still journeying toward faith or are praying for unbelieving family and friends, His patience is good news for all of us.   *SHERIDAN VOYSEY*

I am the vine; you are the branches. If you remain in me and I in you, you will bear much fruit; apart from me you can do nothing.
JOHN 15:5

God has given the world extra time to respond to His offer of forgiveness.

Cleaning House

Read: 1 Peter 1:22–2:5

Rid yourselves of all malice and all deceit, hypocrisy, envy, and slander of every kind. 1 Peter 2:1

Recently, I switched rooms in the home I rent. This took longer than expected, because I didn't want to simply transfer my (extensive) mess to a new room; I wanted a completely fresh and uncluttered start. After hours and hours of cleaning and sorting, bags of stuff sat by the front door to be thrown away, donated, or recycled. But at the end of this exhausting process was a beautiful room I was excited to spend time in.

My housecleaning project gave me a fresh perspective when reading 1 Peter 2:1, as paraphrased in *The Message*: "So, clean house! Make a clean sweep of malice and pretense, envy, and hurtful talk." Interestingly, it's after a joyful confession of their new life in Christ (1:1–12) that Peter urges them to throw away destructive habits (1:13–2:3). When our walk with the Lord feels cluttered and our love for others feels strained, this shouldn't cause us to question our salvation. We don't change our lives to *be* saved, but because we *are* (1:23).

As real as our new life in Christ is, bad habits learned do not disappear overnight. So, on a daily basis, we need to "clean house," throwing away all that prevents us from fully loving others (1:22) and growing (2:2). Then, in that new, clean space, we can experience the wonder of being freshly built (V. 5) by Christ's power and life.   *MONICA BRANDS*

Heavenly Father, thank You for the new life You are building in us through our Lord Jesus. Help us to daily turn to You for cleansing and renewal.

Every day we can reject destructive habits and experience new life in Jesus.

Taking Shortcuts

Read: Luke 9:57–62

Whoever wants to be my disciple must deny themselves and take up their cross daily and follow me. Luke 9:23

Sipping her tea, Nancy gazed out her friend's window and sighed. Spring rains and sunshine had coaxed a riotous expanse of color from a well-groomed flowerbed of lilies, phlox, irises, and evening primrose.

"I want that look," she said wistfully, "without all the work."

Some shortcuts are fine—even practical. Others short-circuit our spirit and deaden our lives. We want romance without the difficulties and messiness of committing to someone so different from ourselves. We want "greatness" without the risks and failures necessary in the adventure of real life. We desire to please God, but not when it inconveniences us.

Jesus made clear to His followers that there is no shortcut that avoids the hard choice of surrendering our lives to Him. He warned a prospective disciple, "No one who puts a hand to the plow and looks back is fit for service in the kingdom of God" (LUKE 9:62). To follow Christ requires a radical altering of our loyalties.

When we turn in faith to Jesus, the work just begins. But it is oh-so-worth-it, for He also told us that no one who sacrifices "for me and the gospel will fail to receive a hundred times as much in this present age . . . and in the age to come eternal life" (MARK 10:29–30). The work of following Christ is difficult, but He's given us His Spirit and the reward is a full, joyful life now and forever.

TIM GUSTAFSON

Father, I will find the strength to do the work You have for me to do, only as I rely on Your Holy Spirit. Help me, please, to be sensitive to that today.

Most things worth doing are difficult.

Destroying the Divides

Read: Joshua 7:1–12

I will not be with you anymore unless you destroy whatever among you is devoted to destruction. Joshua 7:12

A writing deadline loomed over me, while the argument I had with my husband earlier that morning swirled through my mind. I stared at the blinking cursor, fingertips resting on the keyboard. *He was wrong too, Lord.*

When the computer screen went black, my reflection scowled. My unacknowledged wrongs were doing more than hindering the work before me. They were straining my relationship with my husband and my God.

I grabbed my cell phone, swallowed my pride, and asked for forgiveness. Savoring the peace of reconciliation when my spouse apologized as well, I thanked God and finished my article on time.

The Israelites experienced the pain of personal sin and joy of restoration. Joshua warned God's people not to enrich themselves in the battle for Jericho (JOSH. 6:18), but Achan stole captured items and hid them in his tent (7:1). Only after his sin was exposed and dealt with (VV. 4–12) did the nation enjoy reconciliation with their God.

Like Achan, we don't always consider how "tucking sin into our tents" turns our hearts from God and impacts those around us. Acknowledging Jesus as Lord, admitting our sin, and seeking forgiveness provides the foundation for healthy and faithful relationships with God and others. By submitting to our loving Creator and Sustainer daily, we can serve Him and enjoy His presence—together. *XOCHITL DIXON*

Lord, please help us recognize, confess, and turn away from our sin, so that we can nurture loving relationships with You and others.

God can purge our hearts of the sin that destroys our intimacy with Him and others.

Celebrate Freedom

Read: Romans 6:15–23

The law of the Spirit who gives life has set you free from the law of sin and death. Romans 8:2

After being kidnapped, held hostage for thirteen days, and released, New Zealand news cameraman Olaf Wiig, with a broad smile on his face, announced, "I feel more alive now than I have in my entire life."

For reasons difficult to understand, being freed is more exhilarating than being free.

For those who enjoy freedom every day, Olaf's joy was a good reminder of how easily we forget how blessed we are. This is also true spiritually. Those of us who have been Christians for a long time often forget what it's like to be held hostage by sin. We can become complacent and even ungrateful. But then God sends a reminder in the form of a new believer who gives an exuberant testimony of what God has done in his or her life, and once again we see the joy that is ours when we are "free from the law of sin and death" (ROM. 8:2).

If freedom has become boring to you, or if you tend to focus on what you can't do, consider this: Not only are you no longer a slave to sin, but you are freed to be holy and to enjoy eternal life with Christ Jesus! (6:22).

Celebrate your freedom in Christ by taking the time to thank God for the things you are able and free to do as His servant.

JULIE ACKERMAN LINK

Living for Christ brings true freedom.

Could I Say That?

Read: Genesis 45:1–11

It was not you who sent me here, but God. Genesis 45:8

"The perception of favoritism is one of the biggest factors in sibling rivalry," said Dr. Barbara Howard, a developmental behavioral pediatrician ("When Parents Have a Favorite Child" nytimes.com). An example would be the Old Testament character Joseph, who was his father's favorite son, which made his older brothers furious (GEN. 37:3–4). So they sold Joseph to merchants traveling to Egypt and made it appear that a wild animal had killed him (37:12–36). His dreams had been shattered and his future appeared hopeless.

Yet, along Joseph's journey of life, he chose to be true to his God and rely on Him even when it seemed to make his situation worse. After being falsely accused by his employer's wife and imprisoned for something he didn't do, Joseph struggled with the injustice of his situation but kept trusting the Lord.

Years later his brothers came to Egypt to buy grain during a famine and were terrified to discover that their despised younger brother was now the Prime Minister. But Joseph told them, "Do not be distressed and do not be angry with yourselves for selling me here, because it was to save lives that God sent me ahead of you. . . . It was not you who sent me here, but God" (45:5, 8).

Joseph's kind words cause me to wonder if I would be ready for revenge. Or would I be gracious because my heart had confidence in the Lord?   *DAVID MCCASLAND*

Dear Father, give us the faith to trust You today and the ability to see Your hand of good along our road of life.

In the darkest hours of life, only through the eyes of faith can we see the loving hand of God.

Going First

Read: 1 John 4:7–21

We love because he first loved us. 1 John 4:19

We worked patiently to help our son heal and adjust to his new life with our family. Trauma from his early days in an orphanage was fueling some negative behaviors. While I had enormous compassion for the hardships he experienced in his early days, I felt myself begin to withdraw from him emotionally because of those behaviors. Ashamed, I shared my struggle with his therapist. Her gentle reply hit home: "He needs you to go first . . . to show him he's worthy of love before he'll be able to act like it."

John pushes the recipients of his letter to an incredible depth of love, citing God's love as both the source and the reason for loving one another (1 JOHN 4:7, 11). I admit I often fail to show such love to others, whether strangers, friends, or my own children. Yet John's words spark in me renewed desire and ability to do so: *God went first.* He sent His Son to demonstrate the fullness of His love for each of us. I'm so thankful He doesn't respond as we all are prone to do by withdrawing His heart from us.

Though our sinful actions don't invite God's love, He is unwavering in offering it to us (ROM. 5:8). His "go-first" love compels us to love one another in response to, and as a reflection of, that love.   KIRSTEN HOLMBERG

Thank You, Lord, for loving me in spite of my sin. Help me to "go first" in loving others.

God loved us first so we can love others.

The Ultimate Good

Read: Philippians 3:1–11

I consider everything a loss because of the surpassing worth of knowing Christ Jesus my Lord. Philippians 3:8

As I was growing up in Jamaica, my parents raised my sister and me to be "good people." In our home, *good* meant obeying our parents, telling the truth, being successful in school and work, and going to church . . . at least Easter and Christmas. I imagine this definition of being a good person is familiar to many people, regardless of culture. In fact, the apostle Paul, in Philippians 3, used his culture's definition of being good to make a greater point.

Paul, being a devout first-century Jew, followed the letter of the moral law in his culture. He was born into the "right" family, had the "right" education, and practiced the "right" religion. He was the *real deal* in terms of being a good person according to Jewish custom. In verse 4, Paul writes that he could boast in all of his goodness if he wanted to. But, as good as he was, Paul told his readers (and us) that there is something more than being good. He knew that being good, while *good*, was not the same as pleasing God.

Pleasing God, Paul writes in verses 7–8, involves knowing Jesus. Paul considered his own goodness as "garbage" when compared to "the surpassing worth of knowing Christ Jesus." We are good—and we please God—when our hope and faith are in Christ alone, not in our goodness.   *KAREN WOLFE*

Dear God, as I seek to live a good life, help me remember that knowing Jesus is the way to ultimate goodness.

We are good—and we please God—when our hope and faith are in Christ alone, not in our goodness.

A Day to Rest

Read: Exodus 23:10–13

Six days do your work, but on the seventh day do not work.
Exodus 23:12

One Sunday, I stood by the gurgling stream that wends its way through our North London community, delighting in the beauty it brings to our otherwise built-up area. I felt myself relax as I watched the cascading water and listened to the birds chirping. I paused to give the Lord thanks for how He helps us to find rest for our souls.

The Lord instituted a time of Sabbath—a time for rest and renewal—for His people in the ancient Near East because He wanted them to thrive. As we see in the book of Exodus, He tells them to sow their fields for six years and rest on the seventh. So too with working six days and resting on the seventh. His way of life set apart the Israelites from other nations, for not only they but also the foreigners and slaves in their households were allowed to follow this pattern.

We can approach our day of rest with expectancy and creativity, welcoming the chance to worship and do something that feeds our souls, which will vary according to our preferences. Some will like to play games; some to garden; some to share a meal with friends and family; some to take an afternoon nap.

How can we rediscover the beauty and richness of setting apart a day to rest, if that's missing from our lives?

AMY BOUCHER PYE

Lord God, in You we find our rest. Thank You that You've created us both to work and to rest. Please help us to find the right rhythm for our lives.

In our faith and service, rest is as important as work.

A Joyful Heart

Read: 2 Chronicles 7:1–10

Shout for joy to the LORD, all the earth. Psalm 100:1

My granddaughter's favorite tune is one of John Philip Sousa's marches. Sousa, known as "The March King," was a US composer in the late nineteenth century. Moriah isn't in a marching band; she's only twenty months old. She just loves the tune and can even hum a few notes. She associates it with joyful times. When our family gets together, we often hum this song along with claps and other boisterous noises, and the grandchildren dance or parade in circles to the beat. It always ends in dizzy children and lots of laughter.

Our joyful noise reminds me of the psalm that implores us to "worship the LORD with gladness" (PS. 100:2). When King Solomon dedicated the temple, the Israelites celebrated with praises (2 CHRON. 7:5–6). Psalm 100 may have been one of the songs they sang. The psalm declares: "Shout for joy to the LORD, all the earth. Worship the LORD with gladness; come before him with joyful songs. . . . Enter his gates with thanksgiving and his courts with praise; give thanks to him and praise his name" (VV. 1-2, 4). Why? "For the LORD is good and his love endures forever"! (V. 5).

Our good God loves us! In grateful response, let's "shout for joy to the LORD"! (PS. 100:1). *ALYSON KIEDA*

Dear Lord, give us thankful hearts to praise You, because You are good and all that You do is good. Your love endures forever!

Praise is the overflow of a joyful heart.

Getting Away with It

Read: Genesis 4:1–12

By faith Abel still speaks. Hebrews 11:4

In June 2004, at a Vancouver art gallery, Canadian cross-country skier Beckie Scott received an Olympic gold medal. That's interesting, because the Winter Olympics had been held in 2002—in Utah. Scott had won bronze behind two athletes who were disqualified months later when it was learned they had used banned substances.

It's good that Scott eventually received her gold, but gone forever is the moment when she should have stood on the podium to hear her country's national anthem. That injustice couldn't be remedied.

Injustice of any kind disturbs us, and surely there are far greater wrongs than being denied a hard-won medal. The story of Cain and Abel shows an ultimate act of injustice (GEN. 4:8). And at first glance, it might look like Cain got away with murdering his brother. After all, he lived a long, full life, eventually building a city (V. 17).

But God himself confronted Cain. "Your brother's blood cries out to me from the ground," He said (V. 10). The New Testament later recorded Cain as an example to avoid (1 JOHN 3:12; JUDE 1:11). But of Abel we read, "By faith Abel still speaks, even though he is dead" (HEB. 11:4).

God cares deeply about justice, about righting wrongs, and about defending the powerless. In the end, no one gets away with any act of injustice. Nor does God leave unrewarded our work done in faith for Him.   *TIM GUSTAFSON*

Father, as Your Son taught us to pray, we ask that Your kingdom will come, Your will be done to change this broken world. Thank You for redeeming us.

Sin will not ultimately be judged by the way we see it, but by the way God sees it.

Giving in to Jesus

Read: James 4:6–10

In the same way, count yourselves dead to sin but alive to God in Christ Jesus. Romans 6:11

They call it "The Devil's Footprint." It's a foot-shaped impression in the granite on a hill beside a church in Ipswich, Massachusetts. According to local legend the "footprint" happened one fall day in 1740, when the evangelist George Whitefield preached so powerfully that the devil leaped from the church steeple, landing on the rock on his way out of town.

Though it's only a legend, the story calls to mind an encouraging truth from God's Word. James 4:7 reminds us, "Submit yourselves, then, to God. Resist the devil, and he will flee from you."

God has given us the strength we need to stand against our adversary and the temptations in our lives. The Bible tells us that "sin shall no longer be your master" (ROM. 6:14) because of God's loving grace to us through Jesus Christ. As we run to Jesus when temptation comes, He enables us to stand in His strength. Nothing we face in this life can overcome Him, because He has "overcome the world" (JOHN 16:33).

As we submit ourselves to our Savior, yielding our wills to Him in the moment and walking in obedience to God's Word, He is helping us. When we give in to Him instead of giving in to temptation, He is able to fight our battles. In Him we can overcome.

JAMES BANKS

Lord Jesus, I give my will to You today. Help me to stay close to You in every moment, and to love You by obeying You.

The prayer of the feeblest saint . . . is a terror to Satan.
OSWALD CHAMBERS

Approaching God

Read: Hebrews 4:14–16

But as for me, it is good to be near God. I have made the Sovereign
LORD my refuge. Psalm 73:28

A woman desiring to pray grabbed an empty chair and knelt before it. In tears, she said, "My dear heavenly Father, please sit down here; you and I need to talk!" Then, looking directly at the vacant chair, she prayed. She demonstrated confidence in approaching the Lord; she imagined He was *sitting* on the chair and believed He was listening to her petition.

A time with God is an important moment when we engage the Almighty. God comes near to us as we draw near to Him in a mutual involvement (JAMES 4:8). He has assured us, "I am with you always" (MATT. 28:20). Our heavenly Father is always waiting for us to come to Him, always ready to listen to us.

There are times when we struggle to pray because we feel tired, sleepy, sick, and weak. But Jesus sympathizes with us when we are weak or face temptations (HEB. 4:15). Therefore we can "approach God's throne of grace with confidence, so that we may receive mercy and find grace to help us in our time of need" (V. 16).

LAWRENCE DARMANI

Lord, thank You that I can pray to You in all places at all times. Put the desire
to come near to You in my heart. I want to learn to come to You in faith
and in confidence.

God is everywhere, is available every time, and listens always.

Intimate Details

Read: Psalm 139:1–18

You know when I sit and when I rise; you perceive my thoughts from afar. Psalm 139:2

The universe is astonishingly grand. Right now the moon is spinning around us at nearly 2,300 miles an hour. Our Earth is spinning around the sun at 66,000 miles an hour. Our sun is one of 200 billion other stars and trillions more planets in our galaxy, and that galaxy is just one of 100 billion others hurtling through space. Astounding!

In comparison to this vast cosmos, our little Earth is no bigger than a pebble, and our individual lives no greater than a grain of sand. Yet according to Scripture, the God of the galaxies attends to each microscopic one of us in intimate detail. He saw us before we existed (PS. 139:13–16); He watches us as we go about our days and listens for our every thought (VV. 1–6).

It can be hard to believe this sometimes. This tiny "pebble" has big problems like war and famine, and we can question God's care in times of personal suffering. But when King David wrote Psalm 139 he was in the midst of crisis himself (VV. 19–20). And when Jesus said God counts each hair on our heads (MATT. 10:30), He was living in an age of crucifixion. Biblical talk of God's caring attention isn't a naïve wish. It is real-world truth.

The One who keeps the galaxies spinning knows us intimately. That can help us get through the worst of times.

SHERIDAN VOYSEY

Father God, Your eye is on me as much as it is on the stars in the sky. Thank You for Your love, Your care, Your attention.

The God of the cosmos cares for us intimately.

Face to Face

Read: Exodus 33:7–14

The LORD would speak to Moses face to face, as one speaks to a friend.
Exodus 33:11

Although the world is connected electronically like never before, nothing beats time together in person. As we share and laugh together, we can often sense—almost unconsciously—the other person's emotions by watching their facial movements. Those who love each other, whether family or friends, like to share with each other face to face.

We see this face-to-face relationship between the Lord and Moses, the man God chose to lead His people. Moses grew in confidence over the years of following God, and he continued to follow Him despite the people's rebelliousness and idolatry. After the people worshiped a golden calf instead of the Lord (SEE EX. 32), Moses set up a tent outside of the camp in which to meet God, while they had to watch from a distance (33:7–11). As the pillar of cloud signifying God's presence descended to the tent, Moses spoke on their behalf. The Lord promised that His Presence would go with them (V. 14).

Because of Jesus's death on the cross and His resurrection, we no longer need someone like Moses to speak with God for us. Instead, just as Jesus offered to His disciples, we can have friendship with God through Christ (JOHN 15:15). We too can meet with Him, with the Lord speaking to us as one speaks to a friend.

AMY BOUCHER PYE

Face to face! O blissful moment! Face to face—to see and know; face to face with
my Redeemer, Jesus Christ who loves me so!
CARRIE E. BRECK

We can speak to the Lord as a friend.

Are You Being Prepared?

Read: 1 Samuel 17:8, 32–37, 48–50

The LORD who rescued me from the paw of the lion and . . . the bear will rescue me. 1 Samuel 17:37

I worked at a fast-food restaurant for over two years in high school. Some aspects of the job were difficult. Customers verbalized their anger while I apologized for the unwanted slice of cheese on the sandwich I didn't make. Soon after I left, I applied for a computer job at my university. The employers were more interested in my fast-food experience than my computer skills. They wanted to know that I knew how to deal with people. My experience in unpleasant circumstances prepared me for a better job!

Young David persevered through an experience we might well call unpleasant. When Israel was challenged to send someone to fight Goliath, no one was brave enough to step up to the task. No one but David. King Saul was reluctant to send him to fight, but David explained that as a shepherd he had fought and killed a lion and a bear for the sake of the sheep (1 SAM. 17:34–36). Confidently he stated, "The Lord who rescued me from the paw of the lion and . . . the bear will rescue me from the hand of this Philistine" (V. 37).

Being a shepherd didn't earn David much respect, but it prepared him to fight Goliath and eventually become Israel's greatest king. We may be in difficult circumstances, but through them God might be preparing us for something greater!

JULIE SCHWAB

Lord, help me to hold on during the unpleasant times in my life knowing that You may be preparing me for something greater.

God uses present circumstances to prepare us for the future.

Deep Roots

Read: Luke 24:44–49

Then he opened their minds so they could understand the Scriptures.
Luke 24:45

The sequoia tree, one of three species of redwoods, is among the world's largest and most enduring organisms. It can grow to 300 feet in height, weigh over 2.5 million pounds (1.1 million kg), and live for 3,000 years. But the majestic sequoia owes much of its size and longevity to what lies below the surface. A twelve- to fourteen-foot-deep matting of roots, spreading over as much as an acre of earth, firmly grounds its towering height and astonishing weight.

A redwood's expansive root system, however, is small compared to the national history, religion, and anticipation that undergird the life of Jesus. On one occasion He told a group of religious leaders that the Scriptures they loved and trusted told His story (JOHN 5:39). In the synagogue of Nazareth He opened the scroll of Isaiah, read a description of Israel's Messiah, and said, "Today this Scripture is fulfilled in your hearing" (LUKE 4:21).

Later, after His resurrection, Jesus helped His disciples understand how the words of Moses, the prophets, and even the songs of Israel showed why it was necessary for Him to suffer, die, and rise from the dead (24:46).

What grace and grandeur—to see Jesus rooted in the history and Scriptures of a nation, and to see how extensively our own lives are rooted in our need of Him.   *MART DEHAAN*

Father in heaven, please help us never forget that the history of Israel and the inspired words of Scripture ground us in seeing our need of Your Son.

All Scripture helps us see our need of Jesus.

Just Like Dad

Read: John 5:17–20

The Son can do nothing by himself; he can do only what he sees his Father doing, because whatever the Father does the Son also does.
John 5:19

Isn't it endearing to see a child mimicking his parents? How often we've seen the young boy in a car seat, gripping his imaginary steering wheel intently while keeping a close eye on the driver to see what Daddy does next.

I remember doing the same thing when I was young. Nothing gave me greater pleasure than doing exactly what my dad did—and I'm sure he got an even bigger kick watching me copy his actions.

I would like to think God felt the same way when He saw His dearest Son doing exactly what the Father did—reaching out to the lost, helping the needy, and healing the sick. Jesus said, "the Son can do nothing by himself; he can do only what he sees his Father doing, because whatever the Father does the Son also does" (JOHN 5:19).

We too are called to do the same—to "follow God's example, therefore, as dearly loved children and walk in the way of love" (EPH. 5:1-2). As we continue growing to be more like Jesus, may we seek to love like the Father loves, forgive like He forgives, care like He cares, and live in ways that please Him. It is a delight to copy His actions, in the power of the Spirit, knowing that our reward is the affectionate, tender smile of a loving Father.

LESLIE KOH

Jesus, thank You for showing us the way to the Father. Help us to be more and more like You and the Father each day.

The Father gave us the Spirit to make us like the Son.

Beyond Labels

Read: Romans 5:1–11

But God demonstrates his own love for us in this: While we were still sinners, Christ died for us. Romans 5:8

A church in my city has a unique welcome card that captures the love and grace of God for everyone. It says, "If You Are A . . . saint, sinner, loser, winner"—followed by many other terms used to describe struggling people—"alcoholic, hypocrite, cheater, fearful, misfit . . . . You are welcome here." One of the pastors told me, "We read the card aloud together in our worship services every Sunday."

How often we accept labels and allow them to define who we are. And how easily we assign them to others. But God's grace defies labels because it is rooted in His love, not in our self-perception. Whether we see ourselves as wonderful or terrible, capable or helpless, we can receive eternal life as a gift from Him. The apostle Paul reminded the followers of Jesus in Rome that "at just the right time, when we were still powerless, Christ died for the ungodly" (ROM. 5:6).

The Lord does not require us to change by our own power. Instead He invites us to come as we are to find hope, healing, and freedom in Him. "But God demonstrates his own love for us in this: While we were still sinners, Christ died for us" (V. 8). The Lord is ready and willing to receive us just as we are.

DAVID MCCASLAND

Heavenly Father, thank You for Your amazing love in Jesus.

God's forgiveness defies our labels of failure or pride.

Mightier than All

Read: Psalm 93

The LORD reigns, he is robed in majesty; the LORD is robed in majesty and armed with strength. Psalm 93:1

Iguazu Falls, on the border of Brazil and Argentina, is a spectacular waterfall system of 275 falls along 2.7 km (1.67 miles) of the Iguazu River. Etched on a wall on the Brazilian side of the Falls are the words of Psalm 93:4, "Mightier than the thunders of many waters, mightier than the waves of the sea, the Lord on high is mighty!" (RSV). Below it are these words, "God is always greater than all of our troubles."

The writer of Psalm 93, who penned its words during the time that kings reigned, knew that God is the ultimate King over all. "The LORD reigns," he wrote. "Your throne was established long ago; you are from all eternity" (VV. 1–2). No matter how high the floods or waves, the Lord remains greater than them all.

The roar of a waterfall is truly majestic, but it is quite a different matter to be in the water hurtling toward the falls. That may be the situation you are in today. Physical, financial, or relational problems loom ever larger and you feel like you are about to go over the falls. In such situations, the Christian has Someone to turn to. He is the Lord, "who is able to do immeasurably more than all we ask or imagine" (EPH. 3:20) for He is greater than all our troubles.

C. P. HIA

Lord, I know that You are powerful and greater than any trouble that might come my way. I trust You to carry me through.

Never measure God's unlimited power by your limited expectations.

A Time for Everything

Read: Ecclesiastes 3:1–14

There is a time for everything, and a season for every activity under the heavens. Ecclesiastes 3:1

While flying recently, I watched a mother and her children a few rows ahead of me. While the toddler played contentedly, the mother gazed into the eyes of her newborn, smiling at him and stroking his cheek. He stared back with a wide-eyed wonderment. I enjoyed the moment with a touch of wistfulness, thinking of my own children at that age and the season that has passed me by.

I reflected, however, about King Solomon's words in the book of Ecclesiastes about "every activity under the heavens" (V. 1). He addresses through a series of opposites how there is a "time for everything" (V. 1): "a time to be born and a time to die, a time to plant and a time to uproot" (V. 2). Perhaps King Solomon in these verses despairs at what he sees as a meaningless cycle of life. But he also acknowledges the role of God in each season, that our work is a "gift of God" (V. 13) and that "everything God does will endure forever" (V. 14).

We may remember times in our lives with longing, like me thinking of my children as babies. We know, however, that the Lord promises to be with us in every season of our life (ISA. 41:10). We can count on His presence and find that our purpose is in walking with Him.   *AMY BOUCHER PYE*

Lord God, You lead me through the seasons, and whether I'm laughing or crying I know You are with me. May I reach out to someone with Your love today.

God gives us the seasons of our lives.

Dressed Up

Read: Romans 13:11–14

Clothe yourselves with the Lord Jesus Christ. Romans 13:14

In her book *Wearing God*, author Lauren Winner says our clothes can silently communicate to others who we are. What we wear may indicate career, community or identity, moods, or social status. Think of a T-shirt with a slogan, a business suit, a uniform, or greasy jeans and what they might reveal. She writes, "The idea that, as with a garment, Christians might wordlessly speak something of Jesus—is appealing."

According to Paul, we can similarly wordlessly represent Christ. Romans 13:14 tells us to "clothe [ourselves] with the Lord Jesus Christ, and do not think about how to gratify the desires of the flesh." What does this mean? When we become Christians, we take on Christ's identity. We're "children of God through faith" (GAL. 3:26–27). That's our status. Yet each day we need to clothe ourselves in His character. We do this by striving to live for and to be more like Jesus, growing in godliness, love, and obedience and turning our back on the sins that once enslaved us.

This growth in Christ is a result of the Holy Spirit working in us and our desire to be closer to Him through study of the Word, prayer, and time spent in fellowship with other Christians (JOHN 14:26). When others look at our words and attitudes, what statement are we making about Christ? *ALYSON KIEDA*

Dear Lord, we want to be a reflection of You. Help us to look more like You each day. Grow us in godliness, love, joy, and patience.

When others see us, may what they see speak well of the Savior.

"I'm Really Scared . . ."

Read: Philippians 4:4–9

Do not be anxious about anything, but in every situation,
by prayer and petition, with thanksgiving, present your requests to God.
Philippians 4:6

❝ I 'm really scared." This was the poignant note a teenager posted to friends on Facebook as she told them of some upcoming medical tests. She was facing hospitalization and a series of procedures in a city three hours from home and anxiously waited as doctors tried to discover the source of some serious medical problems she was experiencing.

Who of us, in youth or later years, has not felt similar fears when facing unwanted life events that are truly frightening? And where can we turn for help? What comfort can we find from Scripture to give us courage in these kinds of situations?

The reality that God will go with us through our trial can help us to hope. Isaiah 41:13 tells us, "For I am the LORD your God who takes hold of your right hand and says to you, 'Do not fear; I will help you.'"

In addition, God offers indescribable, heart-guarding peace when we present our difficulties to Him in prayer (PHIL. 4:6–7).

Through God's unfailing presence and His peace that "transcends all understanding" (V. 7), we can find the hope and help we need to endure situations in which we are really scared.

DAVE BRANON

Dear heavenly Father, when I am afraid, remind me that You hold my hand and give me peace. I'm grateful that I can lean into Your arms and find help when I'm scared. You are good to me.

God is with us in all our struggles.

Didn't Get Credit?

Read: Colossians 4:7–18

Let your light shine before others, that they may see your good deeds and glorify your Father in heaven. Matthew 5:16

Hollywood musicals were wildly popular during the 1950s and 1960s, and three actresses in particular—Audrey Hepburn, Natalie Wood, and Deborah Kerr—thrilled viewers with their compelling performances. But a huge part of the appeal of these actresses was the breathtaking singing that enhanced their acting. In fact, the classic films' successes were actually due in large part to Marni Nixon, who dubbed the voices for each of those leading ladies and who for a long time went completely uncredited for her vital contribution.

In the body of Christ there are often people that faithfully support others who take a more public role. The apostle Paul depended on exactly that kind of person in his ministry. Tertius's work as a scribe gave Paul his powerful *written* voice (ROM. 16:22). Epaphras's consistent behind-the-scene prayers were an essential foundation for Paul and the early church (COL. 4:12–13). Lydia generously opened her home when the weary apostle needed restoration (ACTS 16:15). Paul's work could not have been possible without the support he received from these fellow servants in Christ (VV. 7–18).

We may not always have highly visible roles, yet we know that God is pleased when we obediently play our essential part in His plan. When we "give [ourselves] fully to the work of the Lord" (1 COR. 15:58), we will find value and meaning in our service as it brings glory to God and draws others to Him (MATT. 5:16).

CINDY HESS KASPER

Lord, help me to obediently do my part in the role You have chosen for me.

The secret of true service is absolute faithfulness wherever God places you.

Mosaic

Read: Ephesians 2:10–22

We are God's handiwork, created in Christ Jesus to do good works.
Ephesians 2:10

For 3 weeks every year, our city becomes an art gallery. Nearly 2,000 artists from around the world display their creations in galleries, museums, hotels, parks, city streets, parking lots, restaurants, churches, and even in the river.

Among my favorite entries are mosaics made from small pieces of colored glass. The winning entry in 2011 was a 9 x 13-foot stained-glass mosaic of the crucifixion by artist Mia Tavonatti. While viewing the artwork, I heard the artist discuss how many times she had cut herself while shaping the pieces of glass for her mosaic.

As I gazed at the beautiful rendition of what was a horrific event, I saw more than a representation of the crucifixion—I saw a picture of the church, the body of Christ. In each piece of glass I saw an individual believer, beautifully shaped by Christ to fit together into the whole (EPHESIANS 2:16,21). In the artist's story, I recognized the shedding of Jesus's blood so that this unity could take place. And in the finished artwork, I saw the act of love required to complete the project despite pain and sacrifice.

We who believe in Christ are a work of art created by God to show the greatness of a Savior who makes something beautiful out of the broken pieces of our lives.   *JULIE ACKERMAN LINK*

Thank You, Father, that You are making something beautiful of our lives.

**Christ gave everything to make something beautiful of
His church.**

What We Bring Back

Read: Psalm 37:1–6, 23–27

I was young and now I am old, yet I have never seen the righteous forsaken or their children begging bread. Psalm 37:25

John F. Burns spent forty years covering world events for *The New York Times*. In an article written after his retirement in 2015, Burns recalled the words of a close friend and fellow journalist who was dying of cancer. "Never forget," his colleague said, "It's not how far you've traveled; it's what you've brought back."

Psalm 37 could be considered David's list of what he "brought back" from his journey of life, from shepherd to soldier and king. The psalm is a series of couplets contrasting the wicked with the righteous, and affirming those who trust the Lord.

"Do not fret because of those who are evil or be envious of those who do wrong; for like the grass they will soon wither" (vv. 1–2).

"The Lord makes firm the steps of the one who delights in him; though he may stumble, he will not fall, for the Lord upholds him with his hand" (vv. 23–24).

"I was young and now I am old, yet I have never seen the righteous forsaken or their children begging bread" (v. 25).

From our experiences in life, what has God taught us? How have we experienced His faithfulness and love? In what ways has the Lord's love shaped our lives?

It's not how far we've traveled in life, but what we've brought back that counts. *DAVID MCCASLAND*

Dear Lord, thank You for walking with me throughout my life. Help me to remember Your faithfulness.

As the years add up, God's faithfulness keeps multiplying.

Out of the Deep

Read: 2 Samuel 22:17–20

He reached down from on high and took hold of me. 2 Samuel 22:17

I scanned the water intently, on alert for signs of trouble. During my six-hour shifts as a lifeguard, I watched from the side of the pool to ensure the safety of those swimming. Leaving my post, or even becoming lax in my attentiveness, could have grave consequences for those in the pool. If a swimmer was in danger of drowning due to injury or lack of skill, it was my responsibility to pluck them from the water and return them to safety on the pool deck.

After experiencing God's aid in battle against the Philistines (2 SAM. 21:15–22), David likens his rescue to being drawn out of "deep waters" (22:17). David's very life—and that of his men—was in serious danger from his enemies. God buoyed David as he was drowning in disaster. While lifeguards are paid to assure the safety of swimmers, God, on the other hand, saved David because of His *delight* in him (V. 20). My heart leaps for joy when I realize that God doesn't watch over and protect me because He's obliged to but because He *wants* to.

When we feel overcome by the troubles of life, we can rest in the knowledge that God, our Lifeguard, sees our struggle and, because of His delight in us, watches over and protects us.

KIRSTEN HOLMBERG

Thank You, Lord, for seeing my struggles and standing ready to save me. Help me to trust Your rescuing love more fully.

God delights in saving His children.

Sweet Company

Read: John 14:15–26

The Spirit of truth . . . lives with you and will be in you. John 14:17

The elderly woman in the nursing home didn't speak to anyone or request anything. It seemed she merely existed, rocking in her creaky old chair. She didn't have many visitors, so one young nurse would often go into her room on her breaks. Without asking the woman questions to try to get her to talk, she simply pulled up another chair and rocked with her. After several months, the elderly woman said to her, "Thank you for rocking with me." She was grateful for the companionship.

Before He went back to heaven, Jesus promised to send a constant companion to His disciples. He told them He would not leave them alone but would send the Holy Spirit to be in them (JOHN 14:17). That promise is still true for believers in Jesus today. Jesus said that the triune God makes His "home" in us (V. 23).

The Lord is our close and faithful companion throughout our entire life. He will guide us in our deepest struggles, forgive our sin, hear each silent prayer, and shoulder the burdens we cannot bear.

We can enjoy His sweet company today.   *ANNE CETAS*

Dear Lord, thank You for giving us Your Spirit as our constant companion.

The Christian's heart is the Holy Spirit's home.

Forgiven!

Read: 1 John 1:1–10

I have strayed like a lost sheep. Seek your servant. Psalm 119:176

My friend Norm Cook sometimes had a surprise for his family when he arrived home from work. He would walk through the front door, and shout, "You're forgiven!" It wasn't that family members had wronged him and needed *his* forgiveness. He was reminding them that though they doubtless had sinned throughout the day, they were by God's grace fully forgiven.

The apostle John supplies this note about grace: "If we walk in the light, as he is in the light, we have fellowship with one another, and the blood of Jesus, his Son, purifies us from all sin. If we claim to be without sin [no inclination to sin], we deceive ourselves and the truth is not in us. If we confess our sins, he is faithful and just and will forgive us our sins and purify us from all unrighteousness" (1 JOHN 1:7–9).

To "walk in the light" is a metaphor for following Jesus. Imitating Jesus with the Spirit's help, John insists, is the sign that we have joined with the apostles in the fellowship of faith. We are authentic Christians. But, he continues, let's not be deceived: We will make wrong choices at times. Nevertheless, grace is given in full measure: We can take what forgiveness we need.

Not perfect; just forgiven by Jesus! That's the good word for today. *DAVID ROPER*

Lord, I know I'm not even close to being perfect. That's why I need You and Your cleansing in my life. I'm lost without You.

Monitor your heart daily to avoid wandering from God's wisdom.

Privileged Access

Read: Hebrews 12:18–24

You have come . . . to the church of the firstborn. Hebrews 12:22–23

Even though it was just a replica, the tabernacle set up in southern Israel was awe-inspiring. Built life-size and as close as possible to the specifications laid out in Exodus 25–27 (without actual gold and acacia wood, of course), it stood tall in the Negev desert.

When our tour group was taken through the "Holy Place" and into the "Most Holy Place" to see the "ark," some of us actually hesitated. Wasn't this the holiest place, where only the high priest was allowed to enter? How could we enter it so casually?

I can imagine how fearful the Israelites must have felt as they approached the tent of meeting with their sacrifices each time, knowing that they were coming into the presence of the Almighty God. And the wonder they must have felt, whenever God had a message for them, delivered through Moses.

Today, you and I can come straight to God with confidence, knowing that Jesus's sacrifice has torn down the barrier between us and God (HEB. 12:22–23). Each of us can talk to God any time we want, and hear from Him directly when we read His Word. We enjoy a direct access that the Israelites could only dream of. May we never take it for granted and cherish this awesome privilege of coming to the Father as His beloved children every day.

LESLIE KOH

Thank You, Father, for this wonderful privilege that Jesus has given us, to be able to come before You knowing we have been forgiven and cleansed by Christ's blood. May we never forget how big a sacrifice it took.

Through prayer, we have instant access to our Father.

All Generations

Read: Psalm 145:1–13

Your kingdom is an everlasting kingdom, and your dominion endures through all generations. Psalm 145:13

My parents married in 1933 during the Great Depression. My wife and I are Baby Boomers, part of the dramatic increase in births following World War II. Our four daughters, born in the seventies and eighties, belong to Generations X and Y. Growing up in such different times, it's not surprising that we have different opinions about many things!

Generations differ widely in their life experiences and values. And this is true among followers of Jesus. But no matter what we wear or the kind of music we enjoy, our spiritual connection is stronger than those differences.

Psalm 145, a mighty song of praise to God, proclaims our bond of faith. "One generation commends your works to another; they tell of your mighty acts. . . . They celebrate your abundant goodness and joyfully sing of your righteousness" (VV. 4, 7). Within a great diversity of age and experience, we come together by honoring the Lord. "They tell of the glory of your kingdom and speak of your might" (V. 11).

While differences and preferences could divide us, shared faith in Jesus Christ the Lord brings us together in mutual trust, encouragement, and praise. Whatever our age and outlook, we need each other! No matter which generation we belong to, we can learn from each other and together honor the Lord—"So that all people may know of [His] mighty acts and the glorious splendor of [His] kingdom" (V. 12).   *DAVID MCCASLAND*

Lord, unite Your people from all generations to honor and praise You as we bear witness of Your love.

God's kingdom is alive and active in all generations.

A "New Man"

Read: Colossians 1:3–14

Continue in your faith, established and firm, and do not move from the hope held out in the gospel. Colossians 1:23

As a group of teenagers visited a home for the elderly in Montego Bay, Jamaica, one young woman noticed a lonely looking man at the end of the room. He appeared to have little left in this world but a bed to sleep on—a bed from which he could not move because of his disability.

The teen began right away to share the story of God's love for us and read some Bible passages to him. "As I shared with him," she would say later, "I started to feel his eagerness to hear more." Responding to his interest, she explained the wonder of Jesus's sacrificial death for us. "It was hard for this man, who had no hope and no family," she recalled, "to understand that Someone he's never met would love him enough to die on the cross for his sins."

She told him more about Jesus—and then about the promise of heaven (including a new body) for all who believe. He asked her, "Will you dance with me up there?" She saw him begin to imagine himself free of his worn-out body and crippling limitations.

When he said he wanted to trust Jesus as his Savior, she helped him pray a prayer of forgiveness and faith. When she asked him if she could get a picture with him, he replied, "If you help me sit up. I'm a new man."

Praise God for the life-changing, hope-giving, available-to-all gospel of Jesus Christ! It offers new life for all who trust Him (COL. 1:5, 23). *DAVE BRANON*

Lord, thank You for the new life we have in Jesus Christ. Help us to share the hope of that new life with others so they can be made new as well.

Jesus offers new life.

Nozomi Hope

Read: 2 Corinthians 4:7–18

We have this treasure in jars of clay to show that this all-surpassing power is from God and not from us. 2 Corinthians 4:7

In 2011, a magnitude 9 earthquake and a resulting tsunami took nearly 19,000 lives and destroyed 230,000 homes in the region northeast of Tokyo. In its aftermath, The Nozomi Project, named for the Japanese word for "hope," was born to provide sustainable income, community, dignity, and hope in a God who provides.

Nozomi women sift through the rubble of homes and furnishings to discover broken china shards that they sand and insert into fittings to form jewelry. The jewelry is sold around the world, providing a livelihood for the women while sharing symbols of their faith in Christ.

In New Testament times, it was customary to hide valuables in the unlikely vessels of simple clay pots. Paul describes how the treasure of the gospel is contained in the human frailty of followers of Christ: jars of clay (2 COR. 4:7). He suggests that the meager—and even at times broken—vessels of our lives actually can reveal God's power in contrast to our imperfections.

When God inhabits the imperfect and broken pieces in our lives, the healing hope of His power is often more visible to others. Yes, His repair work in our hearts often leaves the scars of cracks. But perhaps those lines from our learning are the etchings in our beings that make His character more visible to others.

ELISA MORGAN

Dear God, please show others Your power as I share the treasure of Your gospel in my broken, but beautiful life.

Brokenness can lead to wholeness.

The Professor's Confession

Read: 1 John 3:11–18

This is how we know what love is: Jesus Christ laid down his life for us.
1 John 3:16

Horrified by his students' poor writing habits, renowned author and college professor David Foster Wallace considered how he might improve their skills. That's when a startling question confronted him. The professor had to ask himself why a student would listen to someone "as smug, narrow, self-righteous, [and] condescending" as he was. He knew he had a problem with pride.

That professor could and did change, but he could never become one of his students. Yet when Jesus came to Earth, He showed us what humility looks like by *becoming one of us*. Stepping across all kinds of boundaries, Jesus made himself at home everywhere by serving, teaching, and doing the will of His Father.

Even as He was being crucified, Jesus prayed for forgiveness for His executioners (LUKE 23:34). Straining for every anguished breath, He still granted eternal life to a criminal dying with Him (VV. 42–43).

Why would Jesus do that? Why would He serve people like us to the very end? The apostle John gets to the point. Out of love! He writes, "This is how we know what love is: Jesus Christ laid down his life for us." Then he drives that point home. "And we ought to lay down our lives for our brothers and sisters" (1 JOHN 3:16).

Jesus showed us that His love eradicates our pride, our smugness, our condescension. And He did it in the most powerful way possible. He gave His life.   *TIM GUSTAFSON*

Father, we are so prone to look down on each other. Please forgive us.
Give us the heart of love Your Son showed to us.

Jesus loved us by serving.

Peace and Trust

Read: Isaiah 26:1–9

Peace I leave with you; my peace I give you. I do not give to you as the world gives. Do not let your hearts be troubled and do not be afraid.
John 14:27

When I was six years old I rode a roller coaster for the first time with my older brothers. As soon as we hit a turn at a high speed I started to yell: "Stop this thing *right now*! I want to get off!" Of course the roller coaster didn't stop, and I had to "white knuckle" it, hanging on tight for the rest of the ride.

Sometimes life can feel like an unwanted roller coaster ride, with "downhill" drops and hairpin curves we never see coming. When unexpected difficulties occur, the Bible reminds us that our best recourse is to place our trust in God. It was in a tumultuous time when invasion threatened his country that the prophet Isaiah, inspired by the Spirit, discerned this powerful promise from the Lord: "You will keep in perfect peace those whose minds are steadfast, because they trust in you" (ISA. 26:3).

The peace our Savior gives us as we turn to Him "transcends all understanding" (PHIL. 4:7). I will never forget the words of a woman who was struggling with breast cancer. After a group from our church prayed for her one evening, she said, "I don't know what will happen, but I know that I'll be okay, because the Lord was here with us tonight."

Life will have its difficulties, but our Savior, who loves us more than life, is greater than them all. *JAMES BANKS*

Lord, help me to trust in You so that I may live in peace.

Jesus is our peace.

Training for Life

Read: Psalm 66:8–12

For you, God, tested us; you refined us like silver. Psalm 66:10

My training for the long-distance race was going badly, and the latest run was particularly disappointing. I walked half the time and even had to sit down at one point. It felt like I had failed a mini-test.

Then I remembered that this was the whole point of training. It was not a test to pass, nor was there a grade I had to achieve. Rather, it was something I simply had to go through, again and again, to improve my endurance.

Perhaps you feel bad about a trial you are facing. God allows us to undergo these times of testing to toughen our spiritual muscles and endurance. He teaches us to rely on Him, and purifies us to be holy, so that we become more like Christ.

No wonder the psalmist could praise God for refining the Israelites through fire and water (PS. 66:10–12) as they suffered in slavery and exile. God not only preserved them and brought them to a place of great abundance, but also purified them in the process.

As we go through testing, we can rely on God for strength and perseverance. He is refining us through our toughest moments.

LESLIE KOH

Lord, I know that You allow me to go through trials so that I will be strengthened and purified. Teach me to keep relying on You for Your strength to endure.

Faith-testing times can be faith-strengthening times.

Showing Grace

Read: Colossians 4:2–6

Let your conversation be always full of grace, seasoned with salt, so that you may know how to answer everyone. Colossians 4:6

The US Masters Golf Tournament began in 1934, and since then only three players have won it two years in a row. On April 10, 2016, it appeared that twenty-two-year-old Jordan Spieth would become the fourth. But he faltered on the last nine holes and finished in a tie for second. Despite his disappointing loss, Spieth was gracious toward tournament champion Danny Willett, congratulating him on his victory and on the birth of his first child, something "more important than golf."

Writing in *The New York Times*, Karen Krouse said, "It takes grace to see the big picture so soon after having to sit through a trophy ceremony and watch someone else have his photograph taken." Krouse continued, "Spieth's ball-striking was off all week, but his character emerged unscathed."

Paul urged the followers of Jesus in Colossae to "be wise in the way you act toward outsiders; make the most of every opportunity. Let your conversation be always full of grace, seasoned with salt, so that you may know how to answer everyone" (COL. 4:5–6).

As those who have freely received God's grace, it is our privilege and calling to demonstrate it in every situation of life—win or lose. *DAVID MCCASLAND*

Dear Lord, help me by Your Spirit to be gracious and kind to others and to represent You well.

Gracious words are always the right words.

Reflecting God's Love

Read: Exodus 34:29–35

When Moses came down from Mount Sinai with the two tablets of the covenant law in his hands, he was not aware that his face was radiant because he had spoken with the LORD. Exodus 34:29

I had the privilege of serving as my mom's caregiver during her treatments at a live-in cancer care center. Even on her hardest days, she read Scripture and prayed for others before getting out of bed.

She spent time with Jesus daily, expressing her faith through her dependence on God, her kind deeds, and her desire to encourage and pray for others. Never realizing how much her smiling face glowed with the Lord's loving grace, she shared God's love with the people around her until the day He called her home to heaven.

After Moses spent forty days and forty nights communing with God (EX. 34:28), he descended Mount Sinai. He had no idea his intimate connection with the Lord actually changed his appearance (V. 29). But the Israelites could tell Moses had spoken with the Lord (VV. 30–32). He continued meeting with God and influencing the lives of those around him (VV. 33–35).

We might not be able to see how our experiences with God change us over time, and our transformation will definitely not be as physically apparent as Moses's beaming face. But as we spend time with God and surrender our lives to Him more and more each day, we can reflect His love. God can draw others closer to Him as the evidence of His presence shows in and through us.   *XOCHITL DIXON*

Our intimate moments spent with God can change us and direct others to His love.

Life to the Full

Read: Mark 10:28–31; John 10:9–10

I have come that they may have life, and have it to the full. John 10:10

When I stopped by to visit my sister's family, my nephews eagerly showed me their new chore system, a set of *Choropoly* boards. Each colorful electronic board keeps track of their chores. A job well done means the kids can hit a green button, which adds points to their "spending" account. A misdeed like leaving the back door open results in a fine being deducted from the total. Since a high-points total leads to exciting rewards such as computer time—and misdeeds deduct from that total—my nephews are now unusually motivated to do their work and to keep the door closed!

The ingenious system had me joking that I wished I had such an exciting motivational tool! But of course God *has* given us motivation. Rather than simply commanding obedience, Jesus has promised that a life of following Him, while costly, is also a life of abundance, "life . . . to the full" (JOHN 10:10). Experiencing life in His kingdom is worth "one hundred times" the cost—now and eternally (MARK 10:29–30).

We can rejoice in the fact that we serve a generous God, One who does not reward and punish as we deserve. He generously accepts our weakest efforts—even welcoming and rewarding latecomers to His kingdom as generously as old-timers (SEE MATT. 20:1–16). In light of this reality, let us joyfully serve Him today.

MONICA BRANDS

Lord, help us to remember there is great meaning in following You
and that it is all so worth it.

Following Jesus is the way to a rich and satisfying life.

Available to All

Read: Mark 10:42–52

For even the Son of Man did not come to be served, but to serve, and to give his life as a ransom for many. Mark 10:45

In today's celebrity-obsessed culture, it isn't surprising that entrepreneurs are marketing "celebrities as products . . . allowing them to sell their personal time and attention." Vauhini Vara's article in *The New Yorker* noted that for $15,000, you can have a personal meeting with singer Shakira, while $12,000 will give you and eleven guests lunch with celebrity chef Michael Chiarello at his estate.

Many people treated Jesus like a celebrity as they followed Him from place to place, listened to His teaching, observed His miracles, and sought healing from His touch. Yet Jesus was never self-important or aloof, but available to all. When His followers James and John were privately jockeying for position in His coming kingdom, Jesus reminded all His disciples, "Whoever wants to become great among you must be your servant, and whoever wants to be first must be slave of all" (MARK 10:43–44).

Soon after Jesus said this, He stopped a procession of people following Him to ask a blind beggar, "What do you want me to do for you?" (V. 51) "Rabbi, I want to see," the man replied. He received his sight immediately and followed Jesus (V. 52).

Our Lord "did not come to be served, but to serve, and to give his life as a ransom for many" (V. 45). May we, like Him, be compassionate and available to others today.   *DAVID MCCASLAND*

Lord Jesus, we honor You as the Son of God and Lord of glory who died for all. Help us to demonstrate Your love to others today.

Follow Jesus's example: Reach out to others in need.

The Heart of Christ

Read: Exodus 32:21–32

Please forgive their sin—but if not, then blot me out of the book you have written. Exodus 32:32

An Australian journalist who spent 400 days in an Egyptian jail expressed mixed emotions when he was released. While admitting his relief, he said he accepted his freedom with incredible concern for the friends he was leaving behind. He said he found it extremely hard to say goodbye to fellow reporters who had been arrested and jailed with him—not knowing how much longer they were going to be held.

Moses also expressed great anxiety at the thought of leaving friends behind. When faced with the thought of losing the brother, sister, and nation that had worshiped a golden calf while he was meeting with God on Mount Sinai (EX. 32:11–14), he interceded for them. Showing how deeply he cared, he pled, "But now, please forgive their sin—but if not, then blot me out of the book you have written" (V. 32).

The apostle Paul later expressed a similar concern for family, friends, and nation. Grieving their unbelief in Jesus, Paul said he would be willing to give up his own relationship with Christ if by such love he could save his brothers and sisters (ROM. 9:3).

Looking back, we see that Moses and Paul both expressed the heart of Christ. Yet, the love they could only *feel*, and the sacrifice they could only *offer*, Jesus *fulfilled*—to be with us forever.

MART DEHAAN

Father in heaven, thank You for reminding us how much it is like You to be willing to live—and die—for those who have not yet seen how much You love them.

Caring for others honors Jesus's love for us.

Our Father's Face

Read: Psalm 80

Restore us, O God; make your face shine on us, that we may be saved.
Psalm 80:3

I remember my father's face. It was hard to read. He was a kind man, but stoic and self-contained. As a child, I often searched his face, looking for a smile or other show of affection. Faces are us. A frown, a sullen look, a smile, and crinkly eyes reveal what we feel about others. Our faces are our "tell."

Asaph, the author of Psalm 80, was distraught and wanted to see the Lord's face. He looked north from his vantage point in Jerusalem and saw Judah's sister-state, Israel, collapse under the weight of the Assyrian Empire. With her buffer state gone, Judah was vulnerable to invasion from all sides—Assyria from the north, Egypt from the south, and the Arab nations from the east. She was outnumbered and outmatched.

Asaph gathered up his fears in a prayer, three times repeated (80:3, 7, 19), "Make your face shine on us, that we may be saved." (Or, in other words, let me see Your smile.)

It's good to look away from our fears and search our heavenly Father's face. The best way to see God's face is to look at the cross. The cross is His "tell" (JOHN 3:16).

So know this: When your Father looks at you, He has a great big smile on His face. You're very safe!   *DAVID ROPER*

Ask God to shine His face on you. For further help in prayer,
try praying this Psalm or others.

God's love for us is as expansive as the open arms
of Christ on the cross.

If Only . . .

Read: John 11:21–35

Lord, if you had been here, my brother would not have died. John 11:32

As we exited the parking lot, my husband slowed the car to wait for a young woman riding her bike. When Tom nodded to indicate she could go first, she smiled, waved, and rode on. Moments later, the driver from a parked SUV threw his door open, knocking the young bicyclist to the pavement. Her legs bleeding, she cried as she examined her bent-up bike.

Later, we reflected on the accident: *If only we had made her wait . . . If only the driver had looked before opening his door. If only . . .* Difficulties catch us up in a cycle of second-guessing ourselves. *If only I had known my child was with teens who were drinking . . . If only we had found the cancer earlier . . .*

When unexpected trouble comes, we sometimes question the goodness of God. We may even feel the despair that Martha and Mary experienced when their brother died. *Oh, if Jesus had only come when He first found out that Lazarus was sick!* (JOHN 11:21, 32).

Like Martha and Mary, we don't always understand why hard things happen to us. But we can rest in the knowledge that God is working out His purposes for a greater good. In every circumstance, we can trust the wisdom of our faithful and loving God.

CINDY HESS KASPER

Father, You have carried me through hard circumstances before. Thank You for teaching me to trust Your heart of love even when I don't understand what You are doing in my life.

To trust God in the light is nothing, but to trust Him in the dark—that is faith.
CHARLES HADDON SPURGEON

Grateful for Everything

Read: Deuteronomy 8:6–18

When you have eaten and are satisfied, praise the LORD your God for the good land he has given you. Deuteronomy 8:10

In Australia, it can take hours to drive between towns and fatigue can lead to accidents. So at busy holiday times rest stops are set up on major highways with volunteers offering free coffee. My wife, Merryn, and I grew to enjoy these stops during our long drives there.

On one trip, we pulled in and walked over to order our coffee. An attendant handed the two cups over, and then asked me for two dollars. I asked why. She pointed to the small print on the sign. At this stop, only the *driver* got free coffee; you had to pay for passengers. Annoyed, I told her this was false advertising, paid the two dollars, and walked off. Back at the car, Merryn pointed out my error: I had turned a gift into an entitlement and become ungrateful for what I received. She was right.

When the Israelites were about to enter the Promised Land, Moses urged them to be a grateful people (DEUT. 8:10). Thanks to the blessings of God, the land was abundant, but they could easily treat this prosperity as something they deserved (VV. 17–18). From this, the Jews developed a practice of giving thanks for every meal, no matter how small. For them, it was all a gift.

I went back to the woman and apologized. A free cup of coffee was a gift I didn't deserve—and something for which to be thankful.

SHERIDAN VOYSEY

Blessed are You, O Lord our God, King of the universe, who brings forth bread from the earth.
A JEWISH THANKSGIVING PRAYER FOR MEALS

Be grateful to God for even the smallest gift.

From Fear to Faith

Read: Habakkuk 3:16–19

The Sovereign LORD is my strength; he makes my feet like the feet of a deer. Habakkuk 3:19

The doctor's words landed in her heart with a thud. It was cancer. Her world stopped as she thought of her husband and children. They had prayed diligently, hoping for a different outcome. What would they do? With tears streaming down her face, she said softly, "God, this is beyond our control. Please be our strength."

What do we do when the prognosis is devastating, when our circumstances are beyond our control? Where do we turn when the outlook seems hopeless?

The prophet Habakkuk's situation was out of his control, and the fear that he felt terrified him. The coming judgment would be catastrophic (HAB. 3:16–17). Yet, in the midst of the impending chaos, Habakkuk made a choice to live by his faith (2:4) and rejoice in God (3:18). He did not place his confidence and faith in his circumstances, ability, or resources, but in the goodness and greatness of God. His trust in God compelled him to proclaim: "The Sovereign LORD is my strength; he makes my feet like the feet of a deer, he enables me to tread on the heights" (V. 19).

When we are faced with difficult circumstances—sickness, family crisis, financial trouble—we, too, have only to place our faith and trust in God. He is with us in everything we face.

KAREN WOLFE

Dear God, I thank You that I can always turn to You. When I am faced with the difficulties of life, I can put my trust in You. Thank you that You are my "refuge and strength, a very present help in trouble" (Psalm 46:1).

When faced with difficult circumstances we can trust God to be our strength.

Love for Children

Read: Matthew 18:1–10

Let the children come to me. Don't stop them! For the Kingdom of Heaven belongs to those who are like these children. Matthew 19:14 NLT

Thomas Barnado entered the London Hospital medical school in 1865, dreaming of life as a medical missionary in China. Barnado soon discovered a desperate need in his own front yard—the many homeless children living and dying on the streets of London. Barnado determined to do something about this horrendous situation. Developing homes for destitute children in London's east end, Barnado rescued some 60,000 boys and girls from poverty and possible early death. Theologian and pastor John Stott said, "Today we might call him the patron saint of street kids."

Jesus said, "Let the children come to me. Don't stop them! For the Kingdom of Heaven belongs to those who are like these children" (MATT. 19:14 NLT). Imagine the surprise the crowds—and Jesus's own disciples—must have felt at this declaration. In the ancient world, children had little value and were largely relegated to the margins of life. Yet Jesus welcomed, blessed, and valued children.

James, a New Testament writer, challenged Christ-followers saying, "Pure and lasting religion in the sight of God our Father means that we must care for orphans . . . in their troubles" (JAMES 1:27 NLT). Today, like those first-century orphans, children of every social strata, ethnicity, and family environment are at risk due to neglect, human trafficking, abuse, drugs, and more. How can we honor the Father who loves us by showing His care for these little ones Jesus welcomes?   *BILL CROWDER*

Be an expression of the love of Jesus.

Under His Wings

Read: Psalm 91

He will cover you with his feathers, and under his wings you will find refuge. Psalm 91:4

When I think of protection, I don't automatically think of a bird's feathers. Though a bird's feathers might seem like a flimsy form of protection, there is more to them than meets the eye.

Bird feathers are an amazing example of God's design. Feathers have a smooth part and a fluffy part. The smooth part of the feather has stiff barbs with tiny hooks that lock together like the prongs of a zipper. The fluffy part keeps a bird warm. Together both parts of the feather protect the bird from wind and rain. But many baby birds are covered in a fluffy down and their feathers haven't fully developed. So a mother bird has to cover them in the nest with her own feathers to protect them from wind and rain.

The image of God "[covering] us with his feathers" in Psalm 91:4 and in other Bible passages (SEE PS. 17:8) is one of comfort and protection. The image that comes to mind is a mother bird covering her little ones with her feathers. Like a parent whose arms are a safe place to retreat from a scary storm or a hurt, God's comforting presence provides safety and protection from life's emotional storms.

Though we go through trouble and heartache, we can face them without fear as long as our faces are turned toward God. He is our "refuge" (91:2, 4, 9).   *LINDA WASHINGTON*

Father God, help me trust that You are bigger than any fear I have.

When fear causes hope to fade, flee to God, the refuge you can reach on your knees.

Not Fear but Faith

Read: Numbers 13:25–14:9

The LORD is with us. Do not be afraid of them. Numbers 14:9

"My husband was offered a promotion in another country, but I feared leaving our home, so he reluctantly declined the offer," my friend shared with me. She explained how apprehension over such a big change kept her from embracing a new adventure, and that she sometimes wondered what they missed in not moving.

The Israelites let their anxieties paralyze them when they were called to inhabit a rich and fertile land that flowed "with milk and honey" (EX. 33:3). When they heard the reports of the powerful people in large cities (NUM. 13:28), they started to fear. The majority of the Israelites rejected the call to enter the land.

But Joshua and Caleb urged them to trust in the Lord, saying, "Do not be afraid of the people in the land" for the "LORD is with us" (14:9). Although the people there appeared large, they could trust the Lord to be with them.

My friend wasn't commanded to move to another country like the Israelites were, yet she regretted letting fear close off the opportunity. What about you—do you face a fearful situation? If so, know that the Lord is with you and will guide you. With His never-failing love, we can move forward in faith.

AMY BOUCHER PYE

Loving Father, may I not let my fear stop me from following You, for I know that You will always love me and will never leave me.

Fear can paralyze but faith propels us to follow God.

Promise of a Peaceful Home

Read: Micah 4:1–5

Everyone will sit under their own vine and under their own fig tree, and no one will make them afraid. Micah 4:4

Sixty-five million. That's the number of refugees in our world today—people who have had to leave their homes due to conflict and persecution—and it's higher than it's ever been. The UN has petitioned leaders to work together in receiving refugees so that every child will get an education, every adult will find meaningful work, and every family will have a home.

The dream of making homes for refugees in crisis reminds me of a promise God made to the nation of Judah when ruthless Assyrian armies threatened their homes. The Lord commissioned the prophet Micah to warn the people that they would lose their temple and their beloved city of Jerusalem. But God also promised a beautiful future beyond the loss.

A day will come, said Micah, when God will call the peoples of the world to himself. Violence will end. Weapons of war will become farming tools, and every person who answers God's call will find a peaceful home and a productive life in His kingdom (4:3–4).

For many in the world today, and maybe for you, a safe home remains more a dream than a reality. But we can rely on God's ancient promise of a home for people of all nations, even as we wait and work and pray for those peaceful homes to become a reality.   *AMY PETERSON*

God, thank You for the beautiful promise of a home. Please bring peace to our world, and provide for the needs of all of Your children.

God promises His children a peaceful home in His kingdom.

You're an Original

Read: Psalm 100

Know that the LORD is God. It is he who made us, and we are his.
Psalm 100:3

Each of us is an original from God's hand. There are no self-made men or women. No one ever became talented, buffed, or bright all by himself or herself. God made each of us all by himself. He thought of us and formed us out of His unspeakable love.

God made your body, mind, and soul. And He isn't done with you; He is still making you. His single-minded purpose is our maturity: "He who began a good work in you will carry it on to completion until the day of Christ Jesus" (PHIL. 1:6). God is making you braver, stronger, purer, more peaceful, more loving, less selfish—the kind of person you've perhaps always wanted to be.

"[God's] unfailing love continues forever and his faithfulness continues to each generation" (PS. 100:5 NLT). God has always loved you ("forever" goes both ways), and He will be faithful to you to the end.

You've been given a love that lasts forever and a God who will never give up on you. That's a good reason to have joy and to "come before him with joyful songs"! (V. 2).

If you can't carry a tune, just give Him a shout-out: "Shout for joy to the LORD" (V. 1). *DAVID ROPER*

I'm grateful, Father, that You are at work in me. I find it difficult to change and I wonder sometimes how or if I ever will. Yet I know that You are continuing Your work in me and as I look back I will see the growth You are producing. Thank You!

Spiritual growth occurs when faith is cultivated.

From Grief to Joy

Read: John 16:16–22

You will grieve, but your grief will turn to joy. John 16:20

Kelly's pregnancy brought complications, and doctors were concerned. During her long labor, they decided to whisk her away for a Cesarean section. But despite the ordeal, Kelly quickly forgot her pain when she held her newborn son. Joy had replaced anguish.

Scripture affirms this truth: "A woman giving birth to a child has pain because her time has come; but when her baby is born she forgets the anguish because of her joy that a child is born into the world" (JOHN 16:21). Jesus used this illustration with His disciples to emphasize that though they would grieve because He would be leaving soon, that grief would turn to joy when they saw Him again (VV. 20–22).

Jesus was referring to His death and resurrection—and what followed. After His resurrection, to the disciples' joy, Jesus spent another forty days walking with and teaching them before ascending and leaving them once again (ACTS 1:3). Yet Jesus did not leave them grief-stricken. The Holy Spirit would fill them with joy (JOHN 16:7–15; ACTS 13:52).

Though we have never seen Jesus face to face, as believers we have the assurance that one day we will. In that day, the anguish we face in this earth will be forgotten. But until then, the Lord has not left us without joy—He has given us His Spirit (ROM. 15:13; 1 PETER 1:8–9).   *ALYSON KIEDA*

Dear Lord, we long to be in Your presence, especially when we face pain and sorrow. Yet You have not left us on our own. The Holy Spirit lives within us—and gives us joy.

One day our sorrow will be turned to joy!

The Turn

Read: Esther 8:11–17

For the Jews it was a time of happiness and joy, gladness and honor.
Esther 8:16

As the minister spoke at a funeral for an old military veteran, he mused about where the deceased might be. But then, instead of telling the people how they could know God, he speculated about things not found anywhere in Scripture. *Where is the hope?* I thought.

At last he asked us to turn to a closing hymn. And as we rose to sing "How Great Thou Art," people began to praise God from the depths of their souls. Within moments, the spirit of the entire room had changed. Suddenly, surprisingly, in the middle of the third verse my emotions overwhelmed my voice.

And when I think, that God, His Son not sparing,
Sent Him to die, I scarce can take it in;
That on the Cross, my burden gladly bearing,
He bled and died to take away my sin.

Until we sang that great hymn, I had wondered if God was going to show up at that funeral. In reality, He never leaves. A look at the book of Esther reveals this truth. The Jews were in exile, and powerful people wanted to kill them. Yet at the darkest moment, a godless king granted the right to the enslaved Israelites to defend themselves against those who sought their demise (EST. 8:11–13). A successful defense and a celebration ensued (9:17–19).

It should be no surprise when God shows up in the words of a hymn at a funeral. After all, He turned an attempted genocide into a celebration and a crucifixion into resurrection and salvation!

TIM GUSTAFSON

Our surprising God often shows His presence when we
least expect Him.

Be Still

Read: Psalm 46:1–11

The Lord Almighty is with us, the God of Jacob is our fortress.
Psalm 46:11

"We've created more information in the last five years than in all of human history before it, and it's coming at us all the time" (Daniel Levitin, author of *The Organized Mind: Thinking Straight in the Age of Information Overload*). "In a sense," Levitin says, "we become addicted to the hyperstimulation." The constant barrage of news and knowledge can dominate our minds. In today's environment of media bombardment, it becomes increasingly difficult to find time to be quiet, to think, and to pray.

Psalm 46:10 says, "Be still, and know that I am God," reminding us of the necessity to take time to focus on the Lord. Many people find that a "quiet time" is an essential part of each day—a time to read the Bible, pray, and consider the goodness and greatness of God.

When we, like the writer of Psalm 46, experience the reality that "God is our refuge and strength, an ever-present help in trouble" (V. 1), it drives our fear away (V. 2), shifts our focus from the world's turmoil to God's peace, and creates a quiet confidence that our Lord is in control (V. 10).

No matter how chaotic the world may become around us, we can find quietness and strength in our heavenly Father's love and power. *DAVID MCCASLAND*

Heavenly Father, we bring our noisy lives and our cluttered minds to You so that we can learn to be still and know that You are God.

Each day we need to be still and listen to the Lord.

Ripe for Harvest

Read: John 4:35–38

Open your eyes and look at the fields! They are ripe for harvest.
John 4:35

In late summer, we went for a walk in the New Forest in England and had fun picking the blackberries that grew in the wild while watching the horses frolicking nearby. As I enjoyed the bounty of the sweet fruit planted by others perhaps many years before, I thought of Jesus's words to His disciples: "I sent you to reap what you have not worked for" (JOHN 4:38).

I love the generosity of God's kingdom reflected in those words. He lets us enjoy the fruits of someone else's labors, such as when we share our love for Jesus with a friend whose family—unbeknown to us—has been praying for her for years. I also love the implied limits of Jesus's words, for we may plant seeds that we will never harvest but someone else may. Therefore, we can rest in the tasks before us, not being hoodwinked into thinking that we are responsible for the outcomes. God's work, after all, doesn't depend on us. He has all of the resources for a bountiful harvest, and we are privileged to play a role in it.

I wonder what fields ready for harvest are before you? Before me? May we heed Jesus's loving instruction: "Open your eyes and look at the fields!" (V. 35). *AMY BOUCHER PYE*

Creator God, thank You for Your great generosity in entrusting us to do Your work. May I be alert to the opportunities to share Your good news.

We can reap what others have sown.

Our Guilt Is Gone

Read: Psalm 32:1–11

I said, "I will confess my transgressions to the LORD." And you forgave the guilt of my sin. Psalm 32:5

As a young girl, I invited a friend to browse with me through a gift shop near my home. She shocked me, though, by shoving a handful of colorful crayon-shaped barrettes into my pocket and yanking me out the door of the shop without paying for them. Guilt gnawed at me for a week before I approached my mom—my confession pouring out as quickly as my tears.

Grieved over my bad choice of not resisting my friend, I returned the stolen items, apologized, and vowed never to steal again. The owner told me never to come back. But because my mom forgave me and assured me that I had done my best to make things right, I slept peacefully that night.

King David also rested in forgiveness through confession (PS. 32:1–2). He had hidden his sins against Bathsheba and Uriah (2 SAM. 11–12) until his "strength was sapped" (PS. 32:3–4). But once David refused to "cover up" his wrongs, the Lord erased his guilt (V. 5). God protected him "from trouble" and wrapped him in "songs of deliverance" (V. 7). David rejoiced because the "LORD's unfailing love surrounds the one who trusts in him" (V. 10).

We can't choose the consequences of our sins or control people's responses when we confess and seek forgiveness. But the Lord can empower us to enjoy freedom from the bondage of sin and peace through confession, as He confirms that our guilt is gone—forever. *XOCHITL DIXON*

Lord, when we confess our sins and receive Your forgiveness, please help us believe our guilt is completely and forever wiped away.

When God forgives, our guilt is gone.

The Interests of Others

Read: Philippians 2:1–11

In humility value others above yourselves, not looking to your own interests. Philippians 2:3–4

My friend Jaime works for a huge international corporation. In his early days with the company, a man came by his desk, struck up a conversation, and asked Jaime what he did there. After telling the man about his work, Jaime asked the man his name. "My name is Rich," he replied.

"Nice to meet you," Jaime answered. "And what do you do around here?"

"Oh, I am the owner."

Jaime suddenly realized that this casual, humble conversation was his introduction to one of the richest men in the world.

In this day of self-glorification and the celebration of "me," this little story can serve as a reminder of Paul's important words in the book of Philippians: "Do nothing out of selfish ambition or vain conceit" (2:3). People who turn their attention to others and not on themselves have the characteristics Paul mentions.

When we "value others above [ourselves]," we demonstrate Christlike humility (V. 3). We mirror Jesus, who came not "to be served, but to serve" (MARK 10:45). When we take "the very nature of a servant" (PHIL. 2:7), we have the mindset of Jesus (V. 5).

As we interact with others today, let's not look on our own interests alone but also "to the interests of the others" (V. 4).

DAVE BRANON

Jesus, You gave us the model of humility when You left heaven's splendors to become a humble servant on earth. Help us practice Christlike humility in everything we do.

Serve God by serving others.

Lured Away

Read: James 1:5–6, 12–15

Each person is tempted when they are dragged away by their own evil desire and enticed. James 1:14

In the summer of 2016, my niece convinced me to play Pokémon Go—a game played on a smartphone, using the phone's camera. The object of the game is to capture little creatures called Pokémon. When one appears in the game, a red and white ball also appears on the phone's screen. To capture a Pokémon, the player has to flick the ball toward it with the movement of a finger. Pokémon are more easily caught, however, by using a lure to attract them.

Pokémon characters aren't the only ones who can be lured away. In his New Testament letter to believers, James, the brother of Jesus, reminds us that we "are dragged away by [our] *own* evil desire" (1:14, EMPHASIS ADDED). In other words, our desires work with temptation to lure us down a wrong path. Though we may be tempted to blame God or even Satan for our problems, our real danger lies within.

But there is good news. We can escape the lure of temptation by talking to God about the things that tempt us. Though "God cannot be tempted by evil, nor does he tempt anyone," as James explains in 1:13, He understands our human desire to do what's wrong. We have only to ask for the wisdom God promised to provide (1:1–6).   *LINDA WASHINGTON*

Lord, when I'm tempted, show me the door of escape.

Pray your way past the urge to do wrong.

The Snake and the Tricycle

Read: Luke 1:1–4

I myself have carefully investigated everything from the beginning.
Luke 1:3

For years, I had retold a story from a time in Ghana when my brother and I were toddlers. As I recalled it, he had parked our old iron tricycle on a small cobra. The trike was too heavy for the snake, which remained trapped under the front wheel.

But after my aunt and my mother had both passed away, we discovered a long-lost letter from Mom recounting the incident. In reality, *I* had parked the tricycle on the snake, and my brother had run to tell Mom. Her eyewitness account, written close to the actual event, revealed the reality.

The historian Luke understood the importance of accurate records. He explained how the story of Jesus was "handed down to us by those who from the first were eyewitnesses" (LUKE 1:2). "I too decided to write an orderly account for you," he wrote to Theophilus, "so that you may know the certainty of the things you have been taught" (VV. 3–4). The result was the gospel of Luke. Then, in his introduction to the book of Acts, Luke said of Jesus, "After his suffering, he presented himself to them and gave many convincing proofs that he was alive" (ACTS 1:3).

Our faith is not based on hearsay or wishful thinking. It is rooted in the well-documented life of Jesus, who came to give us peace with God. His Story stands.   *TIM GUSTAFSON*

Father, our hope is in Your Son. Thank You for preserving His story for us in the pages of the Bible.

Genuine faith is rooted in reason.

Earnestly Searching

Read: Isaiah 62:1–12

You will be called Sought After, the City No Longer Deserted.
Isaiah 62:12

Every Saturday our family lines the edges of the racecourse to cheer on my daughter as she runs with her high school cross-country team. After crossing the finish line, the athletes stream out to rejoin their teammates, coaches, and parents. Crowds engulf the finishers—often more than 300 of them—making it difficult to find one person among so many. We scan the crowd excitedly until we find her, eager to put our arms around the *one* athlete we came to watch: our much-loved daughter.

After seventy years of captivity in Babylon, God returned the Jews to Jerusalem and Judah. Isaiah describes the delight God has in them, and the work of preparing the highways for their pilgrimage home and the gates to receive them back. God reaffirms His calling of them as His holy people and restores their honor with a new name, "Sought After, the City No Longer Deserted" (ISA. 62:12). He sought them all from the scattered reaches of Babylon to bring them back to himself.

Like the children of Israel, we too are God's beloved children, earnestly sought after by Him. Though our sin once caused us isolation from Him, Jesus's sacrifice paves our way back to Him. He searches for each of us intently among all the others, waiting expectantly to fold us into a heartfelt embrace.

KIRSTEN HOLMBERG

Thank You, Lord, for seeking me while I was lost and returning me home to You through Jesus Christ.

God seeks His beloved children.

Paying Attention

Read: Psalm 41:1–3

Blessed is he who considers the poor. Psalm 41:1 NKJV

John Newton wrote, "If, as I go home, a child has dropped a halfpenny, and if, by giving it another, I can wipe away its tears, I feel I have done something. I should be glad to do greater things; but I will not neglect this."

These days, it's not hard to find someone in need of comfort: A care-worn cashier in a grocery store working a second job to make ends meet; a refugee longing for home; a single mother whose flood of worries has washed away her hope; a lonely old man who fears he has outlived his usefulness.

But what are we to do? "Blessed is he who considers the poor," wrote David (PS. 41:1 NKJV). Even if we can't alleviate the poverty of those we meet along the way we can *consider* them—a verb that means "to pay attention."

We can let people know we care. We can treat them with courtesy and respect, though they may be testy or tiresome. We can listen with interest to their stories. And we can pray for them or with them—the most helpful and healing act of all.

Remember the old paradox Jesus gave us when He said, "It is more blessed to give than to receive" (ACTS 20:35). Paying attention pays off, for we're happiest when we give ourselves away. Consider the poor. *DAVID ROPER*

Father, as we go through our day, show us the everyday folks who need our attention. Grant us the love and the patience to truly consider them, as You have so patiently loved us.

Only a life given away for love's sake is worth living.
FREDERICK BUECHNER

Overflowing Fruit

Read: Galatians 5:16–25

I chose you and appointed you so that you might go and bear fruit—fruit that will last. John 15:16

During the spring and summer, I admire the fruit growing in our neighbor's yard. Their cultivated vines climb a shared fence to produce large bunches of grapes. Branches dotted with purple plums and plump oranges dangle just within our reach.

Although we don't till the soil, plant the seeds, or water and weed the garden, the couple next door shares their bounty with us. They take responsibility for nurturing their crops and allow us to delight in a portion of their harvest.

The produce from the trees and vines on the other side of our fence reminds me of another harvest that benefits me and the people God places in my life. That harvest is the fruit of the Spirit.

Christ-followers are commissioned to claim the benefits of living by the power of the Holy Spirit (GAL. 5:16–21). As God's seeds of truth flourish in our hearts, the Spirit produces an increase in our ability to express "love, joy, peace, forbearance, kindness, goodness, faithfulness, gentleness and self-control" (VV. 22–23).

Once we surrender our lives to Jesus, we no longer have to be controlled by our self-centered inclinations (V. 24). Over time, the Holy Spirit can change our thinking, our attitudes, and our actions. As we grow and mature in Christ, we can have the added joy of loving our neighbors by sharing the benefits of His generous harvest. *XOCHITL DIXON*

Lord, please cultivate the fruit of the Spirit in our hearts and minds so our neighbors can enjoy Your sweet fragrance in and through our lives.

The fruit of the Spirit changes us so we can impact the lives of those around us.

Made Clean

Read: Ezekiel 36:24–32

I will sprinkle clean water on you, and you will be clean. Ezekiel 36:25

When I opened our dishwasher, I wondered what went wrong. Instead of seeing sparkling clean dishes, I removed plates and glasses that were covered in a chalky dust. I wondered if the hard water in our area was wreaking havoc, or if the machine was broken.

God's cleansing, unlike that faulty dishwasher, washes away all of our impurities. We see in the book of Ezekiel that God is calling His people back to himself as Ezekiel shared God's message of love and forgiveness. The Israelites had sinned as they proclaimed their allegiance to other gods and other nations. The Lord, however, was merciful in welcoming them back to himself. He promised to cleanse them "from all [their] impurities and all [their] idols" (36:25). As He put His Spirit in them (V. 27), He would bring them to a place of fruitfulness, not famine (V. 30).

As in the days of the prophet Ezekiel, today the Lord welcomes us back to Him if we go astray. When we submit ourselves to His will and His ways, He transforms us as He washes us clean from our sins. With His Holy Spirit dwelling within us, He helps us to follow Him day by day.   *AMY BOUCHER PYE*

Lord God, the feeling of being cleansed and forgiven is like no other. Thank You for transforming me into a new person. Teach me to submit to You daily that I might grow more and more closely into the likeness of Jesus.

The Lord makes us clean.

God's Radiant Beauty

Read: Romans 1:18–25

For since the creation of the world God's invisible qualities—his eternal power and divine nature—have been clearly seen, being understood from what has been made. Romans 1:20

Lord Howe Island is a small paradise of white sands and crystal waters off Australia's east coast. When I visited some years ago, I was struck by its beauty. Here, one could swim with turtles and with fish like the shimmering trevally, while moon wrasses drifted nearby, flashing their neon colors like a billboard. In its lagoon I found coral reefs full of bright orange clownfish and yellow-striped butterfly fish that rushed to kiss my hand. Overwhelmed by such splendor, I couldn't help but worship God.

The apostle Paul gives the reason for my response. Creation at its best reveals something of God's nature (ROM. 1:20). The wonders of Lord Howe Island were giving me a glimpse of His own power and beauty.

When the prophet Ezekiel encountered God, he was shown a radiant Being seated on a blue throne surrounded by glorious colors (EZEK. 1:25–28). The apostle John saw something similar: God sparkling like precious stones, encircled by an emerald rainbow (REV. 4:2–3). When God reveals himself, He is found to be not only good and powerful but *beautiful* too. Creation reflects this beauty the way a piece of art reflects its artist.

Nature often gets worshiped instead of God (ROM. 1:25). What a tragedy. Instead, may earth's crystal waters and shimmering creatures point us to the One standing behind them who is more powerful and beautiful than anything in this world.

SHERIDAN VOYSEY

The beauty of creation reflects the beauty of our Creator.

God's Doing Something New

Read: 1 Thessalonians 3:6–13

May the Lord make your love increase and overflow for each other and for everyone else, just as ours does for you. 1 Thessalonians 3:12

"Is God doing something new in your life?" was the question the leader asked in a group I was in recently. My friend Mindy, who is dealing with some difficult situations, responded. She told of needing patience with aging parents, stamina for her husband's health issues, and understanding of her children and grandchildren who have not yet chosen to follow Jesus. Then she made an insightful comment that runs contrary to what we might normally think: "I believe the new thing God is doing is He's expanding my capacity and opportunities to love."

That fits nicely with the apostle Paul's prayer for new believers in Thessalonica: "May the Lord make your love increase and overflow for each other and for everyone else" (1 THESS. 3:12). He had taught them about Jesus but had to leave abruptly because of rioting (ACTS 17:1–9). Now in his letter he encouraged them to continue to stand firm in their faith (1 THESS. 3:7–8). And he prayed that the Lord would increase their love for all.

During difficulties we often choose to complain and ask, *Why?* Or wonder, *Why me?* Another way to handle those times could be to ask the Lord to expand His love in our hearts and to help us take the new opportunities that come to love others.

ANNE CETAS

I've got my own list of things I could worry about, Lord. Change my thinking.
Open my eyes to love.

Our troubles can fill our prayers with love and empathy for others.

Don't Run Alone

Read: Exodus 17:8–13

Since we are surrounded by such a great cloud of witnesses . . . let us run with perseverance the race marked out for us. Hebrews 12:1

My husband, Jack, was on mile 25 out of 26 when his strength failed him.

This was his first marathon, and he was running alone. After stopping for a drink of water at an aid station, he felt exhausted and sat down on the grass beside the course. Minutes passed, and he couldn't get up. He had resigned himself to quitting the race when two middle-aged schoolteachers from Kentucky came by. Although they were strangers, they noticed Jack and asked if he wanted to run with them. Suddenly, he found his strength restored. Jack stood and accompanied by the two women he finished the race.

Those women who encouraged Jack remind me of Aaron and Hur, two friends who helped Moses, the leader of the Israelites, at a key point (EX. 17:8–13). The Israelites were under attack. In battle, they were winning only as long as Moses held his staff up (V. 11). So when Moses's strength began to fail, Aaron and Hur stood on either side of him, holding up his arms for him until sunset (V. 12).

Following God is not a solo endeavor. He did not create us to run the race of life alone. Companions can help us persevere through difficulty as we do what God has called us to do.

AMY PETERSON

God, thank You for relationships that encourage me to continue following You. Help me to be a source of strength for others, as well.

Who can I encourage to persevere through difficulty today?

Priceless Worship

Read: Mark 12:38–44

She, out of her poverty, put in everything—all she had to live on.
Mark 12:44

I use writing to worship and serve God, even more so now that health issues often limit my mobility. So, when an acquaintance said he found no value in what I wrote, I became discouraged. I doubted the significance of my small offerings to God.

Through prayer, study of Scripture, and encouragement from my husband, family, and friends, the Lord affirmed that only He—not the opinions of other people—could determine our motives as a worshiper and the worth of our offerings to Him. I asked the Giver of all gifts to continue helping me develop skills and provide opportunities to share the resources He gives me.

Jesus contradicted our standards of merit regarding our giving (MARK 12:41–44). While the rich tossed large amounts of money into the temple treasury, a poor widow put in coins "worth only a few cents" (V. 42). The Lord declared her gift greater than the rest (V. 43), though her contribution seemed insignificant to those around her (V. 44).

Although the widow's story focuses on financial offerings, every act of giving can be an expression of worship and loving obedience. Like the widow, we honor God with intentional, generous, and sacrificial gifts given from whatever He's already given us. When we present God the best of our time, talents, or treasure with hearts motivated by love, we are lavishing Him with offerings of priceless worship. *XOCHITL DIXON*

Lord, thank You for never comparing us with others when we offer You the best of the gifts You've first given to us.

Sacrificial offerings motivated by our love for God will always be priceless expressions of worship.

Stepping into Strength

Read: 1 Chronicles 16:11–18, 28–36

Devote yourselves to prayer, being watchful and thankful.
Colossians 4:2

"Will we see any snakes?"

Allan, a young boy in our neighborhood, asked that question as we started on a hike by the river near our home.

"We never have before," I answered, "but we might! So let's ask God to keep us safe." We paused, prayed together, and kept walking.

Several minutes later my wife, Cari, suddenly took a quick step backward, narrowly avoiding a poisonous copperhead partially coiled on the path ahead. We waited as the snake left the trail, giving it a wide berth. Then we paused and thanked God nothing had happened. I believe that through Allan's question, God had prepared us for the encounter, and our prayer was part of His providential care.

Our brush with danger that evening brings to mind the importance of David's words: "Look to the LORD and his strength; seek his face always" (1 CHRON. 16:11). This advice was part of a psalm celebrating the return of the ark of the covenant to Jerusalem. It recounts God's faithfulness to His people in their struggles throughout history, reminding them to always praise Him and "cry out" to Him (V. 35).

What does it mean to "seek [God's] face"? It means we turn our hearts toward Him in even the most mundane moments. Sometimes our prayers are answered differently than our asking, but God is faithful come what may. Our Good Shepherd will direct our paths and keeps us in His mercy, strength, and love. May we declare our dependence on Him.   *JAMES BANKS*

Prayer imparts the power to walk and not faint.
OSWALD CHAMBERS

A Little Bit of Paradise

Read: Romans 8:18–23; Revelation 21:1–5

He who was seated on the throne said, "I am making everything new!"
Revelation 21:5

Gazing out my open study window, I hear birds chirping and hear and see the wind gently blowing in the trees. Bales of hay dot my neighbor's newly mowed field, and large, white cumulus clouds stand out in contrast to the brilliant blue sky.

I'm enjoying a little bit of paradise—except for the almost incessant noise of the traffic that runs past our property and the slight ache in my back. I use the word *paradise* lightly because though our world was once completely good, it no longer is. When humanity sinned, we were expelled from the garden of Eden and the ground was "cursed" (SEE GEN. 3). Since then the Earth and everything in it has been in "bondage to decay." Suffering, disease, and our deaths are all a result of humankind's fall into sin (ROM. 8:18–23).

Yet God is making everything new. One day His dwelling place will be among His people in a renewed and restored creation—"a new heaven and a new earth"—where "there will be no more death or mourning or crying or pain, for the old order of things has passed away" (REV. 21:1–4). Until that day we can enjoy the bright splashes and sometimes wide expanses of breathtaking beauty we see around us in this world, which is just a small foretaste of the "paradise" that will be.   *ALYSON KIEDA*

Dear Lord, thank You that in this world that can seem ugly with sin and decay
You allow us to see glimpses of beauty.

God is making all things new.

Give It to God

Read: 2 Kings 19:9–19

Then [Hezekiah] went up to the temple of the LORD and spread it out before the LORD. 2 Kings 19:14

As a teenager, when I became overwhelmed by enormous challenges or high-stakes decisions, my mother taught me the merits of putting pen to paper to gain perspective. When I was uncertain whether to take specific classes or which job to pursue, or how to cope with the frightening realities of adulthood, I learned her habit of writing out the basic facts and the possible courses of action with their likely outcomes. After pouring my heart onto the page, I was able to step back from the problem and view it more objectively than my emotions allowed.

Just as recording my thoughts on paper offered me fresh perspective, pouring our hearts out to God in prayer helps us gain His perspective and remind us of His power. King Hezekiah did just that after receiving a daunting letter from an ominous adversary. The Assyrians threatened to destroy Jerusalem as they had many other nations. Hezekiah spread out the letter before the Lord, prayerfully calling on Him to deliver the people so that the world would recognize He "alone . . . [is] God" (2 KINGS 19:19).

When we're faced with a situation that brings anxiety, fear, or a deep awareness that getting through it will require more than what we have, let's follow in Hezekiah's footsteps and run straight to the Lord. Like him, we too can lay our problem before God and trust Him to guide our steps and calm our uneasy hearts.   *KIRSTEN HOLMBERG*

God is our greatest help in times of distress.

The Ministry of Mourning

Read: Acts 7:54–8:2

Godly men buried Stephen and mourned deeply for him. Acts 8:2

In 2002, a few months after my sister Martha and her husband, Jim, died in an accident, a friend invited me to a "Growing Through Grief" workshop at our church. I reluctantly agreed to attend the first session but had no intention of going back. To my surprise, I discovered a caring community of people trying to come to grips with a significant loss in their lives by seeking the help of God and others. It drew me back week after week as I worked toward acceptance and peace through the process of sharing our grief together.

Like the sudden loss of a loved one or friend, the death of Stephen, a dynamic witness for Jesus, brought shock and sorrow to those in the early church (ACTS 7:57–60). In the face of persecution, "Godly men buried Stephen and mourned deeply for him" (8:2). These men of faith did two things together: They buried Stephen, an act of finality and loss. And they mourned deeply for him, a shared expression of their sorrow.

As followers of Jesus, we need not mourn our losses alone. In sincerity and love we can reach out to others who are hurting, and in humility we can accept the concern of those who stand beside us.

As we grieve together, we can grow in understanding and in the peace that is ours through Jesus Christ, who knows our deepest sorrow.　　　　　　　　　　　　　　　　*DAVID MCCASLAND*

*Father in heaven, help us to "mourn with those who mourn" and grow together
in Your healing love.*

**The ministry of mourning with others helps bring
healing to our hearts.**

Carried Through

Read: Psalm 30:1–12

Weeping may stay for the night, but rejoicing comes in the morning.
Psalm 30:5

I recently stumbled across some of my journals from college and couldn't resist taking time to reread them. Reading the entries, I realized I didn't feel about myself then the same as I do today. My struggles with loneliness and doubts about my faith felt overwhelming at the time, but looking back now I can clearly see how God has carried me to a better place. Seeing how God gently brought me through those days reminded me that what feels overwhelming today will one day be part of a greater story of His healing love.

Psalm 30 is a celebration psalm that similarly looks back with amazement and gratitude on God's powerful restoration: from sickness to healing, from threat of death to life, from feeling God's judgment to enjoying His favor, from mourning to joy (VV. 2–3,11).

The psalm is attributed to David, to whom we owe some of the most pain-filled laments in Scripture. But David also experienced restoration so incredible he was able to confess, "Weeping may stay for the night, but rejoicing comes in the morning" (V. 5). Despite all the pain he had endured, David discovered something even greater—God's powerful hand of healing.

If you are hurting today and need encouragement, recall those times in your past when God carried you through to a place of healing. Pray for trust that He will do so again.

MONICA BRANDS

Lord, when our struggles feel bigger than what we can handle, help us to find comfort and strength in how You've carried us before.

God is lovingly working toward restoration and joy in and through the pain of our lives.

Seeing God

Read: John 14:1–12

Philip said, "Lord, show us the Father and that will be enough for us."
John 14:8

Author and pastor Erwin Lutzer recounts a story about television show host Art Linkletter and a little boy who was drawing a picture of God. Amused, Linkletter said, "You can't do that because nobody knows what God looks like."

"They will when I get through!" the boy declared.

We may wonder, *What is God like? Is He good? Is He kind? Does He care?* The simple answer to those questions is Jesus's response to Philip's request: "Lord, show us the Father." Jesus replied, "Don't you know me, Philip, even after I have been among you such a long time? Anyone who has seen me has seen the Father" (JOHN 14:8–9).

If you ever get hungry to see God, look at Jesus. "The Son is the image of the invisible God," said Paul (COL. 1:15). Read through the four gospels in the New Testament: Matthew, Mark, Luke, and John. Think deeply about what Jesus did and said. "Draw" your own mental picture of God as you read. You'll know much more of what He's like when you're through.

A friend of mine once told me that the only God he could believe in is the one he saw in Jesus. If you look closely, I think you'll agree. As you read about Him your heart will leap, for though you may not know it, Jesus is the God you've been looking for all your life.   *DAVID ROPER*

We're so prone, Lord, to want You to be something You are not. Help us to see You more clearly on the pages of Scripture. Help us reflect Your Son in our lives.

The clearer we see God, the clearer we see ourselves.
ERWIN LUTZER

Writing Letters

Read: 2 Corinthians 3:1–6

You yourselves are our letter, written on our hearts, known and read by everyone. 2 Corinthians 3:2

My mother and her sisters engage in what is increasingly becoming a lost art form—writing letters. Each week they pen personal words to each other with such consistency that one of their mail-carriers worries when he doesn't have something to deliver! Their letters brim with the stuff of life, the joys and heartaches along with the daily happenings of friends and family.

I love to reflect on this weekly exercise of the women in my family. It helps me appreciate even more the apostle Paul's words that those who follow Jesus are "a letter from Christ," who were "written not with ink but with the Spirit of the living God" (2 COR. 3:3). In response to false teachers who wanted to discredit his message (SEE 2 COR. 11), Paul encouraged the church in Corinth to keep on following the true and living God as he had previously taught. In doing so, he memorably described the believers as Christ's letter, with their transformed lives a more powerful witness to the Spirit working through Paul's ministry than any written letter could be.

How wonderful that God's Spirit in us writes a story of grace and redemption! For as meaningful as written words can be, it is our lives that are the best witness to the truth of the gospel, for they speak volumes through our compassion, service, gratitude, and joy. Through our words and actions, the Lord spreads His life-giving love. What message might you send today?

AMY BOUCHER PYE

Lord God, write the story of my life so that I might reflect Your love and goodness to those I encounter today.

We are Christ's letters.

The One Who Understands

Read: John 1:1–18

The Word became flesh and made his dwelling among us. John 1:14

John Babler is the chaplain for the police and fire departments in his Texas community. During a twenty-two-week sabbatical from his job, he attended police academy training so that he could better understand the situations law enforcement officers face. Through spending time with the other cadets and learning about the intense challenges of the profession, Babler gained a new sense of humility and empathy. In the future, he hopes to be more effective as he counsels police officers who struggle with emotional stress, fatigue, and loss.

We know that God understands the situations we face because He made us and sees everything that happens to us. We also know He understands because He has been to earth and experienced life as a human being. He "became flesh and made his dwelling among us" as the person of Jesus Christ (JOHN 1:14).

Jesus's earthly life included a wide range of difficulty. He felt the searing heat of the sun, the pain of an empty stomach, and the uncertainty of homelessness. Emotionally, He endured the tension of disagreements, the burn of betrayal, and the ongoing threat of violence.

Jesus experienced the joys of friendship and family love, as well as the worst problems that we face here on earth. He provides hope. He is the Wonderful Counselor who patiently listens to our concerns with insight and care (ISA. 9:6). He is the One who can say, "I've been through that. I understand."

JENNIFER BENSON SCHULDT

Dear Lord, thank You for caring enough to humble Yourself and come to earth as a human being.

God understands the struggles we face.

Taking the First Step

Read: 2 Corinthians 5:11–21

God was reconciling the world to himself in Christ, not counting people's sins against them. And he has committed to us the message of reconciliation. 2 Corinthians 5:19

Tham Dashu sensed something was missing in his life. So he started going to church—the same church his daughter attended. But they never went together. In earlier days, he had offended her, which drove a wedge between them. So, Tham would slip in when the singing started and leave promptly after the service ended.

Church members shared the gospel story with him, but Tham always politely rejected their invitation to put his faith in Jesus. Still, he kept coming to church.

One day Tham fell gravely ill. His daughter plucked up the courage and wrote him a letter. She shared how Christ had changed her life, and she sought reconciliation with her dad. That night, Tham put his faith in Jesus and the family was reconciled. A few days later, Tham died and entered into the presence of Jesus—at peace with God and his loved ones.

The apostle Paul wrote that we are to "try to persuade others" about the truth of God's love and forgiveness (2 COR. 5:11). He said that it is "Christ's love [that] compels us" to carry out His work of reconciliation (V. 14).

Our willingness to forgive may help others realize that God desires to reconcile us to Himself (V. 19). Would you lean on God's strength to show them His love today?   *POH FANG CHIA*

Is there someone you need to try to reconcile with? What practical first step can you take today?

Our willingness to seek reconciliation with others shows God's heart to them.

Stay Awhile

Read: Hebrews 11:8–13

All these people were still living by faith when they died. They did not receive the things promised; they only saw them and welcomed them from a distance, admitting that they were foreigners and strangers on earth. Hebrews 11:13

During a discussion of *The Lord of the Rings* movie trilogy, a teenager said he prefers his stories in books rather than movies. When asked why, the young man replied, "With a book, I can stay there as long as I want." There is something to be said for the power of lingering in a book, especially the Bible, and "inhabiting" the stories there.

Hebrews 11, often called "the faith chapter" of the Bible, mentions many individuals by name. Each of these people traveled a road of difficulty and doubt, but many of them chose to obey God. Scripture describes those who lived by faith in this way: "All these people were still living by faith when they died. They did not receive the things promised; they only saw them and welcomed them from a distance, admitting that they were foreigners and strangers on earth" (V. 13).

How easy it is to rush through our Bible reading without pondering the people and events in the text. Our self-imposed time schedule robs us of going deeper into God's truth and His plan for our lives. Yet, when we are willing to stay awhile, we find ourselves caught up in the real-life dramas of people like us who chose to stake their lives on God's faithfulness.

When we open God's Word, it's good to recall that we can stay as long as we want. *DAVID MCCASLAND*

Father in heaven, thank You for Your written Word and the examples of people who lived by faith. Help us to follow You as they did.

Linger in God's Word and you'll find stories of faith.

We Have a King!

Read: Judges 2:11–23

In those days Israel had no king; everyone did as they saw fit.
Judges 21:25

After attacking my husband with hurtful words when a situation didn't go my way, I snubbed the Holy Spirit's authority as He reminded me of Bible verses that revealed my sinful attitudes. Was nursing my stubborn pride worth the collateral damage in my marriage or being disobedient to God? Absolutely not. But by the time I asked for forgiveness from the Lord and my spouse, I'd left a wake of wounds behind me—the result of ignoring wise counsel and living as if I didn't have to answer to anyone but myself.

There was a time when the Israelites had a rebellious attitude. After the death of Moses, Joshua led the Israelites into the promised land. Under his leadership, the Israelites served the Lord (JUDG. 2:7). But after Joshua and the generation that outlived him died, the Israelites forgot God and what He'd done (V. 10). They rejected godly leadership and embraced sin (VV. 11–15).

Things improved when the Lord raised up judges (VV. 16–18), who served like kings. But when each judge died, the Israelites returned to defying God. Living as if they didn't have anyone to answer to but themselves, they suffered devastating consequences (VV. 19–22). But that doesn't have to be our reality. We can submit to the sovereign authority of the eternal Ruler we were made to follow—Jesus—because He is our living Judge and King of Kings.   *XOCHITL DIXON*

Jesus, please help us remember You are our living King of Kings and Lord of Lords, almighty and worthy of our loving obedience and trust.

God gives us the power and the privilege to enjoy the rewards of doing things His way.

What's Your Father's Name?

Read: John 8:39–47

To those who believed in his name, he gave the right to become children of God. John 1:12

When I went to buy a cell phone in the Middle East, I was asked the typical questions: name, nationality, address. But then as the clerk was filling out the form, he asked, "What's your father's name?" That question surprised me, and I wondered why it was important. Knowing my father's name would not be important in my culture, but here it was necessary in order to establish my identity. In some cultures, ancestry is important.

The Israelites believed in the importance of ancestry too. They were proud of their patriarch Abraham, and they thought being part of Abraham's clan made them God's children. Their human ancestry was connected, in their opinion, to their spiritual family.

Hundreds of years later when Jesus was talking with the Jews, He pointed out that this was not so. They could say Abraham was their earthly ancestor, but if they didn't love Him—the One sent by the Father—they were not part of God's family.

The same applies today. We don't choose our human family, but we can decide the spiritual family we belong to. If we believe in Jesus's name, God gives us the right to become His children (JOHN 1:12).

Who is your spiritual Father? Have you decided to follow Jesus? Let this be the day you trust in Jesus for the forgiveness of your sins and become part of God's family. *KEILA OCHOA*

Dear Lord, You are my heavenly and eternal Father.
Thank You for Jesus, my Savior.

God is our Eternal Father.

Anger Management

Read: Ephesians 4:15, 26–32

In your anger do not sin: Do not let the sun go down while you are still angry. Ephesians 4:26

As I had dinner with a friend, she expressed how fed up she was with a particular family member. But she was reluctant to say anything to him about his annoying habit of ignoring or mocking her. When she did try to confront him about the problem, he responded with sarcastic remarks. She exploded in anger at him. Both parties wound up digging in their heels, and the family rift widened.

I can relate, because I handle anger the same way. I also have a hard time confronting people. If a friend or family member says something mean, I usually suppress how I feel until that person or someone else comes along and says or does something else mean. After a while, I explode.

Maybe that's why the apostle Paul in Ephesians 4:26 said, "Do not let the sun go down while you are still angry." Providing a time limit on unresolved issues keeps anger in check. Instead of stewing over a wrong, which is a breeding ground for bitterness, we can ask God for help to "[speak] the truth in love" (EPH. 4:15).

Got a problem with someone? Rather than hold it in, hold it up to God first. He can fight the fire of anger with the power of His forgiveness and love. *LINDA WASHINGTON*

Heavenly Father, please guard us from uncontrolled anger. May the words that we speak bring honor to You.

Put out the fire of anger before it blazes out of control.

Removing the Barriers

Read: Philemon 1:8–16

He is very dear to me but even dearer to you, both as a fellow man and as a brother in the Lord. Philemon 1:16

I saw Mary every Tuesday when I visited "the House"—a home that helps former prisoners reintegrate into society. My life looked different from hers: fresh out of jail, fighting addictions, separated from her son. You might say she lived on the edge of society.

Like Mary, Onesimus knew what it meant to live on the edge of society. As a slave, Onesimus had apparently wronged his Christian master, Philemon, and was now in prison. While there, he met Paul and came to faith in Christ (V. 10). Though now a changed man, Onesimus was still a slave. Paul sent him back to Philemon with a letter urging him to receive Onesimus "no longer as a slave, but better than a slave, as a dear brother" (PHILEM. 1:16).

Philemon had a choice to make: He could treat Onesimus as his slave or welcome him as a brother in Christ. I had a choice to make too. Would I see Mary as an ex-convict and a recovering addict—or as a woman whose life is being changed by the power of Christ? Mary was my sister in the Lord, and we were privileged to walk together in our journey of faith.

It's easy to allow the walls of socio-economic status, class, or cultural differences to separate us. The gospel of Christ removes those barriers, changing our lives and our relationships forever.

KAREN WOLFE

Dear God, thank You that the gospel of Jesus Christ changes lives and relationships. Thank You for removing the barriers between us and making us all members of Your family.

The gospel changes people and relationships.

Watch the Conductor

Read: Hebrews 12:1–3

Let us run with perseverance the race marked out for us, fixing our eyes on Jesus, the pioneer and perfecter of faith. Hebrews 12:1–2

World-renowned violinist Joshua Bell has an unusual way of leading the Academy of St. Martin in the Fields, a forty-four-member chamber orchestra. Instead of waving a baton he directs while playing his Stradivarius with the other violinists. Bell told Colorado Public Radio, "Even while I'm playing I can give them all kinds of direction and signals that I think only they would understand at this point. They know by every little dip in my violin, or raise in my eyebrow, or the way I draw the bow. They know the sound I'm looking for from the entire orchestra."

Just as the orchestra members watch Joshua Bell, the Bible instructs us to keep our eyes on Jesus our Lord. After listing many heroes of the faith in Hebrews 11, the writer says, "Therefore, since we are surrounded by such a great cloud of witnesses, let us throw off everything that hinders and the sin that so easily entangles. And let us run with perseverance the race marked out for us, fixing our eyes on Jesus, the pioneer and perfecter of faith" (HEB. 12:1–2).

Jesus promised, "I am with you always, to the very end of the age" (MATT. 28:20). Because He is, we have the amazing privilege of keeping our eyes on Him while He conducts the music of our lives.   *DAVID MCCASLAND*

Lord, our eyes look to You this day so we may follow Your direction and live in harmony with You.

Let us keep our eyes on Jesus our Savior as He directs our lives.

The Best Portion of All

Read: Psalm 73:21–28

I have learned the secret of being content in any and every situation.
Philippians 4:12

"His piece is bigger than mine!"

When I was a boy my brothers and I would sometimes bicker about the size of the piece of homemade pie mom served us. One day Dad observed our antics with a lifted eyebrow, and smiled at Mom as he lifted his plate: "Please just give me a piece as big as your heart." My brothers and I watched in stunned silence as Mom laughed and offered him the largest portion of all.

If we focus on others' possessions, jealousy too often results. Yet God's Word lifts our eyes to something of far greater worth than earthly possessions. The psalmist writes, "You are my portion, LORD; I have promised to obey your words. I have sought your face with all my heart" (PS. 119:57–58). Inspired by the Holy Spirit, the writer conveyed the truth that nothing matters more than closeness to God.

What better portion could we have than our loving and limitless Creator? Nothing on earth can compare with Him, and nothing can take Him away from us. Human longing is an expansive void; one may have "everything" in the world and still be miserable. But when God is our source of happiness, we are truly content. There's a space within us only God can fill. He alone can give us the peace that matches our hearts.   *JAMES BANKS*

Loving Lord, thank You that nothing and no one can meet my
every need like You can.

You have made us for yourself, Lord. Our hearts are restless until they can find rest in You.
AUGUSTINE OF HIPPO

Let's Finish the Race

Read: Ecclesiastes 4:9–12

Two are better than one . . . If either of them falls down, one can help the other up. Ecclesiastes 4:9–10

In the 2016 Rio Olympics, two athletes in the 5,000-meter race caught the world's attention. About 3,200 meters into the race, New Zealander Nikki Hamblin and American Abbey D'Agostino collided and fell. Abbey was quickly up on her feet, but stopped to help Nikki. Moments after the two athletes had started running again, Abbey began faltering, her right leg injured as a result of the fall. It was now Nikki's turn to stop and encourage her fellow athlete to finish the race. When Abbey eventually stumbled across the finish line, Nikki was waiting to embrace her. What a beautiful picture of mutual encouragement!

It reminds me of a passage in the Bible: "Two are better than one. . . . If either of them falls down, one can help the other up. But pity anyone who falls and has no one to help them up" (ECCL. 4:9–10). As runners in a spiritual race, we need one another—perhaps even more so, for we are not racing in competition with each other but as members of the same team. There'll be moments where we falter and need someone to pick us up; at other times, someone may need our encouragement through our prayers or presence.

The spiritual race is not to be run alone. Is God leading you to be a Nikki or Abbey in someone's life? Respond to His prompting today, and let's finish the race!   *POH FANG CHIA*

Dear Lord, thank You for the encouragement of fellow believers to help me on my journey. Help me to look for ways to encourage others.

We need each other to get where God wants us to go.

The Daily Prayer

Read: Ephesians 6:18–19

Pray in the Spirit on all occasions with all kinds of prayers and requests.
Ephesians 6:18

Singer/songwriter Robert Hamlet wrote "Lady Who Prays for Me" as a tribute to his mother who made a point of praying for her boys each morning before they went to the bus stop. After a young mom heard Hamlet sing his song, she committed to praying with her own little boy. The result was heartwarming! Just before her son went out the door, his mother prayed for him. Five minutes later he returned—bringing kids from the bus stop with him! His mom was taken aback and asked what was going on. The boy responded, "Their moms didn't pray with them."

In the book of Ephesians, Paul urges us to pray "on all occasions with all kinds of prayers" (6:18). Demonstrating our daily dependence on God is essential in a family since many children first learn to trust God as they observe genuine faith in the people closest to them (2 TIM. 1:5). There is no better way to teach the utmost importance of prayer than by praying *for* and *with* our children. It is one of the ways they begin to sense a compelling need to reach out personally to God in faith.

When we "start children off" by modeling a "sincere faith" in God (PROV. 22:6; 2 TIM. 1:5), we give them a special gift, an assurance that God is an ever-present part of our lives—continually loving, guiding, and protecting us.   *CINDY HESS KASPER*

Help me to depend more fully on You in every moment of the day and to rest in the assurance that You are always with me.

Daily prayers lessen daily worries.

Sweet and Sour

Read: Job 2:1–10

Shall we accept good from God, and not trouble? Job 2:10

When our toddler first bit into a lemon wedge, he wrinkled his nose, stuck out his tongue, and squeezed his eyes shut. "Sow-wah," he said (*sour*).

I chuckled as I reached for the piece of fruit, intending to toss it into the trash.

"No!" Xavier scampered across the kitchen to get away from me. "Moe-wah!" (*more*). His lips puckered with every juice-squirting bite. I winced when he finally handed me the rind and walked away.

My taste buds accurately reflect my partiality to the sweet moments in life. My preference for avoiding all things bitter reminds me of Job's wife, who seems to have shared my aversion to the sourness of suffering.

Job surely didn't delight in hardship or trouble, yet he honored God through heart-wrenching circumstances (JOB 1:1–22). When painful sores afflicted Job's body, he endured the agony (2:7–8). His wife told him to give up on God (V. 9), but Job responded by trusting the Lord through suffering and afflictions (V. 10).

It's natural to prefer avoiding the bitter bites in life. We can even be tempted to lash out at God when we're hurting. But the Lord uses trials, teaching us how to trust Him, depend on Him, and surrender to Him as He enables us to persevere through difficult times. And like Job, we don't have to enjoy suffering to learn to savor the unexpected sweetness of sour moments—the divine strengthening of our faith.   *XOCHITL DIXON*

Thank You for assuring us that suffering is never wasted when we place our confidence in who You are, what You've done, and what You're capable of doing.

God uses suffering to strengthen our faith.

What Simon Said

Read: Luke 5:1–11

Simon answered, . . . "But because you say so, I will let down the nets."
Luke 5:5

A man named Refuge Rabindranath has been a youth worker in Sri Lanka for more than ten years. He often interacts with the youth late into the night—playing with them, listening to them, counseling and teaching them. He enjoys working with the young people, but it can be disheartening when promising students sometimes walk away from the faith. Some days he feels a bit like Simon Peter in Luke 5.

Simon had been working hard all night but caught no fish (V. 5). He felt discouraged and tired. Yet when Jesus told him to "put out into deep water, and let down the nets for a catch" (V. 4), Simon replied, "Because you say so, I will let down the nets" (V. 5).

Simon's obedience is remarkable. As a seasoned fisherman, he knew that fish move to the bottom of the lake when the sun is up, and the dragnets they used could not go deep enough to catch those fish.

His willingness to trust Jesus was rewarded. Not only did Simon catch a large number of fish, he gained a deeper understanding of who Jesus is. He moved from calling Jesus "Master" (V. 5) to calling Him "Lord" (V. 8). Indeed, "listening" often allows us to see the works of God firsthand and draw closer to Him.

Perhaps God is calling you to "let down your nets again." May we reply to the Lord as Simon did: "Because You say so, I will."

POH FANG CHIA

Father, it is our great privilege to call You "Lord." Help us to obey and trust You, and to learn more of what it means to walk closely with You.

Our obedience to God will guide us through the unknown and draw us closer to Him.

Living in Tents

Read: Genesis 12:4–9

From there he went on towards the hills east of Bethel and pitched his tent. Genesis 12:8

Growing up in Minnesota, a place known for its many beautiful lakes, I loved to go camping to enjoy the wonders of God's creation. But sleeping in a flimsy tent wasn't my favorite part of the experience—especially when a rainy night and a leaky tent resulted in a soggy sleeping bag.

I marvel to think that one of the heroes of our faith spent a *hundred* years in tents. When he was seventy-five years old, Abraham heard God's call to leave his country so the Lord could make him into a new nation (GEN. 12:1–2). Abraham obeyed, trusting that God would follow through on His promise. And for the rest of his life, until he died at 175 (25:7), he lived away from his home country in tents.

We may not have the same call as Abraham did to live nomadically, but even as we love and serve this world and the people in it, we may long for a deeper experience of home, of being rooted here on earth. Like Abraham, when the wind whips our flimsy covering or the rain soaks through, we can look with faith for the city to come, whose "architect and builder is God" (HEB. 11:10). And like Abraham, we can find hope that God is working to renew His creation, preparing a "better country—a heavenly one" to come (V. 16).   *AMY BOUCHER PYE*

Lord God, You are our shelter and our foundation. May we trust You in the big things and small.

God gives us a solid foundation for our lives.

Apart but Not Abandoned

Read: Acts 20:17–20, 35–38

Now I commit you to God and to the word of his grace, which can build you up. Acts 20:32

I had a lump in my throat as I said good-bye to my niece on the eve of her move to Massachusetts to attend graduate school at Boston University. Though she had been away four years as an undergraduate, she hadn't left our state. A two and a one-half-hour drive easily reunited us. Now she would be more than 800 miles away. No longer would we meet regularly to talk. I had to trust that God would take care of her.

Paul likely felt the same way as he said good-bye to the elders of the church in Ephesus. Having established the church and taught them for three years, Paul concluded these elders to be as close as family to him. Now that Paul was headed to Jerusalem, he would not see them again.

But Paul had parting advice for the Ephesians. Though they would no longer have Paul as their teacher, the Ephesians did not have to feel abandoned. God would continue to train them through "the word of his grace" (ACTS 20:32) to lead the church. Unlike Paul, God would always be with them.

Whether it's children we launch from the nest or other family and friends who move away—saying good-bye can be very difficult. They move beyond our influence and into their new lives. When we let go of their hands, we can trust that God has them in His. He can continue to shape their lives and meet their real needs—more than we ever could. *LINDA WASHINGTON*

Lord, help us to trust that Your watchful care extends over those we hold dear who are far away from us.

Though we're far away from those we love, they are never far from God.

From Empty to Full

Read: 2 Kings 4:1–7

When all the jars were full . . . the oil stopped flowing. 2 Kings 4:6

A popular children's book tells the story of a poor, country boy who took off his cap to honor the king. An identical hat appeared instantly in its place on his head, inciting the king's anger for what appeared to be disrespect. Bartholomew removed hat after hat while being escorted to the palace for punishment. Each time, a new one appeared in its place. The hats grew increasingly fancy, bearing precious jewels and feather plumes. The 500th hat was the envy of King Derwin, who pardoned Bartholomew and purchased the hat for 500 pieces of gold. At last, Bartholomew's head was bare; he walked home with freedom *and* money to support his family.

A widow came to Elisha in financial distress, fearing her children would be sold into slavery to pay her debts (2 KINGS 4). She had no assets other than a jar of oil. God multiplied that oil to fill enough borrowed jars to settle the debts plus care for their daily needs (V. 7).

God provided financially for the widow in much the same way He provides salvation for me. I am bankrupted by sin, but Jesus paid my debt—and offers me eternal life as well! Without Jesus, we are each like the poor, country boy with no means to pay our King for our offenses against Him. God miraculously supplies the extravagant ransom for us, and ensures that those who trust in Him will have life abundant forever.   *KIRSTEN HOLMBERG*

Thank You, Lord, for paying my debt through the sacrifice of Jesus Christ. I had nothing; You paid it all for me.

Jesus's sacrifice pays for our spiritual debt.

Clothes for the Climate

Read: Colossians 3:8–17

Over all these virtues put on love, which binds them all together in perfect unity. Colossians 3:14

While removing the price tag from an item of winter clothing I had purchased, I smiled at these words on the back: "WARNING: This innovative product will make you want to go outdoors and stay there." When properly clothed for the climate, a person can survive and even thrive in harsh and changing weather conditions.

The same principle is true in our spiritual lives. As followers of Jesus, our all-weather spiritual wardrobe has been prescribed by the Lord in His Word, the Bible. "As God's chosen people, holy and dearly loved, *clothe* yourselves with compassion, kindness, humility, gentleness and patience. . . . Forgive as the Lord forgave you" (COL. 3:12–13 EMPHASIS ADDED).

These garments that God provides—such as kindness, humility, and gentleness—allow us to meet hostility and criticism with patience, forgiveness, and love. They give us staying power in the storms of life.

When we face adverse conditions at home, school, or work, the "clothing" God tells us to wear protects us and enables us to make a positive difference. "And over all these virtues put on love, which binds them all together in perfect unity" (V. 14).

Dressing according to God's guidelines doesn't change the weather—it equips the wearer.   *DAVID MCCASLAND*

Heavenly Father, help me to put on Your garment of love so that I am prepared for whatever life brings me today.

Kindness is the oil that takes the friction out of life.

The Day I Couldn't Pray

Read: Romans 8:22–26

The Spirit Himself intercedes for us through wordless groans. Romans 8:26

In November 2015, I learned I needed open-heart surgery. Surprised and a little shaken, I was naturally drawn to think about the possibility of death. Were there relationships I needed to mend? Were there financial matters I needed to attend to for my family? Was there work that could be done ahead of time? And what about work that couldn't wait; who should I hand that off to? It was a time to both act and pray.

Except I couldn't do either.

My body was so weary and my mind so fatigued that even the simplest of tasks seemed beyond my strength. Perhaps most surprising, when I tried to pray, my thoughts would drift to the discomfort, or the shallow breathing caused by the damaged heart made me fall asleep. It was frustrating. I couldn't work and I couldn't even ask God to let me live so I could spend more time with my family!

The inability to pray troubled me most. But as with all other human needs, the Creator knew this was happening to me. I would eventually recall He made two preparations for such occurrences: the prayer of the Spirit for us when we can't pray (ROM. 8:26), and the prayer of others on our behalf (JAMES 5:16; GAL. 6:2).

What a comfort it was to know that the Holy Spirit was even then raising my concerns before the Father. What a gift also to hear from friends and family as they prayed for me. Then came another surprise: As my friends and family asked me what to pray for, it became clear that my answers to them were also being heard by God as prayers. What a gift it is in a time of uncertainty to be reminded God hears our heart even when we think we can't call out to Him. *RANDY KILGORE*

God never leaves the voices of His children unheard.

Fresh Faith

Read: John 20:24–29

Let us hold unswervingly to the hope we profess, for he who promised is faithful. Hebrews 10:23

When our son was struggling with heroin addiction, if you had told me God would one day use our experience to encourage other families who face these kinds of battles, I would have had trouble believing it. God has a way of bringing good out of difficult circumstances that isn't always easy to see when you are going through them.

The apostle Thomas also didn't expect God to bring good out of the greatest challenge of his faith—Jesus's crucifixion. Thomas wasn't with the other disciples when Jesus came to them after the resurrection, and in his deep grief he insisted, "Unless I see the nail marks in his hands and put my finger where the nails were . . . I will not believe" (JOHN 20:25). But later, when Jesus appeared to all the disciples together, out of the dust of Thomas's doubts God's Spirit would inspire a striking statement of faith. When Thomas exclaimed, "My Lord and my God!" (V. 28), he was grasping the truth that Jesus was actually God in the flesh, standing right in front of him. It was a bold confession of faith that would encourage and inspire believers in every century that followed.

Our God is able to inspire fresh faith in our hearts, even in moments when we least expect it. We can always look forward to His faithfulness. Nothing is too hard for Him!   *JAMES BANKS*

Thank You, Lord, that Your love is stronger than our greatest difficulties—even our worst doubts or fears!

God can change our doubts into bold statements of faith.

New: Inside and Out

Read: John 3:1–8, 13–16

No one can see the kingdom of God unless they are born again.
John 3:3

A few years ago a publisher made a big mistake. A book had been on the market for several years, so it was time for a makeover. The author rewrote the book to bring it up to date. But when the revision was published, there was a problem. The publisher gave the book a nice new cover but printed the old book inside.

The exterior was fresh and new, but the interior was old and out of date. This "reprint" was not really new at all.

Sometimes that kind of thing happens with people. They realize a change needs to be made in life. Things are heading in the wrong direction. So they may put on a new exterior without making a vital change in their heart. They may change a behavior on the outside but may not realize that it is only God who can change us on the inside.

In John 3, Nicodemus sensed that because Jesus came "from God" (V. 2) He offered something very different. What Jesus told Nicodemus made him realize that He offered nothing short of a rebirth (V. 4): He needed to be "born again," to be made totally new (V. 7).

That change comes only through faith in Jesus Christ. That's when "the old has gone, the new is here" (2 COR. 5:17). Do you need a change? Put your faith in Jesus. He's the one who changes your heart and makes all things new.   *DAVE BRANON*

Lord, I now know that changes on the outside—behavior, looks, attitude—don't change me inside. I put my faith in Jesus, who died on the cross and rose again to forgive my sins. Make me new on the inside—in my soul.

Only God can make us new.

It Takes Time to Grow

Read: Ephesians 4:11–16

Speaking the truth in love, we will grow to become in every respect the mature body of him who is the head, that is, Christ. Ephesians 4:15

On her first day in preschool, young Charlotte was asked to draw a picture of herself. Her artwork featured a simple orb for a body, an oblong head, and two circle eyes. On her last day of preschool, Charlotte was again directed to draw a self-portrait. This one showed a little girl in a colorful dress, a smiling face with distinct features, and a cascade of beautiful red tresses. The school had used a simple assignment to demonstrate the difference that time can make in the level of maturity.

While we accept that it takes time for children to mature, we may grow impatient with ourselves or fellow believers who show slow spiritual growth. We rejoice when we see the "fruit of the Spirit" (GAL. 5:22–23), but are disheartened when we observe a sinful choice. The author of Hebrews spoke of this when he wrote to the church: "Though by this time you ought to be teachers, you need someone to teach you the elementary truths of God's word all over again" (HEB. 5:12).

As we continue to pursue intimacy with Jesus ourselves, let's pray for each other and patiently come alongside those who love God but who seem to struggle with spiritual growth. "Speaking the truth in love," let's continue to encourage one another, so that together we may "grow to become in every respect the mature body of him who is the head, that is, Christ" (EPH. 4:15).

CINDY HESS KASPER

Lord, we love You! In our walk with You, help us to receive and give encouragement.

Words of truth spoken in love can guide us all toward maturity in Christ.

The Perfect Prayer Partner

Read: Romans 8:31–34

[Jesus] is at the right hand of God and is also interceding for us.
Romans 8:34

Few sounds are as beautiful as hearing someone who loves you praying for you. When you hear a friend pray for you with compassion and God-given insight, it's a little like heaven touching earth.

How good it is to know that because of God's kindness to us our prayers can also touch heaven. Sometimes when we pray we may struggle with words and feelings of inadequacy, but Jesus taught His followers that we "should always pray and not give up" (LUKE 18:1). God's Word shows us that one of the reasons we can do this is that Jesus himself "is at the right hand of God and is also interceding for us" (ROM. 8:34).

We never pray alone, because Jesus is praying for us. He hears us as we pray, and speaks to the Father on our behalf. We don't have to worry about the eloquence of our words, because no one understands us like Jesus. He helps us in every way, presenting our needs before God. He also knows when the answers we ask for would not be good for us, handling every request or concern with perfect wisdom and love.

Jesus is the perfect prayer partner—the friend who intercedes for us with immeasurable kindness. His prayers for us are beautiful beyond words, and should encourage us to always pray with thankfulness.   *JAMES BANKS*

Thank You, Lord Jesus, for interceding for me with love. Help me to love and
serve You with my prayers today.

There's no greater privilege than praying with Jesus.

Conceived in Crisis

Read: Psalm 57

I will take refuge in the shadow of your wings until the disaster has passed. Psalm 57:1

Marc recalls a moment from his childhood when his father called the family together. Their car had broken down, and the family would run out of money by the end of the month. Marc's dad paused and prayed. Then he asked the family to expect God's answer.

Today Marc recalls how God's help arrived in surprising ways. A friend repaired their car; unexpected checks arrived; food showed up at the door. Praising God came easily. But the family's gratitude had been forged in a crisis.

Psalm 57 has long provided rich inspiration for worship songs. When David declared, "Be exalted, O God, above the heavens" (v. 11), we might imagine him gazing up at a magnificent Middle Eastern night sky or perhaps singing in a tabernacle worship service. But in reality David, fearful for his life, was hiding in a cave.

"I am in the midst of lions," David said in the psalm. These "ravenous beasts" were "men whose teeth are spears and arrows, whose tongues are sharp swords" (V. 4). David's praise was conceived in crisis. Although he was cornered by enemies who wanted him dead, David could write these amazing words: "My heart, O God, is steadfast . . . . I will sing and make music" (V. 7).

Whatever crisis we face today, we can run to God for help. Then, we can praise Him as we wait expectantly, confident in His infinitely creative care for us.   *TIM GUSTAFSON*

Your next crisis is your next opportunity to trust our unfailing God.

Divine Interruptions

Read: Luke 18:35–43

Jesus asked him, "What do you want me to do for you?" "Lord, I want to see," he replied. Luke 18:40–41

Experts agree that a staggering amount of time is consumed each day by interruptions. Whether at work or at home, a phone call or an unexpected visit can easily deflect us from what we feel is our main purpose.

Not many of us like disruptions in our daily lives, especially when they cause inconvenience or a change of plans. But Jesus treated what appeared to be interruptions in a far different way. Time after time in the Gospels, we see the Lord stop what He is doing to help a person in need.

While Jesus was on His way to Jerusalem where He would be crucified, a blind man begging by the side of the road called out, "Jesus, Son of David, have mercy on me!" (LUKE 18:35–38). Some in the crowd told him to be quiet, but he kept calling out to Jesus. Jesus stopped and asked the man, "'What do you want me to do for you?' 'Lord, I want to see,' he replied. Jesus said to him, 'Receive your sight; your faith has healed you'" (VV. 41–42).

When our plans are interrupted by someone who genuinely needs help, we can ask the Lord for wisdom in how to respond with compassion. What we call an interruption may be a divine appointment the Lord has scheduled for that day.

DAVID MCCASLAND

Lord Jesus, fill us with Your wisdom and compassion that we may respond as You did to people in need.

Interruptions can be opportunities to serve.

Hovering Over Us

Read: Deuteronomy 32:7–12

He shielded him and cared for him . . . like an eagle that . . . hovers over its young. Deuteronomy 32:10–11

Betty's daughter arrived home from an overseas trip feeling unwell. When her pain became unbearable, Betty and her husband took her to the emergency room. The doctors and nurses set to work, and after a few hours one of the nurses said to Betty, "She's going to be okay! We're going to take good care of her and get her healed up." In that moment, Betty felt peace and love flood over her. She realized that while she hovered over her daughter anxiously, the Lord is the perfect parent who nurtures His children, comforting us in difficult times.

In the book of Deuteronomy, the Lord reminded His people how, when they were wandering in the desert, He cared for them as a loving parent who hovers over its young. He never left them, but was like an eagle "that spreads its wings" to catch its children and "carries them aloft" (32:11). He wanted them to remember that although they experienced hardship and strife in the desert, He didn't abandon them.

We too may face challenges of many kinds, but we can take comfort and courage in this reminder that our God will never leave us. When we feel that we are falling, the Lord like an eagle will spread His wings to catch us (V. 11) as He brings us peace.

AMY BOUCHER PYE

Father God, Your love as a parent is greater than anything I can imagine. May my confidence rest in You, and may I share Your love with others.

Our God hovers over us with love.

If I Knew Then . . .

Read: 1 Peter 1:3–9

In his great mercy [God] has given us new birth into a living hope through the resurrection of Jesus Christ from the dead. 1 Peter 1:3

On the way to work, I listened to the song "Dear Younger Me," which asks: If you could go back, knowing what you know now, what would you tell your younger self? As I listened, I thought about the bits of wisdom I might give my younger, less-wise self. Most of us have thought about how we might do things differently—if only we could do it all over again.

But the song illustrates that even though we have regrets from our past, all our experiences have shaped who we are. We can't change the consequences of our choices or sin. Praise God we don't have to carry the mistakes around with us. Because of what Jesus has done! "In his great mercy he has given us new birth into a living hope through the resurrection of Jesus Christ from the dead"! (1 PETER 1:3).

If we turn to Him in faith and sorrow for our sins, He will forgive us. On that day we're made brand new and begin the process of being spiritually transformed (2 COR. 5:17). It doesn't matter what we've done (or haven't done), we are forgiven because of what *He's* done. We can move forward, making the most of today and anticipating a future with Him. In Christ, we're free!

ALYSON KIEDA

Dear Lord, I'm so thankful that through You we can be free of the burdens of the past—the mistakes, the pain, the sins—that hang so heavy. We don't need to carry around regret or shame. We can leave them with You.

Leave your heavy burdens with God.

How Long?

Read: Habakkuk 1:2–11

How long, LORD, must I call for help? Habakkuk 1:2

When I married, I thought I would have children immediately. That did not happen, and the pain of infertility brought me to my knees. I often cried out to God, "How long?" I knew God could change my circumstance. Why wasn't He?

Are you waiting on God? Are you asking, How long, Lord, before justice prevails in our world? Before there is a cure for cancer? Before I am no longer in debt?

The prophet Habakkuk was well acquainted with that feeling. In the seventh century BC, he cried out to the Lord: "How long, LORD, must I call for help, but you do not listen? Or cry out to you, 'Violence!' but you do not save? Why do you make me look at injustice? Why do you tolerate wrongdoing?" (HAB. 1:2-3). He prayed for a long time, struggling to reconcile how a just and powerful God could allow wickedness, injustice, and corruption to continue in Judah. As far as Habakkuk was concerned, God should have already intervened. *Why was God doing nothing?*

There are days when we too feel as if God is doing nothing. Like Habakkuk, we have continuously asked God, "How long?"

Yet, we are not alone. As with Habakkuk, God hears our burdens. We must continue to cast them on the Lord because He cares for us. God hears us and, in His time, will give an answer.

KAREN WOLFE

Lord, thank You for bearing my burdens. I know that You hear my cries and will answer in accordance to Your perfect plan and purposes.

Don't despair because of evil; God will have the last word.

Enough

Read: 2 Kings 4:42–44

They ate and had some left over, according to the word of the LORD.
2 Kings 4:44

When my husband and I were first asked to host a small group in our home, my immediate reaction was to decline. I felt inadequate. We didn't have seats for everyone; our home was small and couldn't hold many people. I didn't know whether we had the skills to facilitate the discussion. I worried that I'd be asked to prepare food, something for which I lacked both passion and funds. I didn't feel like we had "enough" to do it. I didn't feel *I* was "enough" to do it. But we wanted to give to God and our community, so despite our fears, we agreed. Over the next five years we found great joy in welcoming the group into our living room.

I observe similar reluctance and doubt in the man who brought bread to God's servant, Elisha. Elisha had instructed him to give it to the people, but the man questioned whether twenty loaves could feed so many—one hundred men. He seems to have been tempted to withhold the food because—in his human understanding—it wouldn't be sufficient. Yet it was *more* than enough (2 KINGS 4:44), because God took his gift, given in obedience, and made it enough.

When we feel inadequate, or think what we have to offer isn't sufficient, let's remember that God asks us to give what we have in faithful obedience. He is the one who makes it "enough."

KIRSTEN HOLMBERG

Lord, when I fear what I have to give is insufficient, help me to give to You anyway and trust You to make it "enough."

An offering given in faithful obedience is just right.

From Worms to War

Read: Judges 6:11–16, 36–40

The LORD said to [Gideon], "Peace! Do not be afraid. You are not going to die." Judges 6:23

It was ten-year-old Cleo's first time fishing, and as he looked into the container of bait he seemed hesitant to get started. Finally he said to my husband, "Help me, I-S-O-W!" When my husband asked him what the problem was, Cleo responded, "I-S-O-W! I'm scared of worms!" His fear had made him unable to act.

Fear can paralyze grown men too. Gideon must've been afraid when the angel of the Lord came to him as he was threshing wheat in secret, hiding from his Midianite enemies (JUDG. 6:11). The angel told him he had been chosen by God to lead His people in battle (VV. 12–14).

Gideon's response? "Pardon me, my lord, . . . but how can I save Israel? My clan is the weakest in Manasseh, and I am the least in my family" (V. 15). After being assured of the Lord's presence, Gideon still seemed fearful and asked for signs that God would use him to save Israel as He promised (VV. 36–40). And God responded to Gideon's requests. The Israelites were successful in battle and then enjoyed peace for forty years.

We all have fears of various kinds—from worms to wars. Gideon's story teaches us that we can be confident of this: If God asks us to do something, He'll give us the strength and power to do it.   *ANNE CETAS*

Lord, thank You for the assurance that You are with us.

To take the fear out of living, put your faith in the living God.

Wake-Up Call!

Read: Revelation 3:1–6

Wake up! Strengthen what remains and is about to die, for I have found your deeds unfinished in the sight of my God. Revelation 3:2

During the years when I traveled frequently and stayed in a different city every night, I always scheduled a wake-up call when I checked into a hotel. Along with a personal alarm, I needed a jangling telephone to help get me out of bed and moving in the morning.

The book of Revelation contains a spiritual wake-up call in the apostle John's letters to the seven churches in the province of Asia. To the church in Sardis he wrote this message from Jesus himself: "I know your deeds; you have a reputation of being alive, but you are dead. Wake up! Strengthen what remains and is about to die, for I have found your deeds unfinished in the sight of my God" (REV. 3:1–2).

In the midst of spiritual fatigue, we may fail to notice the lethargy that creeps into our relationship with God. But the Lord tells us to "remember . . . what you have received and heard; hold it fast, and repent" (V. 3).

Many people find that scheduling some extra time each morning to read the Bible and talk to the Lord in prayer helps them stay spiritually alert. It's not a job but a joy to spend time with Jesus and know that He prepares us for whatever lies ahead that day.   *DAVID MCCASLAND*

Lord, enable us to hear and respond to Your wake-up call today.

Spending time with Jesus is a joy!

Two-Winged Sun

Read: Isaiah 38:1–8

[The Lord says:] I have heard your prayer and seen your tears.
Isaiah 38:5

For five years, an ancient clay seal remained in a closet in Jerusalem's Institute of Archaeology. After the seal was dug up at the foot of the southern part of Jerusalem's old city wall, initial examination failed to establish the significance of the nearly 3,000-year-old object. But then a researcher carefully scrutinized the letters on the seal, resulting in a major discovery. The inscription, written in ancient Hebrew, reads: "Belonging to Hezekiah [son of] Ahaz king of Judah."

At the center of the seal is a two-winged sun surrounded by two images symbolizing life. The archaeologists who discovered the seal believe that King Hezekiah began using this seal as a symbol of God's protection after the Lord healed him from a life-threatening illness (ISA. 38:1–8). Hezekiah had been pleading with the Lord to heal him. And God heard his prayer. He also gave Hezekiah a sign that He would indeed do what He had promised, saying, "I will cause the sun's shadow to move ten steps backward" (V. 8 NLT).

The facts related to this archeological artifact give us an encouraging reminder that the people in the Bible were learning, as we are, to call on the Lord who hears us when we cry out to Him for help. And even when His answers are not what we want or expect, we can rest assured that He is compassionate and He is powerful. The One who orders the movement of the sun can certainly move in our hearts.   *POH FANG CHIA*

Dear God, You are great and powerful, yet You care for me. Help me to believe in Your power and love, and to seek Your help always.

Call out to God; He is wanting to hear from you.

The Good Shepherd

Read: Isaiah 40:6–11

He gathers the lambs in his arms and carries them close to his heart.
Isaiah 40:11

I sat in the hospital room with my husband, waiting anxiously. Our young son was having corrective eye surgery and I felt the butterflies jostle in my stomach as I fretted and worried. I tried to pray, asking God to give me His peace. As I leafed through my Bible, I thought about Isaiah 40, so I turned to the familiar passage, wondering if anything fresh would strike me.

As I read, I caught my breath, for the words from so many years ago reminded me that the Lord "tends his flock like a shepherd" as He "gathers the lambs in his arms and carries them close to his heart" (v. 11). In that moment my anxiety left me as I realized the Lord was holding us, leading us, and caring for us. *That was just what I needed, Lord,* I breathed silently. I felt enveloped in God's peace during and after the surgery (which thankfully went well).

The Lord promised His people through the prophet Isaiah that He would be their shepherd, guiding them in their daily lives and giving them comfort. We too can know His gentle tending as we tell Him our anxious thoughts and seek His love and peace. We know that He is our Good Shepherd, holding us close to His heart and carrying us in His everlasting arms.　　*AMY BOUCHER PYE*

Lord Jesus Christ, You are the Good Shepherd who lays down His life for His sheep. Thank You for the gift of Your sacrificial love and for the peace that passes all understanding.

The Good Shepherd cares for His sheep.

A New Name

Read: John 1:35–42

Jesus looked at him, and said, . . . "You will be called Cephas" (which, when translated, is Peter). John 1:42

In the article "Leading by Naming," Mark Labberton wrote about the power of a name. He said: "I can still feel the impact of a musical friend who one day called me 'musical.' No one had ever called me that. I didn't really play an instrument. I was no soloist. Yet . . . I instantly felt known and loved. . . . [He] noticed, validated, and appreciated something deeply true about me."

Perhaps this is what Simon felt when Jesus renamed him. After Andrew was convinced that Jesus was the Messiah, he immediately found his brother Simon and brought him to Jesus (JOHN 1:41–42). Jesus peered into his soul and validated and appreciated something deeply true about Simon. Yes, Jesus saw the failure and impetuous nature that would get him into trouble. But more than that He saw the potential of Simon to become a leader in the church. Jesus named him Cephas—Aramaic for Peter—a rock (JOHN 1:42; SEE MATT. 16:18).

And so it is with us. God sees our pride, anger, and lack of love for others, but He also knows who we are in Christ. He calls us justified and reconciled (ROM. 5:9–10); forgiven, holy, and beloved (COL. 2:13; 3:12); chosen and faithful (REV. 17:14). Remember how God sees you and seek to let that define who you are.

MARVIN WILLIAMS

Lord, thank You for knowing me fully, yet loving me like no other. Help me to see others through Your eyes.

No one can steal your identity in Christ.

Held by God

Read: Psalm 131

I have calmed and quieted myself, I am like a weaned child with its mother; like a weaned child I am content. Psalm 131:2

As I was nearing the end of lunch with my sister and her children one afternoon, my sister told my three-year-old niece, Annica, it was time to get ready for her nap. Her face filled with alarm. "But Aunt Monica did not hold me yet today!" she objected, tears filling her eyes. My sister smiled. "Okay, she may hold you first—how long do you need?" "Five minutes," she replied.

As I held my niece, I was grateful for how, without even trying, she constantly reminds me what it looks like to love and be loved. I think sometimes we forget that our faith journey is one of learning to experience love—God's love—more fully than we can imagine (EPH. 3:18). When we lose that focus, we can find ourselves, like the older brother in Jesus's parable of the prodigal son, trying desperately to win God's approval while missing out on all He has already given us (LUKE 15:25–32).

Psalm 131 is one prayer in Scripture that can help us to "become like little children" (MATT. 18:3) and to let go of the battle in our mind over what we don't understand (PS. 131:1). Instead, through time with Him we can return to a place of peace (V. 2), finding the hope we need (V. 3) in His love—as calm and quiet as if we were children again in our mothers' arms (V. 2).

MONICA BRANDS

Lord, we are so grateful for those in our lives who remind us what it means to love and be loved. Help us to be ever more deeply rooted in Your love.

Like children, we can learn to rest in the love of God.

Creation Care

Read: Genesis 1:26–31

The highest heavens belong to the LORD, but the earth he has given to mankind. Psalm 115:16

The "big browns" are spawning in the Owyhee River—brown trout beginning their fall nesting ritual. You can see them excavating their nests in the gravelly shallows.

Wise fishermen know that fish are spawning and try not to disturb them. They avoid walking on gravel bars where they might trample the eggs, or wading upstream from the nests where they might dislodge debris that can smother them. And they don't fish for these trout, though it's tempting to do so as they rest near their nests.

These precautions are part of an ethic that governs responsible fishing. But there is a deeper and a better cause.

The Scriptures stress the fact that God has given us the earth (GEN. 1:28–30). It is ours to use, but we must use it as those who love it.

I muse on the work of God's hands: a partridge calling across a canyon, a bull elk bugling up a fight, a herd of antelope far off in the distance, a brook trout and its kaleidoscopic rose moles, a mother otter playing in a stream with her pups—I love all these things, for they have been given to me for my delight, out of my Father's great love.

And what I love, I protect. *DAVID ROPER*

Heavenly Father, You have put us here to enjoy and ponder Your marvelous creation. May everything You have made remind us of Your goodness, love, and care.

Care for creation honors the Creator.

Room 5020

Read: Genesis 50:15–20

You intended to harm me, but God intended it for good to accomplish what is now being done. Genesis 50:20

Jay Bufton turned his hospital room into a lighthouse.

The fifty-two-year-old husband, father, high school teacher, and coach was dying of cancer, but his room—Room 5020—became a beacon of hope for friends, family, and hospital workers. Because of his joyful attitude and strong faith, nurses wanted to be assigned to Jay. Some even came to see him during off-hours.

Even as his once-athletic body was wasting away, he greeted anyone and everyone with a smile and encouragement. One friend said, "Every time I visited Jay he was upbeat, positive, and filled with hope. He was, even while looking cancer and death in the face, living out his faith."

At Jay's funeral, one speaker noted that Room 5020 had a special meaning. He pointed to Genesis 50:20, in which Joseph says that although his brothers sold him into slavery, God turned the tables and accomplished something good: "the saving of many lives." Cancer invaded Jay's life, but by recognizing God's hand at work Jay could say that "God intended it for good." That's why Jay could use even the ravages of cancer as an open door to tell others about Jesus.

What a legacy of unwavering trust in our Savior even as death was knocking at the door! What a testimony of confidence in our good and trustworthy God!   *DAVE BRANON*

Lord, difficult things come into our lives so often. Please help us to trust You enough to see that nothing is beyond Your control. Help us to tell of Your love even in the tough times.

By God's grace, we can have our best witness in the worst of times.

Invisible Influence

Read: 1 Thessalonians 5:16–24

Do not quench the Spirit. 1 Thessalonians 5:19

On a visit to the National Gallery of Art in Washington, DC, I saw a masterpiece called *The Wind*. The painting showed a storm moving through a wooded area. Tall, thin trees leaned to the left. Bushes thrashed in the same direction.

In an even more powerful sense, the Holy Spirit is able to sway believers in the direction of God's goodness and truth. If we go along with the Spirit, we can expect to become more courageous and more loving. We will also become more discerning about how to handle our desires (2 TIM. 1:7).

In some situations, however, the Spirit nudges us toward spiritual growth and change, but we respond with a "no." Continually stonewalling this conviction is what Scripture calls "quench[ing] the Spirit" (1 THESS. 5:19). Over time, things we once considered wrong appear not to be quite as bad.

When our relationship with God seems distant and disconnected, this may be because the Spirit's conviction has been repeatedly brushed aside. The longer this goes on, the harder it is to see the root of the problem. Thankfully, we can pray and ask God to show us our sin. If we turn away from sin and recommit ourselves to Him, God will forgive us and revive the power and influence of His Spirit within us. *JENNIFER BENSON SCHULDT*

God, show me how I have resisted Your Holy Spirit. Help me to listen when You speak. I want to be right with You again.

Yielding to the Holy Spirit leads to right living.

An Encounter with Stones

Read: Isaiah 53:1–6

He was pierced for our transgressions, he was crushed for our iniquities.
Isaiah 53:5

After centuries of war and destruction, the modern city of Jerusalem is literally built on its own rubble. During a family visit, we walked the Via Dolorosa (the Way of Sorrow), the route tradition says Jesus followed on His way to the cross. The day was hot, so we paused for a rest and descended to the cool basement of the Convent of the Sisters of Zion. There I was intrigued by the sight of ancient pavement stones unearthed during recent construction—stones etched with games played by Roman soldiers during their idle moments.

Those particular stones, even though likely from a period later than Jesus, caused me to ponder my spiritual life at the time. Like a bored soldier passing time in idle moments, I had become complacent and uncaring toward God and others. I was deeply moved by remembering that near the place I was standing, the Lord was beaten, mocked, insulted, and abused as He took all of my failure and rebellion on himself.

"He was pierced for our transgressions, he was crushed for our iniquities; the punishment that brought us peace was on him, and by his wounds we are healed" (ISA. 53:5).

My encounter with the stones still speaks to me of Jesus's loving grace that is greater than all my sin.   *DAVID MCCASLAND*

Lord Jesus, through Your great sacrifice for us, we find forgiveness, healing, and hope. Thank You that we live today and forever in Your love.

Our sin is great—God's grace is greater.

We've Got the Power!

Read: Romans 7:14–25

Since we live by the Spirit, let us keep in step with the Spirit.
Galatians 5:25

The loud crackling noise startled me. Recognizing the sound, I raced to the kitchen. I'd accidently tapped the start button on the *empty* coffee maker. Unplugging the appliance, I grabbed the handle of the carafe. Then I touched the bottom of the container to ensure it wasn't too hot to place on the tile counter. The smooth surface burned my fingertips, blistering my tender skin.

As my husband nursed my wound, I shook my head. I knew the glass would be hot. "I honestly do not know why I touched it," I said.

My response after making such a mistake reminded me of Paul's reaction to a more serious issue in Scripture—the nature of sin.

The apostle admits to not knowing why he does things he knows he shouldn't do and doesn't want to do (ROM. 7:15). Affirming that Scripture determines right and wrong (V. 7), he acknowledges the real, complex war constantly waging between the flesh and the spirit in the struggle against sin (VV. 15–23). Confessing his own weaknesses, he offers hope for victory now and forever (VV. 24–25).

When we surrender our lives to Christ, He gives us His Holy Spirit who empowers us to choose to do right (8:8–10). As He enables us to obey God's Word, we can avoid the searing sin that separates us from the abundant life God promises those who love Him.   *XOCHITL DIXON*

Lord, thanks for breaking the chains that used to bind us to a life controlled by our sinful nature.

The Holy Spirit transforms us through His love and by His grace.

When Beauty Never Ends

Read: Psalm 27:1–4

Because your love is better than life, my lips will glorify you. Psalm 63:3

I love looking at the Grand Canyon. Whenever I stand at the canyon rim I see new brushstrokes of God's handiwork that take my breath away.

Even though it's just a (very large) "hole" in the ground, the Grand Canyon causes me to reflect on heaven. A very honest twelve-year-old asked me once, "Won't heaven be boring? Don't you think we'll get tired of praising God all the time?" But if a "hole in the ground" can be so overwhelmingly beautiful we can't stop looking at it, we can only imagine the joy of one day seeing the very Source of beauty—our loving Creator—in all of the pristine wonder of the new creation.

David expressed this longing when he wrote, "One thing I ask from the Lord, this only do I seek: that I may dwell in the house of the Lord all the days of my life, to gaze on the beauty of the Lord" (PS. 27:4). There's nothing more beautiful than the presence of God, which draws near to us on this earth as we seek Him by faith, looking forward to seeing Him face to face.

On that day we'll never tire of praising our amazing Lord, because we will never come to an end of fresh, new discoveries of His exquisite goodness and the wonders of the works of His hands. Every moment in His presence will bring a breathtaking revelation of His beauty and His love.   *JAMES BANKS*

Beautiful Savior, please help me to seek You every day and to live even now in
Your presence and Your love.

We were created to enjoy God forever.

Your Safe Place

Read: Proverbs 18:10–11

The name of the LORD is a fortified tower; the righteous run to it and are safe. Proverbs 18:10

My daughter and I were arranging to attend an extended family gathering. Because she was nervous about the trip, I offered to drive. "Okay. But I feel safer in my car. Can you drive it?" she asked. I assumed she preferred her more spacious vehicle to my compact one so I responded, "Is my car too cramped?" "No, it's just that my car is my safe place. Somehow I feel protected there."

Her comment challenged me to consider my own personal "safe place." Immediately I thought of Proverbs 18:10, "The name of the LORD is a fortified tower; the righteous run to it and are safe." In Old Testament times, the walls and watchtower of a city provided warning of danger from without and shielding for its citizens within. The writer's point is that God's name, which stands for His character, person, and everything that He is, provides true protection for His people.

Certain physical places promise longed-for safety in moments that seem dangerous. A sturdy roof overhead in the midst of a storm. A hospital offering medical care. The embrace of a loved one.

What is your "safe place"? Wherever we seek safety, it is God's presence with us in that place that provides the strength and protection we really need. *ELISA MORGAN*

Dear God, thank You that no matter what worries and concerns we have today, when we think about You, we find safety in Your presence.

God is a safe place in life's storms.

Love of Another Kind

Read: John 15:9–17

My command is this: Love each other as I have loved you. John 15:12

One of my favorite churches started several years ago as a ministry to ex-prisoners who were transitioning back into society. Now the church flourishes with people from all walks of life. I love that church because it reminds me of what I picture heaven will be like—filled with different kinds of people, all redeemed sinners, all bound together by the love of Jesus.

Sometimes, though, I wonder if church seems more like an exclusive club than a safe haven for forgiven sinners. As people naturally gravitate into groups of "a certain kind" and cluster around those they feel comfortable with, it leaves others feeling marginalized. But that's not what Jesus had in mind when He told His disciples to "love each other as I have loved you" (JOHN 15:12). His church was to be an extension of His love mutually shared with all.

If hurting, rejected people can find loving refuge, comfort, and forgiveness in Jesus, they should expect no less from the church. So let's exhibit the love of Jesus to everyone we encounter—especially those who are not like us. All around us are people Jesus wants to love through us. What a joy it is when people unite to worship together in love—a slice of heaven we can enjoy here on earth! *JOE STOWELL*

Lord, remind me today that while I was a sinner You embraced me with Your deep and unconditional love and brought me into the fellowship of Your grace. Lead me to someone I can love as You loved me.

Share Christ's love with another.

Brother to Brother

Read: Genesis 33:1–11

A new command I give you: Love one another. John 13:34

My brother and I, less than a year apart in age, were quite "competitive" growing up (translation: we *fought!*). Dad understood. He had brothers. Mom? Not so much.

Our story could have fit in the book of Genesis, which might well be subtitled *A Brief History of Sibling Rivalry*. Cain and Abel (GEN. 4); Isaac and Ishmael (21:8–10); Joseph and everyone not named Benjamin (CH. 37). But for brother-to-brother animosity, it's hard to beat Jacob and Esau.

Esau's twin brother had cheated him twice, so he wanted to kill Jacob (27:41). Decades later Jacob and Esau would reconcile (CH. 33). But the rivalry continued on in their descendants, who became the nations of Edom and Israel. When the people of Israel prepared to enter the Promised Land, Edom met them with threats and an army (NUM. 20:14–21). Much later, as Jerusalem's citizens fled invading forces, Edom slaughtered the refugees (OBAD. 1:10–14).

Happily for us, the Bible contains not just the sad account of our brokenness but the story of God's redemption as well. Jesus changed everything, telling His disciples, "A new command I give you: Love one another" (JOHN 13:34). Then He showed us what that means by dying for us.

As my brother and I got older, we became close. That's the thing with God. When we respond to the forgiveness He offers, His grace can transform our sibling rivalries into brotherly love.

TIM GUSTAFSON

Lord, we invite You to transform our relationships with Your healing love.

Sibling rivalry is natural. God's love is supernatural.

Jesus in Disguise

Read: Matthew 25:31–40

Whatever you did for one of the least of these . . . you did for me.
Matthew 25:40

When a friend cared for her housebound mother-in-law, she asked her what she longed for the most. Her mother-in-law said, "For my feet to be washed." My friend admitted, "How I hated that job! Each time she asked me to do it I was resentful, and would ask God to hide my feelings from her."

But one day her grumbling attitude changed in a flash. As she got out the bowl and towel and knelt at her mother-in-law's feet, she said, "I looked up, and for a moment I felt like I was washing the feet of Jesus himself. She was Jesus in disguise!" After that, she felt honored to wash her mother-in-law's feet.

When I heard this moving account, I thought of Jesus's story about the end of time that He taught on the slopes of the Mount of Olives. The King welcomes into His kingdom His sons and daughters, saying that when they visited the sick or fed the hungry, "Whatever you did for one of the least of these brothers and sisters of mine, you did for me" (MATT. 25:40). We too serve Jesus himself when we visit those in prison or give clothes to the needy.

Today, might you echo my friend, who now wonders when she meets someone new, "Are you Jesus in disguise?"

AMY BOUCHER PYE

Lord Jesus Christ, You can transform the most mundane of tasks. Help me to love others in Your name.

When we serve others, we serve Jesus.

Surviving in the Wilderness

Read: Exodus 17:1–7

The message they heard was of no value to them, because they did not share the faith of those who obeyed. Hebrews 4:2

In the 1960s, the Kingston Trio released a song called "Desert Pete." The ballad tells of a thirsty cowboy who is crossing the desert and finds a hand pump. Next to it, Desert Pete has left a note urging the reader not to drink the water in the jar left there but to use its contents to prime the pump.

The cowboy resists the temptation to drink and uses the water as the note instructs. In reward for his obedience, he receives an abundance of cold, satisfying water. Had he not acted in faith, he would have had only a jar of unsatisfying, warm water to drink.

This reminds me of Israel's journey through the wilderness. When their thirst became overwhelming (EX. 17:1-7), Moses sought the Lord. He was told to strike the rock of Horeb with his staff. Moses believed and obeyed, and water gushed from the stone.

Sadly, Israel would not consistently follow Moses's example of faith. Ultimately, "the message they heard was of no value to them, because they did not share the faith of those who obeyed" (HEB. 4:2).

Sometimes life can seem like an arid desert. But God can quench our spiritual thirst in the most unlikely circumstances. When by faith we believe the promises of God's Word, we can experience rivers of living water and grace for our daily needs.

DENNIS FISHER

Help us to place our trust in You, Lord. You are what our heart thirsts after.

Only Jesus, the Living Water, can satisfy our thirst for God.

Exceedingly Better

Read: 1 Chronicles 17:1–5

He is the one who will build a house for me, and I will establish his throne forever. 1 Chronicles 17:12

My birthday is the day after my mother's. As an adolescent, I would scramble to think of a gift that delighted my mom yet fit in my budget. She always received my purchases with appreciation, and on the following day, my birthday, she would present her gift to me. Without fail, her gift vastly outshone mine. Her intention wasn't to diminish what I'd given her; she simply gave generously from her resources, which far exceeded my own.

My desire to give to my mother reminds me of David's wish to build a home for God. Struck by the contrast between his palace and the tent where God revealed himself, David longed to build God a temple. Instead of granting David's wish to give, God responded by giving David an exceedingly better gift. God promised that not only would one of David's children (Solomon) build the temple (1 CHRON. 17:11), but that He would build David a house, a dynasty. That promise began with Solomon but found its ultimate fulfillment in Jesus, whose throne was indeed "established forever" (V. 12). David wanted to give from his finite resources, but God promised something infinite.

Like David, may we always be moved to give to God out of gratitude and love. And may we always see how much more abundantly He has given to us in Jesus. *KIRSTEN HOLMBERG*

Father God, I thank You for Your astounding gift to me in Jesus Christ. Your love overwhelms me.

God's gift to us in Jesus Christ exceeds all gifts.

God Provides

Read: Deuteronomy 24:19–22

Those who work their land will have abundant food. Proverbs 12:11

Outside my office window, the squirrels are in a race against winter to bury their acorns in a safe, accessible place. Their commotion amuses me. An entire herd of deer can go through our back yard and not make a sound, but one squirrel sounds like an invasion.

The two creatures are different in another way as well. Deer do not prepare for winter. When the snow comes they eat whatever they can find along the way (including ornamental shrubs in our yard). But squirrels would starve if they followed that example. They would be unable to find suitable food.

The deer and the squirrel represent ways that God cares for us. He enables us to work and save for the future, and He meets our need when resources are scarce. As the wisdom literature teaches, God gives us seasons of plenty so that we can prepare for seasons of need (PROV. 12:11). And as Psalm 23 says, the Lord leads us through perilous places to pleasant pastures.

Another way that God provides is by instructing those with plenty to share with those in need (DEUT. 24:19). So when it comes to provision, the message of the Bible is this: Work while we can, save what we can, share what we can, and trust God to meet our needs.   *JULIE ACKERMAN LINK*

Thank You, Lord, for the promise that You will meet our needs. Help us not to fear or doubt. We're grateful that You're watching over us and that our cries for help reach Your ear.

Our needs will never exhaust God's supply.

Rooted in God

Read: Jeremiah 17:5–8

They will be like a tree planted by the water . . . its leaves are always green. Jeremiah 17:8

When friends moved into a new home, they planted wisteria near their fence and looked forward to the lavender blossom that would appear after five years of growth. Over two decades they enjoyed this plant, carefully pruning and tending it. But suddenly the wisteria died, for their neighbors had poured some weed killer by the other side of the fence. The poison seeped into the wisteria's roots and the tree perished—or so my friends thought. To their surprise, the following year some shoots came through the ground.

We see the image of trees flourishing and perishing when the prophet Jeremiah relates them to God's people who either trust in the Lord or ignore His ways. Those who follow God will send their roots into soil near water and will bear fruit (JER. 17:8), but those who follow their own hearts will be like a bush in the desert (VV. 5–6). The prophet yearns that God's people would rely on the true and living God, that they would be "a tree planted by the water" (V. 8).

We know the "Father is the gardener" (JOHN 15:1) and that in Him we can trust and have confidence (JER. 17:7). May we follow Him with our whole heart as we bear fruit that lasts.

AMY BOUCHER PYE

Loving Lord, I want to follow You completely, whether in times of drought or abundance. Help me turn to You for help and hope.

When we follow God, He makes us to flourish.

Trust Tally

Read: Deuteronomy 1:21–33

See, the LORD your God has given you the land. . . . Do not be afraid; do not be discouraged. Deuteronomy 1:21

Before my husband and I surrendered our lives to Christ, we seriously considered divorce. But after committing to love and obey God, we recommitted to each other. We sought wise counsel and invited the Holy Spirit to transform us individually and as a couple. Our heavenly Father continues to help us develop healthy communication skills. He's teaching us how to love and trust Him—and one another—no matter what happens.

Yet, even as we head toward celebrating our twenty-fifth anniversary, I occasionally forget everything God has done in and through our trials. Sometimes, I struggle with a deep-seated fear of the unknown—experiencing unnecessary anxiety instead of relying on God's track record.

In Deuteronomy 1, Moses affirmed the Lord's reliability. He encouraged the Israelites to move forward in faith so they could enjoy their inheritance (V. 21). But God's people demanded details about what they'd be up against and what they'd receive before committing to trust Him with their future (VV. 22–33).

Followers of Christ are not immune to succumbing to fear or anxiety. Worrying about what difficulties we may or may not encounter can keep us from depending on faith, and may even damage our relationships with God and others. But the Holy Spirit can help us create a trust tally of the Lord's past faithfulness. He can empower us with courageous confidence in God's trustworthiness yesterday, today, and forever.   *XOCHITL DIXON*

Lord, thank You for affirming that we don't need to know everything that lies ahead when we know You. We know You never change.

God's past faithfulness proves His everlasting dependability.

Unraveling the Mysteries

Read: Psalm 119:97–104

I gain understanding from your precepts; therefore I hate every wrong path. Psalm 119:104

I have always enjoyed the wit and insight of *Peanuts* creator Charles Schulz. One of my favorite cartoons drawn by him appeared in a book about young people in the church. It shows a young man holding a Bible as he tells a friend on the phone, "I think I've made one of the first steps toward unraveling the mysteries of the Old Testament . . . I'm starting to read it!" (*Teen-Ager Is Not a Disease*).

Psalm 119 overflows with the writer's hunger to understand and experience the power of God's Word each day. "Oh, how I love your law! I meditate on it all day long" (V. 97). This eager pursuit leads to growing wisdom, understanding, and obedience to the Lord (VV. 98–100).

The Bible doesn't contain a magic formula for "unraveling the mysteries" in its pages. The process is more than mental and requires a response to what we read. While some passages may remain puzzling to us, we can embrace those truths we clearly understand, and say to the Lord, "How sweet are your words to my taste, sweeter than honey to my mouth! I gain understanding from your precepts; therefore I hate every wrong path" (VV. 103–104).

A wonderful journey of discovery awaits us in God's Word.

DAVID MCCASLAND

Lord, thank You for the Bible, which gives us wisdom and understanding to follow Your pathway of life today.

A commitment to read and follow God's Word begins a daily journey of discovering His love and power.

Ruth's Story

Read: Romans 10:1–13

Everyone who calls on the name of the Lord will be saved.
Romans 10:13

Ruth cannot tell her story without tears. In her mid-eighties and unable to get around much anymore, Ruth may not appear to be a central figure in our church's life. She depends on others for rides, and because she lives alone she doesn't have a huge circle of influence.

But when she tells us her story of salvation—as she does often—Ruth stands out as a remarkable example of God's grace. Back when she was in her thirties, a friend invited her to go to a meeting one night. Ruth didn't know she was going to hear a preacher. "I wouldn't have gone if I knew," she says. She already had "religion," and it wasn't doing her any good. But go she did. And she heard the good news about Jesus that night.

Now, more than fifty years later, she cries tears of joy when she talks of how Jesus transformed her life. That evening, she became a child of God. Her story never grows old.

It doesn't matter if our story is similar to Ruth's or not. What does matter is that we take the simple step of putting our faith in Jesus and His death and resurrection. The apostle Paul said, "If you declare with your mouth, 'Jesus is Lord,' and believe in your heart that God raised him from the dead, you will be saved" (ROM. 10:9).

That's what Ruth did. You can do that too. Jesus redeems, transforms, and gives us new life.   *DAVE BRANON*

Belonging to Christ is not rehabilitation; it's re-creation.

Who Is This?

Read: Mark 4:35–41

They were terrified and asked each other, "Who is this? Even the wind and the waves obey him!" Mark 4:41

"Remove everything from your desks, take out a piece of paper and pencil." When I was a student these dreaded words announced that "test time" had come.

In Mark 4, we read that Jesus's day, which started with teaching by the seaside (V. 1), ended with a time of testing on the sea (V. 35). The boat that had been used as a teaching platform was used to transport Jesus and a handful of His followers to the other side of the sea. During the journey (while an exhausted Jesus slept in the back of the boat), they encountered a swirling storm (V. 37). Drenched disciples woke Jesus with the words, "Teacher, don't you care if we drown?" (V. 38). Then it happened. The One who had exhorted the crowds to "Listen!" earlier in the day (V. 3) uttered a simple, powerful command to the winds of nature—"Quiet! Be still!" (V. 39).

The wind obeyed and the wonder of fear-filled disciples was displayed with the words, "Who is this?" (V. 41). The question was a good one but it would take them a while to honestly and correctly conclude that Jesus was God's Son. Sincere, honest, open-hearted questions and experience lead people to the same conclusion today. He is more than a teacher to listen to; He is the God to be worshiped.   *ARTHUR JACKSON*

Father, thank You for Your Word that helps us to see Jesus as Your Son. Please help me to listen to You and to trust that You are in control.

"Teacher, I will follow you wherever you go."
MATTHEW 8:19

Living Anonymously

Read: Romans 12:1–13

Let us have real warm affection for one another as between [family].
Romans 12:10 PHILLIPS

My well-worn and often-read copy of Jane Yolen's essay "Working Up to Anon" (Anonymous) was clipped from *The Writer* magazine many years ago. "The best writers," she says, "are the ones who really, in their heart of hearts, aspire to the byline Anon. The story told is important, not the storyteller."

The story we tell is about Jesus, the Savior, who gave His life for us. Together with other believers we live for Him and share His love with others.

Romans 12:3–21 describes the attitude of humility and love that should permeate our relationships with each other as followers of Jesus. "Don't cherish exaggerated ideas of yourself or your importance, but try to have a sane estimate of your capabilities by the light of the faith that God has given to you all. . . . Let us have real warm affection for one another as between [family], and a willingness to let the other [person] have the credit" (vv. 3, 10 J.B. PHILLIPS NEW TESTAMENT).

Pride in our past accomplishments can blind us to the gifts of others. Arrogance can poison the future.

John the Baptist, whose mission was to pave the way for Jesus, said, "He must become greater; I must become less" (JOHN 3:30).

That's a good motto for us all. *ANONYMOUS*

I admit, Lord, that I have a lot to learn about humility. Help me to see You for who You are so You and others have their rightful place in my life.

Always be humble before God and allow Him to be your all in all.
OSWALD CHAMBERS

Powerful Baby

Read: Psalm 13

How long, LORD? Will you forget me forever? . . . But I trust in your unfailing love. Psalm 13:1, 5

The first time I saw him, I cried. He looked like a perfect newborn asleep in his crib. But we knew he would never wake up. Not until he was in the arms of Jesus.

He clung to life for several months. Then his mother told us of his death in a heart-wrenching email. She wrote of "that deep, deep pain that groans inside you." Then she said, "How deeply God carved His work of love into our hearts through that little life! What a powerful life it was!"

Powerful? How could she say that?

This family's precious little boy showed them—and us—that we must depend on God for everything. Especially when things go horribly wrong! The hard yet comforting truth is that God meets us in our pain. He knows the grief of losing a Son.

In our deepest pain, we turn to the songs of David because he writes out of his own grief. "How long must I wrestle with my thoughts and day after day have sorrow in my heart?" he asked (PS. 13:2). "Give light to my eyes, or I will sleep in death" (V. 3). Yet David could give his biggest questions to God. "But I trust in your unfailing love; my heart rejoices in your salvation" (V. 5).

Only God can bring ultimate significance to our most tragic events.   *TIM GUSTAFSON*

Where do I turn when a crisis hits me? Do I ever get angry with God when facing grief and loss? Am I afraid to share my true emotions with Him? Have I ever asked God for His peace?

God can do the most with what we think is least.

That Famous Smile

Read: Psalm 28:6–9

The prospect of the righteous is joy. Proverbs 10:28

After my wife and I had the privilege of visiting the Louvre in Paris, I called our eleven-year-old granddaughter Addie on the phone. When I mentioned seeing da Vinci's famous painting *Mona Lisa*, Addie asked, "Is she smiling?"

Isn't that the big question surrounding this painting? More than 600 years after Leonardo captured this subject in oil, we still don't know if the lady was smiling or not. Though enraptured by the painting's beauty, we are unsure about Mona Lisa's demeanor.

The "smile" is part of the intrigue of the painting. But how important is this anyway? Is smiling something the Bible mentions? In reality, the word appears less than five times in Scripture, and never as something we are told to do. However, the Bible does suggest for us an attitude that leads to smiles—and that is the word *joy*. Nearly 250 times we read about joy: "My heart leaps for joy," David says as he thinks about the Lord (PS. 28:7). We are to "sing joyfully to the LORD" (PS. 33:1); God's statutes are "the joy of [our] heart" (119:111); and we are "filled with joy" because "the LORD has done great things for us" (126:3).

Clearly, the joy God provides through everything He has done for us can bring a smile to our face. *DAVE BRANON*

You are a good Father, dear God, and You do make us smile. You provide joy that is beyond what anything the world can offer. Help us show that joy to others by our countenance.

Hope in the heart puts a smile on the face.

Joy and Justice

Read: Psalm 67

You rule the peoples with equity and guide the nations of the earth.
Psalm 67:4

At a conference in Asia, I had two eye-opening conversations in the span of a few hours. First, a pastor told of spending eleven years in prison for a wrongful murder conviction before he was cleared. Then, a group of families shared how they had spent a fortune to escape religious persecution in their homeland, only to be betrayed by the very people they had paid to bring about their rescue. Now, after years in a refugee camp, they wonder if they will ever find a home.

In both cases, victimization was compounded by an absence of justice—just one evidence of our world's brokenness. But this vacuum of justice is not a permanent condition.

Psalm 67 calls on God's people to make Him known to our hurting world. The result will be joy, not only as a response to God's love but also because of His justice. "May the nations be glad and sing for joy," says the psalmist, "for you rule the peoples with equity and guide the nations of the earth" (V. 4).

Although the Bible writers understood that "equity" (fairness and justice) is a key component of God's love, they also knew that it will only be fully realized in the future. Until then, in our world of injustice, we can serve to point others to our God's divine justice. His coming will see "justice roll on like a river, righteousness like a never-failing stream!" (AMOS 5:24).   *BILL CROWDER*

Father, help us to work for Your justice now where we live, even as we await the day when You will make everything right. We long for that day.

Work for justice; pray for mercy.

Our Prayers, God's Timing

Read: Luke 1:5–17

Now to him who is able to do immeasurably more than all we ask or imagine, according to his power that is at work within us.
Ephesians 3:20

Sometimes God takes His time in answering our prayers, and that isn't always easy for us to understand.

That was the situation for Zechariah, a priest whom the angel Gabriel appeared to one day near an altar in the temple in Jerusalem. Gabriel told him, "Do not be afraid, Zechariah; *your prayer has been heard.* Your wife Elizabeth will bear you a son, and you are to call him John" (LUKE 1:13, ITALICS ADDED).

But Zechariah had probably asked God for a child years before, and he struggled with Gabriel's message because Elizabeth was now well beyond the expected age for childbirth. Still, God answered his prayer.

God's memory is perfect. He is able to remember our prayers not only for years but also for generations beyond our lifetime. He never forgets them and may move in response long after we first brought our requests to Him. Sometimes His answer is "no," other times it is "wait"—but His response is always measured with love. God's ways are beyond us, but we can trust that they are good.

Zechariah learned this. He asked for a son, but God gave him even more. His son John would grow up to be the very prophet who would announce the arrival of the Messiah.

Zechariah's experience demonstrates a vital truth that should also encourage us as we pray: God's timing is rarely our own, but it is always worth waiting for.   *JAMES BANKS*

When we cannot see God's hand at work, we can still trust His heart.

Second Chances

Read: Ruth 4:13–17

He has not stopped showing his kindness. Ruth 2:20

"How can you be so kind if you don't even know me!"

By making some wrong decisions, Linda had ended up in jail in a country not her own. For six years she remained in prison, and when she was set free she didn't have anywhere to go. She thought her life was over! While her family gathered money to buy her ticket home, a kind couple offered her lodging, food, and a helping hand. Linda was so touched by their kindness that she willingly listened as they told her the good news of a God who loves her and wants to give her a second chance.

Linda reminds me of Naomi, a widow in the Bible who lost her husband and two sons in a foreign land and thought her life was over (RUTH 1). However, the Lord hadn't forgotten Naomi, and through the love of her daughter-in-law and the compassion of a godly man named Boaz, Naomi saw God's love and was given a second chance (4:13–17).

The same God cares for us today. Through the love of others we can be reminded of His presence. We can see God's grace in the helping hand of people we may not even know well. But above all, God is willing to give us a fresh start. We just need, like Linda and Naomi, to see God's hand in our everyday lives and realize He never stops showing us His kindness. *KEILA OCHOA*

Dear Lord, thank You that You let us begin again and again.

God gives us second chances.

Think Before You Speak

Read: Psalm 141

Set a guard over my mouth, LORD; keep watch over the door of my lips.
Psalm 141:3

Cheung was upset with his wife for failing to check the directions to the famous restaurant where they hoped to dine. The family had planned to round out their holiday in Japan with a scrumptious meal before catching the flight home. Now they were running late and would have to miss that meal. Frustrated, Cheung criticized his wife for her poor planning.

Later Cheung regretted his words. He had been too harsh, plus he realized that he could have checked the directions himself and he had failed to thank his wife for the other seven days of great planning.

Many of us may identify with Cheung. We are tempted to blow up when angry and to let words fly without control. Oh, how we need to pray as the psalmist did: "Set a guard over my mouth, LORD; keep watch over the door of my lips" (PS. 141:3).

But how can we do that? Here's a helpful tip: Think before you speak. Are your words good and helpful, gracious and kind? (SEE EPH. 4:29–32.)

Setting a guard over our mouth requires that we keep our mouth shut when we're irritated and that we seek the Lord's help to say the right words with the right tone or, perhaps, not speak at all. When it comes to controlling our speech, it's a lifelong work. Thankfully, God is working in us, giving us "the desire and the power to do what pleases him" (PHIL. 2:13 NLT).

POH FANG CHIA

Dear Lord, help us always to think before speaking. Give us the words to say and the wisdom to know when to keep silent.

Gracious words are a honeycomb, sweet to the soul and healing to the bones.
PROVERBS 16:24

A Good Ending

Read: Revelation 22:1–5

The throne of God and of the Lamb will be in the city, and his servants will serve him. They will see his face. Revelation 22:3–4

As the lights dimmed and we prepared to watch *Apollo 13*, my friend said under his breath, "Shame they all died." I watched the movie about the 1970 spaceflight with apprehension, waiting for tragedy to strike, and only near the closing credits did I realize I'd been duped. I hadn't known or remembered the end of the true story—that although the astronauts faced many hardships, they made it home alive.

In Christ, we can know the end of the story—that we too will make it home alive. By that I mean we will live forever with our heavenly Father, as we see in the book of Revelation. The Lord will create a "new heaven and a new earth" as He makes all things new (21:1, 5). In the new city, the Lord God will welcome His people to live with Him, without fear and without the night. We have hope in knowing the end of the story.

What difference does this make? It can transform times of extreme difficulty, such as when people face the loss of a loved one or even their own death. Though we recoil at the thought of dying, yet we can embrace the joy of the promise of eternity. We long for the city where no longer will there be any curse, where we'll live forever by God's light (22:5).   *AMY BOUCHER PYE*

Lord Jesus Christ, give me unfailing hope, that I might rest in Your promises and welcome Your life eternal.

God promises His people a good end to the story.

The Hand of Comfort

Read: 2 Corinthians 1:3–7

Praise be to the God and Father of our Lord Jesus Christ, . . . who comforts us in all our troubles. 2 Corinthians 1:3–4

"Patient is combative," the nurse's notes read.

What she didn't realize until later was that I was having an allergic reaction as I awakened after a complicated open-heart surgery. I was a mess, with a tube down my throat. My body began shaking violently, straining against the straps on my arms, which were there to keep me from suddenly pulling out my breathing tube. It was a frightening and painful episode. At one point, a nurse's assistant to the right side of my bed reached down and simply held my hand. It was an unexpected move, and it struck me as especially gentle. I began to relax, which caused my body to stop shaking so badly.

Having experienced this with other patients, the nurse's assistant knew that a hand of comfort could minister to me as well. It was a vivid example of how God uses comfort when His children suffer.

Comfort is a powerful and memorable tool for any caregiver, and Paul tells us in 2 Corinthians 1:3–4 it's an important part of God's toolbox. Not only that, but God also multiplies the impact of His comfort by calling us to use the memory of the comfort He gives us to comfort others in similar situations (VV. 4–7). It is but another sign of His great love; and one we can share with others—sometimes in the simplest of gestures.   *RANDY KILGORE*

Thank You, Father, for the comfort You provide to us, either directly or through the acts of Your children. Help us to see where we can apply that same comfort to others in and for Your name.

Simple gestures can bring powerful comfort.

Before the Beginning

Read: Genesis 1

Father, glorify me in your presence with the glory I had with you before the world began. John 17:5

When he was a teenager, my son asked me one of those questions that make you earn your pay as a parent. "Dad," Steve inquired, "if God has existed for eternity, what was He doing before He created the universe?"

So, what was happening in the eons before "God created the heavens and the earth"? (GENESIS 1:1). For one thing, we know that there was "wisdom" before creation itself, which came from God's character. Wisdom, personified in Proverbs 8:23, said, "I have been established from everlasting, from the beginning, before there was ever an earth."

Also, we know that God's salvation plan of grace was in the works before the world was hung in its place. In 2 Timothy 1:9, we read that grace "was given us in Christ Jesus before the beginning of time." Likewise, Titus 1:2 says that eternal life was promised "before the beginning of time." We also know that Jesus was glorified and loved in God's presence "before the world was" (John 17:5; see also v. 24).

These tiny glimpses of God before He created the earth help us see a little of the essence and magnitude of our awesome, eternal God. We see His majesty and greatness. Amazing, isn't it? We worship a God who existed from the beginning . . . and beyond.

DAVE BRANON

Great God of the universe, we stand amazed that You are the Alpha and Omega—the Beginning and the End—and so much more. Thank You that we can worship and magnify You.

The created world is but a small parenthesis in eternity.
SIR THOMAS BROWNE

What's the Best Gift?

Read: 2 Chronicles 2:1–10

The temple I am going to build will be great, because our God is greater than all other gods. 2 Chronicles 2:5

My husband recently celebrated a milestone birthday, the kind that ends in a zero. I thought hard about the best way to honor him on this important occasion. I discussed my many ideas with our children to help me home in on the best one. I wanted our celebration to reflect the significance of a new decade and how precious he is to our family. I wanted our gift to be in keeping with the importance of this milestone in his life.

King Solomon wanted to give to God a much greater gift than a "big birthday" would merit. He wished for the temple he built to be worthy of God's presence in it. To secure raw materials, he messaged the king of Tyre. In his letter, he remarked that the temple would be great "because our God is greater than all other gods" (2 CHRON. 2:5). He acknowledged that God's vastness and goodness far exceeded what could ever be built with human hands, yet set about the task anyway out of love and worship.

Our God is indeed greater than all other gods. He has done wondrous things in our lives, prompting our hearts to bring Him a loving and precious offering, regardless of its external value. Solomon knew his gift wouldn't match God's worth, yet joyfully set his offering before Him; we can too.   *KIRSTEN HOLMBERG*

Lord, You are indeed a great God, matchless in worth. May my offerings be pleasing in Your sight.

The most treasured gift we can give to God is our love.

Multiplied Generosity

Read: 2 Corinthians 8:1–9

See that you also excel in this grace of giving. 2 Corinthians 8:7

Cheryl was in for a surprise as she pulled up to deliver her next pizza. Expecting to arrive at a home, she instead found herself outside a church. Cheryl confusedly carried the pepperoni pizza inside, where she was met by the pastor.

"Is it fair to say life hasn't been easy for you?" the pastor asked her. Cheryl agreed it hadn't. With that, he brought out two offering plates that church members had filled with money. The pastor then poured over $750 into Cheryl's delivery bag as a tip! Unbeknownst to Cheryl, the pastor had asked the pizza shop to send their most financially strapped driver over. Cheryl was stunned. She could now pay some bills.

When the first Christians in Jerusalem faced poverty, it was a church that rushed to their aid. Though in need themselves, the Macedonian Christians gave sacrificially, considering it a privilege to do so (2 COR. 8:1-4). Paul cited their generosity as an example for the Corinthians, and us, to follow. When we use our plenty to supply another's need, we reflect Jesus, who gave away His riches to meet our own spiritual poverty (V. 9).

Cheryl told all her customers about the church's kindness that day, and, following its example, donated the rest of the day's tips to others in need. An act of generosity multiplied. And Christ was glorified. *SHERIDAN VOYSEY*

Lord, You meet our needs in surprising ways sometimes.
Use us to do that for others as well.

Our generosity meets needs and glorifies Jesus.

Great Love

Read: 1 John 3:1–8

See what great love the Father has lavished on us, that we should be called children of God! And that is what we are! 1 John 3:1

Recently, we took our twenty-two-month-old granddaughter, Moriah, overnight for the first time without her older brothers. We lavished lots of loving, undivided attention on her, and had fun doing the things she likes to do. The next day after dropping her off, we said our goodbyes and headed out the door. As we did, without a word Moriah grabbed her overnight bag (still sitting by the door) and began following us.

The picture is etched in my memory: Moriah in her diaper and mismatched sandals ready to depart with Grandma and Grandpa again. Every time I think of it, I smile. She was eager to go with us, ready for more individualized time.

Although she is as yet unable to vocalize it, our granddaughter feels loved and valued. In a small way, our love for Moriah is a picture of the love God has for us, His children. "See what great love the Father has lavished on us, that we should be called children of God! And that is what we are!" (1 JOHN 3:1).

When we believe in Jesus as our Savior, we become His children and begin to understand the lavish love He bestowed on us by dying for us (V. 16). Our desire becomes to please Him in what we say and do (V. 6)—and to love Him, eager to spend time with Him.   *ALYSON KIEDA*

Dear Lord, thank You for loving us so much that You died for us and rose again that we might have eternal life with You. Help us to be examples of Your love to all we meet.

How deep is the Father's love for us!

How Much More!

Read: Luke 11:5–13

If you then, though you are evil, know how to give good gifts to your children, how much more will your Father in heaven give the Holy Spirit to those who ask him! Luke 11:13

In October 1915, during World War I, Oswald Chambers arrived at Zeitoun Camp, a military training center near Cairo, Egypt, to serve as a YMCA chaplain to British Commonwealth soldiers. When he announced a weeknight religious service, 400 men packed the large YMCA hut to hear Chambers's talk titled, "What Is the Good of Prayer?" Later, when he spoke individually with men who were trying to find God in the midst of war, Oswald often quoted Luke 11:13, "If you then, though you are evil, know how to give good gifts to your children, how much more will your Father in heaven give the Holy Spirit to those who ask him!"

The free gift of God through His Son, Jesus, is forgiveness, hope, and His living presence in our lives through the Holy Spirit. "For everyone who asks receives; the one who seeks finds; and to the one who knocks, the door will be opened" (V. 10).

On November 15, 1917, Oswald Chambers died unexpectedly from a ruptured appendix. To honor him, a soldier led to faith in Christ by Oswald purchased a marble carving of a Bible with the message of Luke 11:13 on its open page and placed it beside his grave: "How much more will your Father in heaven give the Holy Spirit to those who ask Him!" This amazing gift from God is available to each of us today.   *DAVID MCCASLAND*

Father, You are the giver of all good gifts. We thank You for the great gift of the Holy Spirit who lives in us and guides us in Your truth today.

God's gift of the Holy Spirit in our lives is available to each of us today.

In His Presence

Read: Psalm 89:1–17

Blessed are those who have learned to acclaim you, who walk in the light of your presence, LORD. Psalm 89:15

The seventeenth-century monk Brother Lawrence, before a day's work as cook in his community, would pray, "O my God . . . grant me your grace to stay in your presence. Help me in my labors. Possess all my affections." As he worked, he kept talking to God, listening for His leading and dedicating his work to Him. Even when he was busiest, he would use intervals of relative calm to ask for His grace. No matter what was happening, he sought for and found a sense of his Maker's love.

As Psalm 89 confesses, the fitting response to the Creator of all who rules the oceans and is worshiped by hosts of angels is to lift up our lives—our whole lives to Him. When we understand the beauty of who God is we "hear the joyful call to worship"—whenever and wherever we are, "all day long" (VV. 15–16 NLT).

Whether it's standing in store or airport lines, or waiting on hold minute after minute, our lives are full of moments like these, times when we could get annoyed. Or these can be times when we catch our breath and see each of these pauses as an opportunity to learn to "walk in the light of [God's] presence" (V. 15).

The "wasted" moments of our lives, when we wait or lay ill or wonder what to do next, are all possible pauses to consider our lives in the light of His presence.   *HAROLD MYRA*

Every moment can be lived in God's presence.

Serve and Be Served

Read: Philippians 4:10–19

You were concerned, but you had no opportunity to show it.
Philippians 4:10

Marilyn had been ill for many weeks, and many people had encouraged her through this difficult time. *How will I ever repay all their kindnesses?* she worried. Then one day she read the words of a written prayer: "Pray that [others] will develop humility, allowing them not only to serve, but also to be served." Marilyn suddenly realized there was no need to balance any scale, but just to be thankful and allow others to experience the joy of serving.

In Philippians 4, the apostle Paul expressed his gratitude for all those who shared "in [his] troubles" (V. 14). He depended on people to support him as he preached and taught the gospel. He understood that the gifts provided for him when he was in need were simply an extension of people's love for God: "[Your gifts] are a fragrant offering, an acceptable sacrifice, pleasing to God" (V. 18).

It may not be easy to be the one on the receiving end—especially if you've usually been the first one to help other people. But with humility, we can allow God to gently care for us by a variety of means when we need help.

Paul wrote, "My God will meet all your needs" (V. 19). It was something he had learned during a life of trials. God is faithful and His provision for us has no limits.   *CINDY HESS KASPER*

Dear Lord, thank You for caring for us through Your people. May we graciously give and receive help.

Receive love. Give love. Repeat.

Hide and Seek

Read: Ezekiel 8

In his great mercy he has given us new birth into a living hope through the resurrection of Jesus Christ from the dead. 1 Peter 1:3

"You can't see me!"

When small children play "hide and seek," they sometimes believe they're hiding just by covering their eyes. If they can't see you, they assume you can't see them.

Naïve as that may seem to adults, we sometimes do something similar with God. When we find ourselves desiring to do something we know is wrong, our tendency may be to shut God out as we willfully go our own way.

The prophet Ezekiel discovered this truth in the vision God gave him for his people, exiled in Babylon. The Lord told him, "Have you seen what the elders of Israel are doing in the darkness, each at the shrine of his own idol? They say, 'The LORD does not see us'" (EZEK. 8:12).

But God misses nothing, and Ezekiel's vision was proof of it. Yet even though they had sinned, God offered His repentant people hope through a new promise: "I will give you a new heart and put a new spirit in you" (36:26).

For us, God met the brokenness and rebellion of sin with His tender mercy at the cross, paying the ultimate penalty for it. Through Jesus Christ, God not only offers us a new beginning, but He also works within us to change our hearts as we follow Him. How good is God! When we were lost and hiding in our sinfulness, God drew near through Jesus, who "came to seek and to save" us (LUKE 19:10; ROM. 5:8).   *JAMES BANKS*

Thank You for Your kindness to me, Lord. Help me to seek You and follow You faithfully today.

God knows us completely . . . and loves us just as much.

Seeing Masterpieces

Read: Psalm 139:11–18

You knit me together in my mother's womb. Psalm 139:13

My father creates custom quivers designed for archers to carry their arrows. He carves elaborate wildlife pictures into pieces of genuine leather, before stitching the material together.

During a visit, I watched him construct one of his works of art. His careful hands applied just the right pressure as he pressed a sharp blade into the supple leather, creating various textures. Then he dipped a rag into crimson dye and covered the leather with even strokes, magnifying the beauty of his creation.

As I admired my dad's confident craftsmanship, I realized how often I fail to acknowledge and appreciate my heavenly Father's creativity manifested in others and even in myself. Reflecting on the Lord's magnificent workmanship, I recalled King David's affirmation that God creates our "inmost being" and that we're "fearfully and wonderfully made" (PS. 139:13–14).

We can praise our Creator in confidence because we know His "works are wonderful" (V. 14). And we can be encouraged to respect ourselves and others more, especially when we remember that the Maker of the Universe knew us inside and out and planned our days "before one of them came to be" (VV. 15–16).

Like the pliable leather carved by my father's skilled hands, we are each beautiful and valuable simply because we are God's one-of-a-kind creations. Each one of us, intentionally designed to be unique and purposed as God's beloved masterpieces, contributes to reflect God's magnificence. *XOCHITL DIXON*

Lord, thank You for creating us in Your perfect love. Please help us to see ourselves, and others, as Your unique masterpieces.

God masterfully creates each person with uniqueness and purpose.

Take a Number

Read: John 14:15–27

Peace I leave with you; my peace I give to you. John 14:27

We have an ancient cherry tree in our backyard that had seen better days and looked like it was dying, so I called in an arborist. He checked it out and declared that it was "unduly stressed" and needed immediate attention. "Take a number," my wife, Carolyn, muttered to the tree as she walked away. It had been one of those weeks.

Indeed, we all have anxious weeks—filled with worries over the direction our culture is drifting or concerns for our children, our marriages, our businesses, our finances, our personal health and well-being. Nevertheless, Jesus has assured us that despite disturbing circumstances we can be at peace. He said, "My peace I give to you" (JOHN 14:27).

Jesus's days were filled with distress and disorder: He was beleaguered by His enemies and misunderstood by His family and friends. He often had no place to lay His head. Yet there was no trace of anxiety or fretfulness in His manner. He possessed an inner calm, a quiet tranquility. *This is the peace He has given us*—freedom from anxiety concerning the past, present, and future. The peace He exhibited; *His* peace.

In any circumstances, no matter how dire or trivial, we can turn to Jesus in prayer. There in His presence we can make our worries and fears known to Him. Then, Paul assures us, the peace of God will come to "guard [our] hearts and [our] minds in Christ Jesus" (PHIL. 4:7). Even if we've had "one of those weeks," we can have *His* peace.   *DAVID ROPER*

Dear Lord, thank You that I can come to You with every care and Your peace will guard my mind.

In the midst of troubles, peace can be found in Jesus.

Helicopter Seeds

Read: John 12:23–33

Unless a kernel of wheat falls to the ground and dies, it remains only a single seed. But if it dies, it produces many seeds. John 12:24

When our children were young, they loved trying to catch the "helicopter seeds" that fell from our neighbor's silver maple trees. Each seed resembles a wing. In late spring they twirl to the ground like a helicopter's rotor blades. The seeds' purpose is not to fly, but to fall to earth and grow into trees.

Before Jesus was crucified, He told His followers, "The hour has come for the Son of Man to be glorified. . . . [U]nless a kernel of wheat falls to the ground and dies, it remains only a single seed. But if it dies, it produces many seeds" (JOHN 12:23–24).

While Jesus's disciples wanted Him to be honored as the Messiah, He came to give His life so we could be forgiven and transformed through faith in Him. As Jesus's followers, we hear His words, "Anyone who loves their life will lose it, while anyone who hates their life in this world will keep it for eternal life. Whoever serves me must follow me; and where I am, my servant also will be. My Father will honor the one who serves me" (VV. 25–26).

Helicopter seeds can point us to the miracle of Jesus, the Savior, who died that we might live for Him.

DAVID MCCASLAND

Lord Jesus, we are amazed by Your love. Give us grace to serve You today as we long to do.

Jesus calls us to give our lives in serving Him.

Make a Joyful Noise

Read: Psalm 98

Shout for joy to the LORD, all the earth, burst into jubilant song with music. Psalm 98:4

Back when I was searching for a church to attend regularly, a friend invited me to a service at her church. The worship leaders led the congregation in a song I particularly loved. So I sang with gusto, remembering my college choir director's advice to "Project!"

After the song, my friend's husband turned to me and said, "You really sang loud." This remark was not intended as a compliment! After that, I self-consciously monitored my singing, making sure I sang softer than those around me and always wondering if the people around me judged my singing.

But one Sunday, I noticed the singing of a woman in the pew beside me. She seemed to sing with adoration, without a trace of self-consciousness. Her worship reminded me of the enthusiastic, spontaneous worship that David demonstrated in his life. In Psalm 98, in fact, David suggests that "all the earth" should "burst into jubilant song" in worship (v. 4).

Verse one of Psalm 98 tells us why we should worship joyfully, reminding us that "[God] has done marvelous things." Throughout the psalm, David recounts these marvelous things: God's faithfulness and justice to all nations, His mercy, and salvation. Dwelling on who God is and what He's done can fill our hearts with praise.

What "marvelous things" has God done in your life? Thanksgiving is the perfect time to recall His wondrous works and give God thanks. Lift your voice and sing!

LINDA WASHINGTON

Lord, thank You for who You are and for what You've done.

Worship takes the focus off us and places it where it belongs—on God.

Our Powerful God

Read: Amos 4:12–13

[He] who creates the wind, . . . the LORD God Almighty is his name.
Amos 4:13

One day by the seaside, I delighted in watching some kite surfers as they bounced along the water, moved by the force of the wind. When one came to shore, I asked him if the experience was as difficult as it looked. "No," he said, "It's actually easier than regular surfing because you harness the power of the wind."

Afterward as I walked by the sea, thinking about the wind's ability not only to propel the surfers but also to whip my hair into my face, I paused to wonder at our God the Creator. As we see in the Old Testament book of Amos, He who "forms the mountains" and "creates the wind" can turn "dawn to darkness" (V. 13).

Through this prophet, the Lord reminded His people of His power as He called them back to himself. Because they had not obeyed Him, He said He would reveal himself to them (V. 13). Although we see His judgment here, we know from elsewhere in the Bible of His sacrificial love in sending His Son to save us (SEE JOHN 3:16).

The power of the wind on this breezy day in the South of England reminded me of the sheer immensity of the Lord. If you feel the wind today, why not stop and ponder our all-powerful God?   *AMY BOUCHER PYE*

Father, thank You for Your power and love. Help us to daily rely on You.

God through His love created the world. Praise Him!

The Heart's True Home

Read: Ecclesiastes 3:10–11

[God] has . . . set eternity in the human heart. Ecclesiastes 3:11

We had a West Highland Terrier for a number of years. "Westies" are tough little dogs, bred to tunnel into badger holes and engage the "enemy" in its lair. Our Westie was many generations removed from her origins, but she still retained that instinct, put into her through years of breeding. On one occasion she became obsessed by some "critter" under a rock in our backyard. Nothing could dissuade her. She dug and dug until she tunneled several feet under the rock.

Now consider this question: Why do we as humans pursue, pursue, pursue? Why must we climb unclimbed mountains, ski near-vertical slopes? Run the most difficult and dangerous rapids, challenge the forces of nature? Part of it is a desire for adventure and enjoyment, but it's much more. It's an instinct for God that has been implanted in us. We cannot *not* want to find God.

We don't know that, of course. We only know that we long for something. "You don't know what it is you want," Mark Twain said, "but you want it so much you could almost die."

God is our heart's true home. As church father Augustine said in that most famous quotation: "You have made us for Yourself, O Lord, and our hearts are restless until they rest in You."

And what is the heart? A deep void within us that only God can fill.   *DAVID ROPER*

Help me, Lord, to recognize my deep longing for You. Then fill me with the knowledge of You. Draw me near.

Beneath all our longings is a deep desire for God.

Being Human Beings

Read: 1 Peter 2:11–17; 3:8–9

All of you, be like-minded, be sympathetic, love one another, be compassionate and humble. 1 Peter 3:8

When asked to define his role in a community that was sometimes uncooperative with law enforcement, a sheriff didn't flash his badge or respond with the rank of his office. Rather he offered, "We are human beings who work with human beings in crisis."

His humility—his stated equality with his fellow human beings—reminds me of Peter's words when writing to first-century Christians suffering under Roman persecution. Peter directs: "All of you, be like-minded, be sympathetic, love one another, be compassionate and humble" (1 PETER 3:8). Perhaps Peter was saying that the best response to humans in crisis is to be human, to be aware that we are all the same. After all, isn't that what God himself did when He sent His Son—became human in order to help us? (PHIL. 2:7).

Gazing only at the core of our fallen hearts, it's tempting to disdain our human status. But what if we consider our humanness to be part of our offering in our world? Jesus teaches us how to live fully human, as servants recognizing we are all the same. "Human" is how God made us, created in His image and redeemed by His unconditional love.

Today we're sure to encounter folks in various struggles. Imagine the difference we might make when we respond humbly—as fellow humans who work together with other humans in crisis.   *ELISA MORGAN*

Father, help us to be humble as we respond to one another, human being to human being.

Humility is the result of knowing God and knowing yourself.

God Knows

Read: Matthew 6:1–4

Your Father, who sees what is done in secret, will reward you.
Matthew 6:4

When Denise met a hurting young woman in her church, her heart went out to her and she decided to see if she could help. Every week she spent time counseling her and praying with her. Denise became her mentor. However, some church leaders didn't notice Denise's efforts and decided to assign a church staff member to mentor the woman. No one, they commented, seemed to be taking care of her.

While she was not expecting any credit, Denise couldn't help but feel a little discouraged. "It's as if I wasn't doing anything at all," she told me.

One day, however, the young woman told Denise how grateful she was for her comfort. Denise felt encouraged. It was as if God was telling her, "I know you're there for her." Denise still meets with the woman regularly.

Sometimes, we feel unappreciated when our efforts don't get recognized. Scripture, however, reminds us that God knows what we're doing. He sees what others don't. And it pleases Him when we serve for His sake—not for man's praise.

Perhaps that's why Jesus gave us an example by telling us to do our giving "in secret," so that "your Father, who sees what is done . . . will reward you" (MATT. 6:4). We need not look to others for recognition and praise; we can take heart that God knows when we're faithful in serving Him and others. *LESLIE KOH*

Lord, forgive me for the times when I crave others' recognition and praise. Help me to serve for Your glory alone.

God sees everything we do for Him.

Knowing Better

Read: 2 Kings 22:1–4, 8–13

When the king heard the words of the Book of the Law, he tore his robes. 2 Kings 22:11

When we brought our adoptive son home from overseas, I was eager to shower him with love and provide what he had lacked over the preceding months, especially quality food, since he had a nutritional deficit. But despite our best efforts, including consulting specialists, he grew very little. After nearly three years, we learned he had some severe food intolerances. After removing those items from his diet, he grew five inches in just a few months. While I grieved at how long I'd unwittingly fed him foods that impaired his growth, I rejoiced at this surge in his health!

I suspect Josiah felt similarly when the Book of the Law was discovered after having been lost in the temple for years. Just as I grieved having unintentionally hindered my son's growth, Josiah grieved having ignorantly missed God's fullest and best intentions for His people (2 KINGS 22:11). Although he is commended for doing what was right in the eyes of the Lord (V. 2), he learned better how to honor God after finding the Law. With his newfound knowledge, he led the people to worship again as God had instructed them (23:22–23).

As we learn through the Bible how to honor Him, we may grieve the ways we've fallen short of God's will for us. Yet we can be comforted that He heals and restores us, and leads us gently into deeper understanding. *KIRSTEN HOLMBERG*

Thank You, God, for showing me how to live in a way that pleases You. I'm sorry for the ways I've not done that in the past. Help me to honor and obey You now.

God gives us a new start.

Harvest and Thanksgiving

Read: Genesis 8:15–9:3

Celebrate the Festival of Harvest with the firstfruits of the crops you sow in your field. Exodus 23:16

Several thousand years ago, God spoke directly to Moses and instituted a new festival for His people. In Exodus 23:16, according to Moses's record, God said, "Celebrate the Festival of Harvest with the firstfruits of the crops you sow in your field."

Today countries around the world do something similar by celebrating the land's bounty. In Ghana, the people celebrate the Yam Festival as a harvest event. In Brazil, *Dia de Ação de Graças* is a time to be grateful for the crops that yielded their food. In China, there is the Mid-Autumn (Moon) Festival. In the United States and Canada: Thanksgiving.

To understand the fitting goal of a harvest celebration, we visit Noah right after the flood. God reminded Noah and his family—and us—of His provision for our flourishing existence on the earth. Earth would have seasons, daylight and darkness and "seedtime and harvest" (GEN. 8:22). Our gratitude for the harvest, which sustains us, goes to God alone.

No matter where you live or how you celebrate your land's bounty, take time today to express gratitude to God—for we would have no harvest to celebrate without His grand creative design.   *DAVE BRANON*

Dear Creator God, thank You so much for the wondrous way You fashioned this world—with seasons, with harvest-time, with everything we need to exist. Please accept our gratitude.

Gratitude is the memory of a glad heart.

The Power of Empathy

Read: Hebrews 2:14–18; 13:1–3

Remember those in prison as if you were together with them in prison.
Hebrews 13:3

Put on the R70i Age Suit and you immediately feel forty years older as you experience impaired vision, hearing loss, and reduced mobility. The Age Suit was designed to help caregivers better understand their patients. *Wall Street Journal* correspondent Geoffrey Fowler wore one and wrote, "The unforgettable, and at times distressing, experience shed light not just on aging, but also how virtual reality equipment can teach empathy and shape our perceptions of the world around us."

Empathy is the power to understand and share the feelings of another. During a time of severe persecution against the followers of Jesus, the writer of Hebrews urged fellow believers to "continue to remember those in prison as if you were together with them in prison, and those who are mistreated as if you yourselves were suffering" (13:3).

This is exactly what our Savior has done for us. Jesus was made like us, "fully human in every way . . . that he might make atonement for the sins of the people. Because he himself suffered when he was tempted, he is able to help those who are being tempted" (2:17–18).

Christ the Lord, who became like us, calls us to stand with others "as if [we] were together with them" during their time of need. *DAVID MCCASLAND*

Lord Jesus, we marvel at Your willingness to share our flesh and blood in order to purchase our salvation. Give us grace to stand with others who are in need today.

Jesus calls us to stand with others as if we were in their place.

Imperfect, Yet Loved

Read: Luke 7:36–50

God demonstrates his own love for us in this: While we were still sinners, Christ died for us. Romans 5:8

In Japan, food products are immaculately prepared and packaged. Not only must they taste good but they must look good too. Often I wonder if I am purchasing the food or the packaging! Because of the Japanese emphasis on good quality, products with slight defects are often discarded. However, in recent years *wakeari* products have gained popularity. *Wakeari* means "there is a reason" in Japanese. These products are not thrown away but are sold at a cheap price "for a reason"—for example, a crack in a rice cracker.

My friend who lives in Japan tells me that *wakeari* is also a catchphrase for people who are obviously less than perfect.

Jesus loves all people—including the *wakeari* who society casts aside. When a woman who had lived a sinful life learned that Jesus was eating at a Pharisee's house, she went there and knelt behind Jesus at His feet, weeping (LUKE 7:37-38). The Pharisee labeled her "a sinner" (V. 39), but Jesus accepted her. He spoke gently to her, assuring her that her sins were forgiven (V. 48).

Jesus loves imperfect, *wakeari* people—which includes you and me. And the greatest demonstration of His love for us is that "while we were still sinners, Christ died for us" (ROM. 5:8). As recipients of His love, may we be conduits of His love to the flawed people around us so they too may know that they can receive God's love despite their imperfections.   *ALBERT LEE*

I know I'm not perfect, Lord, so help me not to be hypocritical and pretend I have it all together. Open my heart to others in acceptance and love so that they might know Jesus's concern for them.

Broken people are made whole by God's love.

The Last Will Be First

Read: Mark 9:33–37

Those who humble themselves will be exalted. Matthew 23:12

Recently I was among the last in line to board a large passenger jet with unassigned seating. I located a middle seat beside the wing, but the only spot for my bag was the overhead compartment by the very last row. This meant I had to wait for everyone to leave before I could go back and retrieve it.

I laughed as I settled into my seat and a thought occurred to me that seemed to be from the Lord: "It really won't hurt you to wait. It will actually do you good." So I resolved to enjoy the extra time, helping other passengers lower their luggage after we landed and assisting a flight attendant with cleaning. By the time I was able to retrieve my bag, I laughed again when someone thought I worked for the airline.

That day's experience made me ponder Jesus's words to His disciples: "Anyone who wants to be first, must be the very last, and the servant of all" (MARK 9:35).

I waited because I had to, but in Jesus's "upside down" kingdom, there's a place of honor for those who voluntarily set themselves aside to attend to others' needs.

Jesus came into our hurried, me-first world not "to be served, but to serve, and to give his life as a ransom for many" (MATT. 20:28). We serve Him best by serving others. The lower we bend, the closer we are to Him. *JAMES BANKS*

Loving Lord, help me to follow You into the needs of others and serve You there.

Jesus's kingdom is upside-down.

Ham and Eggs

Read: 2 Chronicles 16:1–9

The eyes of the LORD range throughout the earth to strengthen those whose hearts are fully committed to him. 2 Chronicles 16:9

In the fable of the chicken and the pig, the two animals discuss opening a restaurant together. As they plan their menu, the chicken suggests they serve ham and eggs. The pig swiftly objects saying, "No thanks. I'd be committed, but you would only be involved."

Although the pig didn't care to put himself on the platter, his understanding of commitment is instructive to me as I learn to better follow God with my whole heart.

To protect his kingdom, Asa, king of Judah, sought to break up a treaty between the kings of Israel and Aram. To accomplish this, he sent personal treasure along with "silver and gold out of the treasuries of the Lord's temple" to secure favor with Ben-Hadad, the king of Aram (2 CHRON. 16:2). Ben-Hadad agreed and their joint forces repelled Israel.

But God's prophet Hanani called Asa foolish for relying on human help instead of God who had delivered other enemies into their hands. Hanani asserted, "The eyes of the LORD range throughout the earth to strengthen those whose hearts are fully committed to him" (V. 9).

As we face our own battles and challenges, let's remember that God is our best ally. He strengthens us when we're willing to "serve up" a whole-hearted commitment to Him.

KIRSTEN HOLMBERG

Lord, I want to rely on You more fully. Sometimes I see only what is around me. Please help me to look up and to trust You more.

When we are abandoned to God, He works through us all the time.
OSWALD CHAMBERS

Waiting

Read: Micah 5:2–4

Bethlehem . . . out of you will come for me one who will be ruler over Israel. Micah 5:2

"How much longer until it's Christmas?" When my children were little, they asked this question repeatedly. Although we used a daily Advent calendar to count down the days to Christmas, they still found the waiting excruciating.

We can easily recognize a child's struggle with waiting, but we might underestimate the challenge it can involve for all of God's people. Consider, for instance, those who received the message of the prophet Micah, who promised that out of Bethlehem would come a "ruler over Israel" (5:2) who would "stand and shepherd his flock in the strength of the LORD" (V. 4). The initial fulfillment of this prophecy came when Jesus was born in Bethlehem (MATT. 2:1) —after the people had waited some 700 years. But some of the prophecy's fulfillment is yet to come. For we wait in hope for the return of Jesus, when all of God's people will "live securely" and "his greatness will reach to the ends of the earth" (MIC. 5:4). Then we will rejoice greatly, for our long wait will be over.

Most of us don't find waiting easy, but we can trust that God will honor His promises to be with us as we wait (MATT. 28:20). For when Jesus was born in little Bethlehem, He ushered in life in all its fullness (SEE JOHN 10:10)—life without condemnation. We enjoy His presence with us today while we eagerly wait for His return.   *AMY BOUCHER PYE*

We wait, Father God, and we hope. We wait, dear Jesus, as we long for peace to break out. We wait, comforting Spirit, for all the world to experience Your love.

We wait for God's promises, believing they will come true.

Christmas at MacPherson

Read: Luke 1:68–75

Praise be to the Lord, the God of Israel, because he has come to his people and redeemed them. Luke 1:68

About 230 families and individuals live at MacPherson Gardens, Block 72 in my neighborhood. Each person has his or her own life story. On the tenth floor resides an elderly woman whose children have grown up, gotten married, and moved out. She lives by herself now. Just a few doors away from her is a young couple with two kids—a boy and a girl. And a few floors below lives a young man serving in the army. He has been to church before; maybe he will visit again on Christmas Day. I met these people last Christmas when our church went caroling in the neighborhood to spread Christmas cheer.

Every Christmas—as on the first Christmas—there are many people who do not know that God has entered into our world as a baby whose name is Jesus (LUKE 1:68; 2:21). Or they do not know the significance of that event—it is "good news that will cause great joy for all the people" (2:10). Yes, all people! Regardless of our nationality, culture, gender, or financial status, Jesus came to die for us and offer us complete forgiveness so that we can be reconciled with Him and enjoy His love, joy, peace, and hope. All people, from the woman next door to the colleagues we have lunch with, need to hear this wonderful news!

On the first Christmas, the angels were the bearers of this joyous news. Today, God desires to work through us to take the story to others. *POH FANG CHIA*

Lord, use me to touch the lives of others with the news of Your coming.

The good news of Jesus's birth is a source of joy for all people.

Jesus Loves Maysel

Read: 1 John 4:7–16

This is love: not that we loved God, but that he loved us. 1 John 4:10

When my sister Maysel was little, she would sing a familiar song in her own way: "Jesus loves me, this I know, for the Bible tells Maysel." This irritated me to no end! As one of her older, "wiser" sisters, I knew the words were "me so," not "Maysel." Yet she persisted in singing it *her* way.

Now I think my sister had it right all along. The Bible does indeed tell Maysel, and all of us, that Jesus loves us. Over and over again we read that truth. Take, for example, the writings of the apostle John, "the disciple whom Jesus loved" (JOHN 21:7, 20). He tells us about God's love in one of the best-known verses of the Bible: John 3:16, "For God so loved the world that he gave his one and only Son, that whoever believes in him shall not perish but have eternal life."

John reinforces that message of love in 1 John 4:10: "This is love: not that we loved God, but that he loved us and sent his Son as an atoning sacrifice for our sins." Just as John knew Jesus loved him, we too can have that same assurance: Jesus *does* love us. The Bible tells us so.   *ALYSON KIEDA*

Dear Lord, thank You for the assurance that You love us. We are filled with gratitude that You love us so much that You died for us.

Jesus loves me! This I know.

Trusting God Even If

Read: Daniel 3:13–25

The God we serve is able to deliver us. Daniel 3:17

Due to an injury that occurred in 1992, I suffer from chronic pain in my upper back, shoulders, and neck. During the most excruciating and disheartening moments, it's not always easy to trust or praise the Lord. But when my situation feels unbearable, God's constant presence comforts me. He strengthens me and reassures me of His unchanging goodness, limitless power, and sustaining grace. And when I'm tempted to doubt my Lord, I'm encouraged by the determined faith of Shadrach, Meshach, and Abednego. They worshiped God and trusted He was with them, even when their situation seemed hopeless.

When King Nebuchadnezzar threatened to throw them into a blazing furnace if they didn't turn away from the true God to worship his golden statue (DAN. 3:13–15), these three men displayed courageous and confident faith. They never doubted the Lord was worthy of their worship (V. 17), "even if" He didn't rescue them from their current predicament (V. 18). And God didn't leave them alone in their time of need; He joined and protected them in the furnace (VV. 24–25).

God doesn't leave us alone either. He remains with us through trials that can feel as destructive as Nebuchadnezzar's furnace. Even if our suffering doesn't end on this side of eternity, God is and always will be mighty, trustworthy, and good. We can rely on His constant and loving presence. *XOCHITL DIXON*

Lord, thank You for being with us, no matter what we're going through.

Faith relies on our Almighty God's unchanging character, not on our circumstances.

First Things First

Read: 1 Timothy 4:12–16

Watch your life and doctrine closely. 1 Timothy 4:16

When you travel by air, before the flight takes off an airline employee presents a safety briefing, which explains what to do if there is a loss of cabin pressure. Passengers are told that oxygen masks will drop from the compartment above and they are to put one on themselves before helping others. Why? Because before you can help anyone else, you need to be physically alert yourself.

When Paul wrote to Timothy, he stressed the importance of maintaining his own spiritual health before helping and serving others. He reminded Timothy of his many responsibilities as a pastor: There were false teachings to contend with (1 TIM. 4:1–5) and wrong doctrines to correct (VV. 6–8). But to discharge his duties well, what was most important was to "watch [his] life and doctrine closely [and] persevere in them" (V. 16). He needed to take care of his own relationship with the Lord first before he could attend to others.

What Paul told Timothy applies to us too. Each day we encounter people who do not know the Lord. When we tank up on our spiritual oxygen first through time in God's Word, prayer, and the enabling of the Holy Spirit, we keep our relationship right with God. Then we will be spiritually alert to help others.

C. P. HIA

Lord, open Your Word to me now. Let me breathe in its freshness before I go out to be Your light to the world.

A Christian's life is the window through which others can see Jesus.

Unexpected Grace

Read: Acts 9:1–19

In a vision, he has seen a man named Ananias come and place his hands on him to restore his sight. Acts 9:12

It was an early Saturday morning in my sophomore year of high school, and I was eager to get to my job at the local bowling lanes. The evening before, I had stayed late to mop the muddy tile floors because the janitor called in sick. I hadn't bothered to tell the boss about the janitor so I could surprise him. After all, *What could go wrong?* I thought.

Plenty, as it turns out.

Stepping in the door, I saw inches of standing water, with bowling pins, rolls of toilet paper, and boxes of paper scoresheets bobbing on top. Then I realized what I had done: *While doing the floors, I had left a large faucet running overnight!* Incredibly, my boss greeted me with a huge hug and a big smile—"for trying," he said.

Saul was actively punishing and harassing Christians (ACTS 9:1–2) when he came face to face with Jesus on the road to Damascus (VV. 3–4). Jesus confronted the soon-to-be-called apostle Paul with his sinful actions. Blinded by the experience, Saul/Paul would need a Christian—Ananias—to restore his sight to him in an act of courage *and* grace (V. 17).

Both Saul and I received *unexpected* grace.

Most people know they're messed up. Instead of lectures, they need a hope for redemption. Stern faces or sharp words can block their view of that hope. Like Ananias, or even my boss, followers of Jesus must become the face of grace in these life-changing encounters with others.   *RANDY KILGORE*

A Christian's grace-filled actions can smooth someone's path to the Savior's presence.

Outside In?

Read: Galatians 3:23–29

All of you who were baptized into Christ have clothed yourselves with Christ. Galatians 3:27

"Change: From the Inside Out or the Outside In?" the headline read, reflecting a popular trend today—the idea that outward changes like a makeover or better posture can be an easy way to change how we feel on the inside—and even change our lives.

It's an appealing concept—who wouldn't want improving our lives to be as easy as a new look? Many of us have learned the hard way that changing deep-rooted habits can seem nearly impossible. Focusing on simple external changes offers hope that there is a quicker path toward improving our lives.

But although such changes can improve our lives, Scripture invites us to seek a deeper transformation—one that is impossible on our own. In fact, in Galatians 3 Paul argued that even God's law—a priceless gift that revealed His will—couldn't heal the brokenness of God's people (VV. 19–22). True healing and freedom required them to, through faith, be "clothed" in Christ (V. 27) through His Spirit (5:5). Set apart and shaped through Him, they would find their true identity and worth—every believer equally an heir to all of God's promises (3:28–29).

We could easily devote much energy to self-improvement techniques. But the deepest and most satisfying changes in our hearts come in knowing the love that surpasses knowledge (EPH. 3:17–19)—the love that changes everything.   *MONICA BRANDS*

Lord, we're so grateful we don't have to rely on ourselves. Thank You for Your Spirit renewing us every day and drawing us closer to You and Your love.

In Jesus, true and lasting transformation is possible.

Restored Failures

Read: Psalm 145:1–16

The LORD upholds all who fall and lifts up all who are bowed down.
Psalm 145:14

A guest band was leading praise and worship at our church, and their passion for the Lord was moving. We could see—and feel—their enthusiasm.

Then the musicians revealed that they were all ex-prisoners. Suddenly their songs took on special meaning, and I saw why their words of praise meant so much to them. Their worship was a testimony of lives broken and restored.

The world may embrace success. But stories of past failure offer people hope too. They assure us that God loves us no matter how many times we have failed. Pastor Gary Inrig says that what we call the Hall of Faith in Hebrews 11 could well be entitled God's Hall of Reclaimed Failures. "There is scarcely an individual in that chapter without a serious blemish in his or her life," he observes. "But God is in the business of restoring failures. . . . That is a great principle of God's grace."

I love the comfort of Psalm 145, which speaks of God's "wonderful works" (VV. 5–6) and glorious kingdom (V. 11). It describes His compassion (VV. 8–9) and faithfulness (V. 13)—then immediately tells us that He lifts up those who have fallen (V. 14). All His attributes are expressed when He picks us up. He is indeed in the business of restoration.

Have you failed before? We all have. Have you been restored? All who have been redeemed are stories of God's grace.

LESLIE KOH

Our stories of failure can be God's stories of success.

It's All a Gift!

Read: Ephesians 2:1–9

For it is by grace you have been saved, through faith—and this is not from yourselves, it is the gift of God. Ephesians 2:8

London's Café Rendezvous has nice lighting, comfortable couches, and the smell of coffee in the air. What it doesn't have are prices. Originally started as a business by a local church, the café was transformed a year after it started. The managers felt that God was calling them to do something radical—make everything on the menu free. Today you can order a coffee, cake, or sandwich without cost. There isn't even a donation jar. It's all a gift.

I asked the manager why they were so generous. "We're just trying to treat people the way God treats us," he said. "God gives to us whether we thank him or not. He's generous to us beyond our imaginations."

Jesus died to rescue us from our sins and reconcile us with God. He rose from the grave and is alive now. Because of this, every wrong thing we've done can be forgiven, and we can have new life today (EPH. 2:1–5). And one of the most amazing things about this is that it is all free. We can't buy the new life Jesus offers. We can't even donate toward the cost (VV. 8–9). It's all a gift.

As the folks at Café Rendezvous serve their cakes and coffees, they give people a glimpse of God's generosity. You and I are offered eternal life for free because Jesus has paid the bill.

SHERIDAN VOYSEY

Let the one who is thirsty come; and let the one who wishes take the free gift of the water of life.
REVELATION 22:17

Eternal life is a free gift ready to be received.

The Cure for Anxiety

Read: Philippians 4:1–9

Do not be anxious about anything, but in every situation,
by prayer and petition, with thanksgiving, present your requests to God.
Philippians 4:6

We were excited about moving for my husband's job. But the unknowns and challenges left me feeling anxious. Thoughts of sorting and packing up belongings. Looking for a place to live. My finding a new job too. Making my way around a new city, and getting settled. It was all . . . unsettling. As I thought about my "to-do" list, words written by the apostle Paul echoed in my mind: *Don't worry, but pray* (PHIL. 4:6–7).

If anyone could have been anxious about unknowns and challenges, it would have been Paul. He was shipwrecked. He was beaten. He was jailed. In his letter to the Philippian church, he encouraged his friends who also were facing unknowns, telling them, "Do not be anxious about anything, but in every situation, by prayer and petition, with thanksgiving, present your requests to God" (V. 6).

Paul's words encourage me. Life is not without uncertainties—whether they come in the form of a major life transition, family issues, health scares, or financial trouble. What I continue to learn is that God cares. He invites us to let go of our fears of the unknown by giving them to Him. When we do, He, who knows all things, promises that His peace, "which transcends all understanding, will guard" our heart and mind in Christ Jesus (V. 7).

KAREN WOLFE

Dear God, what a blessing to know we do not have to be anxious about anything!
Remind us that we can come to You and tell You about everything. Thank You for
who You are and what You are doing in our lives.

God's care for me eases my mind.

It Isn't Me

Read: 1 Corinthians 15:1–11

I no longer live, but Christ lives in me. Galatians 2:20

As one of the most celebrated orchestral conductors of the twentieth century, Arturo Toscanini is remembered for his desire to give credit to whom credit is due. In David Ewen's *Dictators of the Baton*, the author describes how members of the New York Philharmonic Orchestra rose to their feet and cheered Toscanini at the end of a rehearsal of Beethoven's *Ninth Symphony*. When there was a lull in the ovation, and with tears in his eyes, Arturo's broken voice could be heard exclaiming as he spoke: "It isn't me . . . it's Beethoven! . . . Toscanini is nothing."

In the apostle Paul's New Testament letters, he also refused to take credit for his spiritual insight and influence. He knew he was like a spiritual father and mother to many who had put their faith in Christ. He admitted he had worked hard and suffered much to encourage the faith, hope, and love of so many (1 COR. 15:10). But he could not, in good conscience, accept the applause of those who were inspired by his faith, love, and insight.

So for his readers' sake, and for ours, Paul said, in effect, "It isn't me, brothers and sisters. It's Christ . . . Paul is nothing." We are only messengers of the One who deserves our cheers.

MART DEHAAN

Father in heaven, without You we would have nothing. Without Your grace we would be hopeless. Without the Spirit of Your Son we would be helpless. Please show us how to give You the honor You deserve.

Wise is the person who would rather give honor than receive it.

With God's Help

Read: Joshua 14:7–15

So here I am today, eighty-five years old! . . . I'm just as vigorous to go out to battle now as I was then. Joshua 14:10–11

As I've grown older, I've noticed more joint pain, especially when cold weather hits. Some days, I feel less like a conqueror and more like someone conquered by the challenges of becoming a senior citizen.

That's why my hero is an older man named Caleb—the former spy sent by Moses to scout out Canaan, the Promised Land (NUM. 13–14). After the other spies gave an unfavorable report, Caleb and Joshua were the only spies out of the twelve whom God favored to enter Canaan. Now, in Joshua 14, the time for Caleb to receive his portion of land had come. But there were enemies still to drive out. Not content to retire and leave the battle to the younger generation, Caleb declared, "You yourself heard then that the Anakites were there and their cities were large and fortified, but, the LORD helping me, I will drive them out just as he said" (JOSH. 14:12).

"The LORD helping me." That's the kind of mindset that kept Caleb battle-ready. He focused on God's power, not his own, nor on his advanced age. God would help him do whatever needed to be done.

Most of us don't think of taking on anything monumental when we reach a certain age. But we can still do great things for God, no matter how old we are. When Caleb-sized opportunities come our way, we don't have to shy away from them. With the Lord helping us, we can conquer!   *LINDA WASHINGTON*

Heavenly Father, thank You for giving me the strength to get through each day. Help me to do Your will.

I can do all this through him who gives me strength.
PHILIPPIANS 4:13

More Than a Hero

Read: John 1:1–5, 9–14

We have seen his glory, the glory of the one and only Son, who came from the Father, full of grace and truth. John 1:14

As *Star Wars* fans around the world eagerly await the release of Episode 8, "The Last Jedi," people continue to analyze the remarkable success of these films dating back to 1977. Frank Pallotta, media reporter for CNNMoney, said that *Star Wars* connects with many who long for "a new hope and a force of good at a time when the world needs heroes."

At the time of Jesus's birth, the people of Israel were oppressed and longing for their long-promised Messiah. Many anticipated a hero to deliver them from Roman tyranny, but Jesus did not come as a political or military hero. Instead, He came as a baby to the town of Bethlehem. As a result, many missed who He was. The apostle John wrote, "He came to that which was his own, but his own did not receive him" (JOHN 1:11).

More than a hero, Jesus came as our Savior. He was born to bring God's light into the darkness and to give His life so that everyone who receives Him could be forgiven and freed from the power of sin. John called Him "the one and only Son, who came from the Father, full of grace and truth" (V. 14).

"To all who did receive him, to those who believed in his name, he gave the right to become children of God" (V. 12). Indeed, Jesus is the one true hope the world needs.

DAVID MCCASLAND

Lord Jesus, You are our Savior, and we praise You for coming to die that we might live.

At Bethlehem, God demonstrated that to love is to give.

Big World, Bigger God

Read: Colossians 1:12–17

For by [Jesus] all things were created. Colossians 1:16 NASB

As we drove through northern Michigan, Marlene exclaimed, "It's unbelievable how big the world is!" She made her comment as we passed a sign marking the 45th parallel—the point halfway between the equator and the North Pole. We talked about how small we are and how vast our world is. Yet, compared to the size of the universe, our tiny planet is only a speck of dust.

If our world is great, and the universe is vastly greater, how big is the One who powerfully created it? The Bible tells us, "For by [Jesus] all things were created, *both* in the heavens and on earth, visible and invisible, whether thrones or dominions or rulers or authorities—all things have been created through Him and for Him" (COL. 1:16 NASB).

This is good news because this same Jesus who created the universe is the One who has come to rescue us from our sin for every day and forever. The night before He died, Jesus said, "These things I have spoken to you, so that in Me you may have peace. In the world you have tribulation, but take courage; I have overcome the world" (JOHN 16:33 NASB).

When facing the large and small challenges of life, we call on the One who made the universe, died and rose again, and won victory over this world's brokenness. In our times of struggle, He powerfully offers us His peace.   *BILL CROWDER*

*Lord, I'm grateful that You are greater than my mind could ever comprehend.
Help me to trust You today.*

God's grace is immeasurable, His mercy inexhaustible, His peace inexpressible.

Gentleness

Read: Ephesians 4:1–6

Be completely humble and gentle. Ephesians 4:2

The troubles of life can make us cranky and out of sorts, but we should never excuse these bouts of bad behavior, for they can wither the hearts of those we love and spread misery all around us. We have not fulfilled our duty to others until we have learned to be pleasant.

The New Testament has a word for the virtue that corrects our unpleasantness—*gentleness*, a term that suggests a kind and gracious soul. Ephesians 4:2 reminds us, "Be completely humble and gentle."

Gentleness is a willingness to accept limitations and ailments without taking out our aggravation on others. It shows gratitude for the smallest service rendered and tolerance for those who do not serve us well. It puts up with bothersome people—especially noisy, boisterous little people; for kindness to children is a crowning mark of a good and gentle person. It speaks softly in the face of provocation. It can be silent; for calm, unruffled silence is often the most eloquent response to unkind words.

Jesus is "gentle and humble in heart" (MATT. 11:29). If we ask Him, He will, in time, recreate us in His image. Scottish author George MacDonald says, "[God] would not hear from [us] a tone to jar the heart of another, a word to make it ache . . . . From such, as from all other sins, Jesus was born to deliver us."

DAVID ROPER

Dear Lord, I want to be a gentle person. Please help me to be kind and gracious to others today.

Humility toward God will make us gentle toward others.

Everlasting Hope

Read: Psalm 146

Blessed are those whose help is the God of Jacob, whose hope is in the Lord their God. Psalm 146:5

The week before Christmas, two months after my mom died, holiday shopping and decorating sat at the bottom of my priority list. I resisted my husband's attempts to comfort me as I grieved the loss of our family's faith-filled matriarch. I sulked as our son, Xavier, stretched and stapled strands of Christmas lights onto the inside walls of our home. Without a word, he plugged in the cord before he and his dad left for work.

As the colorful bulbs blinked, God gently drew me out of my darkness. No matter how painful the circumstances, my hope remained secure in the light of God's truth, which always reveals His unchanging character.

Psalm 146 affirms what God reminded me on that difficult morning: My endless "hope is in the Lord," my helper, my mighty and merciful God (V. 5). As Creator of all, He "remains faithful forever" (V. 6). He "upholds the cause of the oppressed," protecting us and providing for us (V. 7). "The Lord lifts up those who are bowed down" (V. 8). He "watches over" us, "sustains" us, and will always be King (VV. 9–10).

Sometimes, when Christmas rolls around, our days will overflow with joyful moments. Sometimes, we'll face loss, experience hurt, or feel alone. But at all times, God promises to be our light in the darkness, offering us tangible help and everlasting hope.

XOCHITL DIXON

Father God, thanks for inviting us to know and rely on Your unchanging character as the source of our eternal hope.

God secures our hope in His unchanging character.

Extreme Measures

Read: Luke 19:1–10

The Son of Man came to seek and to save the lost. Luke 19:10

A few years ago, a friend of mine lost track of her young son while walking through a swarm of people at Union Station in Chicago. Needless to say, it was a terrifying experience. Frantically, she yelled his name and ran back up the escalator, retracing her steps in an effort to find her little boy. The minutes of separation seemed like hours, until suddenly—thankfully—her son emerged from the crowd and ran to the safety of her arms.

Thinking of my friend who would have done anything to find her child fills me with a renewed sense of gratitude for the amazing work God did to save us. From the time God's first image-bearers—Adam and Eve—wandered off in sin, He lamented the loss of fellowship with His people. He went to great lengths to restore the relationship by sending His one and only Son "to seek and to save the lost" (LUKE 19:10). Without the birth of Jesus, and without His willingness to die to pay the price for our sin and to bring us to God, we would have nothing to celebrate at Christmastime.

So this Christmas, let's be thankful that God took extreme measures by sending Jesus to reclaim our fellowship with Him. Although we once were lost, because of Jesus we have been found! *JOE STOWELL*

Heavenly Father, in the midst of all the joy of Christmas, remind me that the true meaning of this season lies in the depth of Your love. Thank You for sending Jesus to reclaim undeserving people like me!

Christmas is about God taking extreme measures to reclaim those who were lost.

The Son Is Given

Read: Luke 1:26–33

To us a child is born, to us a Son is given. Isaiah 9:6

One of my favorite portions of Handel's *Messiah* is the joyous movement "For unto us a Child is born," from the first part of the oratorio. I especially love how the chorus rises to the phrase, "Unto us a Son is given." Those words, of course, are taken from Isaiah 9:6, "To us a child is born, unto us a son is given." Handel's majestic music soars with adoration for the Son who came to us in human flesh that first Christmas.

The New Testament clarifies even further who this Son is. In Luke 1, the angelic messenger appeared to Mary and identified the Christ-child in four ways. He would be the son of Mary, making Him fully human (1:31). He would be the Son of the Highest, which made Him fully divine (1:32). He would also be the Son of David, giving Him royal lineage (1:32). And He would bear the title of Son of God (1:35), giving Him equality with the Father in all things. All of the roles the Messiah was called to fill are made possible in these distinct expressions of His Sonship.

As we worship Him this Christmas, may our celebrations be filled with joy and wonder at the fullness of what it means. Our heavenly Father has given us His perfect, sufficient Son. O come, let us adore Him!   *BILL CROWDER*

We come and bow down to adore You, Christ the Lord!

O come, let us adore Him!

Home for Christmas

Read: Genesis 28:10–17

I am with you and will watch over you wherever you go, and I will bring you back to this land. Genesis 28:15

One year Christmas found me on assignment in a place many of my friends couldn't locate on a map. Trudging from my worksite back to my room, I braced against the chill wind blowing off the bleak Black Sea. I missed home.

When I arrived at my room, I opened the door to a magical moment. My artistic roommate had completed his latest project—a nineteen-inch ceramic Christmas tree that now illuminated our darkened room with sparkling dots of color. If only for a moment, I was home again!

As Jacob fled from his brother Esau, he found himself in a strange and lonely place too. Asleep on the hard ground, he met God in a dream. And God promised Jacob a home. "I will give you and your descendants the land on which you are lying," He told him. "All peoples on earth will be blessed through you and your offspring" (GEN. 28:13–14).

From Jacob, of course, would come the promised Messiah, the One who left His home to draw us to himself. "I will come back and take you to be with me that you also may be where I am," Jesus told His disciples (JOHN 14:3).

That December night I sat in the darkness of my room and gazed at that Christmas tree. Perhaps inevitably I thought of the Light that entered the world to show us the way home.

TIM GUSTAFSON

Lord, no matter where we are today, we can thank You for preparing a place for us to be with You. And we have the presence of Your Spirit today!

Home is not so much a place on a map, as it is a place to belong. God gives us that place.

Silent Night of the Soul

Read: 2 Corinthians 5:14–21

If anyone is in Christ, the new creation has come: The old has gone; the new is here! 2 Corinthians 5:17

Long before Joseph Mohr and Franz Gruber created the familiar carol "Silent Night," Angelus Silesius had written:

Lo! in the silent night a child to God is born,
And all is brought again that ere was lost or lorn.
Could but thy soul, O man, become a silent night
God would be born in thee and set all things aright.

Silesius, a Polish monk, published the poem in 1657 in *The Cherubic Pilgrim*. During our church's annual Christmas Eve service, the choir sang a beautiful rendition of the song titled "Could but Thy Soul Become a Silent Night."

The twofold mystery of Christmas is that God became one of us so that we might become one with Him. Jesus suffered everything that was wrong so that we could be made right. That's why the apostle Paul could write, "If anyone is in Christ, the new creation has come: The old has gone; the new is here! All this is from God who reconciled us to himself through Christ" (2 COR. 5:17–18).

Whether our Christmas is filled with family and friends or empty of all we long for, we know that Jesus came to be born in us.

Ah, would thy heart but be a manger for the birth,
God would once more become a child on earth.

DAVID MCCASLAND

Lord Jesus, thank You for being born into this dark world so that we might be born again into Your life and light.

God became one of us so that we might become one with Him.

God with Us

Read: Matthew 1:18–23

The virgin will conceive and give birth to a son, and they will call him Immanuel. Matthew 1:23

"Christ with me, Christ before me, Christ behind me, Christ within me, Christ beneath me, Christ above me, Christ at my right, Christ at my left . . ." These hymn lyrics, written by the fifth-century Celtic Christian St. Patrick, echo in my mind when I read Matthew's account of Jesus's birth. They feel like a warm embrace, reminding me that I'm never alone.

Matthew's account tells us that God dwelling with His people is at the heart of Christmas. Quoting Isaiah's prophecy of a child who would be called Immanuel, meaning "God with us" (ISA. 7:14), Matthew points to the ultimate fulfillment of that prophecy—Jesus, the One born by the power of the Holy Spirit to be God with us. This truth is so central that Matthew begins and ends his gospel with it, concluding with Jesus's words to His disciples: "And surely I am with you always, to the very end of the age" (MATT. 28:20).

St. Patrick's lyrics remind me that Christ is with believers always through His Spirit living within. When I'm nervous or afraid, I can hold fast to His promises that He will never leave me. When I can't fall asleep, I can ask Him to give me His peace. When I'm celebrating and filled with joy, I can thank Him for His gracious work in my life.

Jesus, Immanuel—God with us.   *AMY BOUCHER PYE*

Father God, thank You for sending Your Son to be God with us. May we experience Your presence this day.

God's love became Incarnate at Bethlehem.

A Thrill of Hope

Read: Luke 2:11–20

Today in the town of David a Savior has been born to you; he is the Messiah, the Lord. Luke 2:11

Reginald Fessenden had been working for years to achieve wireless radio communication. Other scientists found his ideas radical and unorthodox, and doubted he would succeed. But he claims that on December 24, 1906, he became the first person to ever play music over the radio.

Fessenden held a contract with a fruit company which had installed wireless systems on roughly a dozen boats to communicate about the harvesting and marketing of bananas. That Christmas Eve, Fessenden said that he told the wireless operators on board all ships to pay attention. At 9 o'clock they heard his voice.

He reportedly played a record of an operatic aria, and then he pulled out his violin, playing "O Holy Night" and singing the words to the last verse as he played. Finally, he offered Christmas greetings and read from Luke 2 the story of angels announcing the birth of a Savior to shepherds in Bethlehem.

Both the shepherds in Bethlehem over two thousand years ago and the sailors on board the United Fruit Company ships in 1906 heard an unexpected, surprising message of hope on a dark night. And God still speaks that same message of hope to us today. A Savior has been born for us—Christ the Lord! (LUKE 2:11). We can join the choir of angels and believers through the ages who respond with "Glory to God in the highest heaven, and on earth peace to those on whom his favor rests" (V. 14).

AMY PETERSON

God, we give You glory and thank You for sending Your Son Jesus Christ to be our Savior!

Without Christ there is no hope.
CHARLES SPURGEON

Traditions and Christmas

Read: Luke 2:1–10

I bring you good news that will cause great joy . . . a Savior has been born to you. Luke 2:10–11

As you savor a candy cane this Christmas, say "danke schön" to the Germans, for that confectionary treat was first created in Cologne. As you admire your poinsettia, say "gracias" to Mexico, where the plant originated. Say "merci beaucoup" to the French for the term *noël*, and give a "cheers" to the English for your mistletoe.

But as we enjoy our traditions and festivities of the Christmas season—customs that have been collected from around the world—let's save our most sincere and heartfelt "thank you" for our good, merciful, and loving God. From Him came the reason for our Christmas celebration: the baby born in that Judean manger more than 2,000 years ago. An angel announced the arrival of this gift to mankind by saying, "I bring you good news that will cause great joy . . . a Savior has been born to you" (LUKE 2:10–11).

This Christmas, even in the light of the sparkling Christmas tree and surrounded by newly opened presents, the true excitement comes when we turn our attention to the baby named Jesus, who came to "save his people from their sins" (MATT. 1:21). His birth transcends tradition: It is our central focus as we send praises to God for this indescribable Christmas gift.

DAVE BRANON

Lord, we thank You for coming to join us on that first Christmas. During a time of the year filled with many traditions, help us to keep You first.

May the God of hope fill you with all joy and peace as you trust in him.
ROMANS 15:13

DECEMBER 26

What on Earth?

Read: Matthew 17:24–27

My God will meet all your needs according to the riches of his glory in Christ Jesus. Philippians 4:19

When Andrew Cheatle lost his cell phone at the beach, he thought it was gone forever. About a week later, however, fisherman Glen Kerley called him. He had pulled Cheatle's phone, still functional after it dried, out of a 25-pound cod.

Life is full of odd stories, and we find more than a few of them in the Bible. One day tax collectors came to Peter demanding to know, "Doesn't your teacher pay the temple tax?" (MATT. 17:24). Jesus turned the situation into a teaching moment. He wanted Peter to understand His role as king. Taxes weren't collected from the children of the king, and the Lord made it clear that neither He nor His children owed any temple tax (VV. 25–26).

Yet Jesus wanted to be careful not to "cause offense" (V. 27), so He told Peter to go fishing. (This is the odd part of the story.) Peter found a coin in the mouth of the first fish he caught.

What on earth is Jesus doing here? A better question is, "What in God's kingdom is Jesus doing?" He is the rightful King—even when many do not recognize Him as such. When we accept His role as Lord in our lives, we become His children.

Life will still throw its various demands at us, but Jesus will provide for us. As former pastor David Pompo put it, "When we're fishing for our Father, we can depend on Him for all we need."

TIM GUSTAFSON

Lord, teach us to bask in the wonderful realization that You provide everything we need.

We are children of the King!

Thanks Journal

Read: Psalm 117

Praise the Lᴏʀᴅ, all you nations; extol him, all you peoples. Psalm 117:1

When I was a new believer in Jesus, a spiritual mentor encouraged me to keep a thanks journal. It was a little booklet I carried with me everywhere I went. Sometimes I would record a thanksgiving right away. Other times, I would pen it at the end of the week during a time of reflection.

Taking note of praise items is a good habit—one I'm considering re-establishing in my life. It would help me to be mindful of God's presence and grateful for His provision and care.

In the shortest of all the psalms, Psalm 117, the writer encourages everyone to praise the Lord because "great is his love toward us" (V. 2).

Think about it: How has the Lord shown His love toward you today, this week, this month, and this year? Don't just look for the spectacular. His love is seen in the ordinary, everyday circumstances of life. Then consider how He has shown His love toward your family, your church, and to others. Let your mind soak up the extent of His love for all of us.

The psalmist added that "the faithfulness of the Lᴏʀᴅ *endures* forever" (v. 2, emphasis added). In other words, He will continue to love us! So we will continue to have many things to praise God for in the coming days. As His dearly loved children, may praising and thanking God characterize our lives!   *POH FANG CHIA*

Father, if we were to record all of Your blessings, we could not complete the task in a lifetime. But we can pause this moment to say a simple "Thank You" for Your faithfulness and goodness.

Remember to thank God for the ordinary as well as the extraordinary.

Everyday Moments

Read: Proverbs 15:13–15

A happy heart makes the face cheerful, but heartache crushes the spirit.
Proverbs 15:13

I piled groceries in my car and carefully exited my parking spot. Suddenly a man darted across the pavement just in front of me, not noticing my approach. I slammed on my brakes, just missing him. Startled, he looked up and met my gaze. In that moment, I knew I had a choice: respond with rolled-eye frustration or offer a smiling forgiveness. I smiled.

Relief flickered across his face, raising the edges of his own lips in gratefulness.

Proverbs 15:13 says, "A happy heart makes the face cheerful, but heartache crushes the spirit." Is the writer directing us to cheery grins in the face of every interruption, disappointment, and inconvenience life brings? Surely not! There are times for genuine mourning, despair, and even anger at injustice. But in our everyday moments, a smile can offer relief, hope, and the grace needed to continue.

Perhaps the point of the proverb is that a smile naturally results from the condition of our inner beings. A "happy heart" is at peace, content, and yielded to God's best. With such a heart, happy from the inside out, we can respond to surprising circumstances with a genuine smile, inviting others to embrace the hope and peace they too can experience with God.

ELISA MORGAN

Dear Father, today as I cross paths with others around me, make my heart happy that I may share with them the hope only You can offer.

Encourage one another and build each other up.
1 THESSALONIANS 5:11

What Remains in the Eye

Read: Psalm 104:24–35

How many are your works, LORD! Psalm 104:24

The hummingbird gets its English name from the hum made by its rapidly beating wings. In other languages, it is known as the "flower-kisser" (Portuguese) or "flying jewels" (Spanish). One of my favorite names for this bird is *biulu*, "what remains in the eye" (Mexican Zapotec). In other words, once you see a hummingbird, you'll never forget it.

G. K. Chesterton wrote, "The world will never starve for want of wonders, but only for want of wonder." The hummingbird is one of those wonders. What is so fascinating about these tiny creatures? Maybe it is their small size (averaging two to three inches) or the speed of their wings that can flap from 50 to 200 times per second.

We aren't sure who wrote Psalm 104, but the psalmist was certainly captivated by nature's beauty. After describing many of creation's wonders, like the cedars of Lebanon and the wild donkeys, he sings, "May the LORD rejoice in his works" (V. 31). Then he prays, "May my meditation be pleasing to him" (V. 34).

Nature has plenty of things that can remain in the eye because of their beauty and perfection. How can we meditate on them and please God? We can observe, rejoice, and thank God as we contemplate His works and recapture the wonder.   *KEILA OCHOA*

Father, help me to reflect on the wonders of nature and meditate on them with thankfulness for all You have done!

Wonder leads to gratitude.

Times of Completion

Read: Acts 14:21–28

They sailed back to Antioch, where they had been committed to the grace of God for the work they had now completed. Acts 14:26

At the end of the year, the burden of uncompleted tasks can weigh us down. Responsibilities at home and work may seem never-ending, and those unfinished today roll into tomorrow. But there are times in our journey of faith when we should pause and celebrate God's faithfulness and the tasks completed.

After the first missionary journey of Paul and Barnabas, "they sailed back to Antioch, where they had been committed to the grace of God for the work they had now completed" (ACTS 14:26). While much work remained in sharing the message of Jesus with others, they took time to give thanks for what had been done. "They gathered the church together and reported all that God had done through them and how he had opened a door of faith to the Gentiles" (V. 27).

What has God done through you during the past year? How has He opened the door of faith for someone you know and love? In ways we can't imagine, He is at work through us in tasks that may seem insignificant or incomplete.

When we feel painfully aware of our unfinished tasks in serving the Lord, let's not forget to give thanks for the ways He has worked through us. Rejoicing over what God has done by His grace sets the stage for what is to come!   *DAVID MCCASLAND*

Lord, as this year comes to a close, we give thanks for all You have accomplished in and through us. By Your grace, lift our eyes to see what is to come!

God is always at work in and through us.

Faith-Building Memories

Read: Lamentations 3:19–26

Great is your faithfulness. Lamentations 3:23

As I stepped into the music-filled sanctuary, I looked around at the crowd that had gathered for a New Year's Eve party. Joy lifted my heart with hope, as I recalled the prayers of the previous year. Our congregation had collectively grieved over wayward children, deaths of loved ones, job losses, and broken relationships. But we'd also experienced God's grace as we recalled changed hearts and healed personal connections. We'd celebrated victories, weddings, graduations, and baptisms into God's family. We'd welcomed children born, adopted, or dedicated to the Lord, and more—so much more.

Reflecting over the history of trials our church family faced, much like Jeremiah remembered his "affliction" and his "wandering" (LAM. 3:19), I believed that "because of the LORD's great love we are not consumed, for his compassions never fail" (V. 22). As the prophet reassured himself of God's past faithfulness, his words comforted me: "The LORD is good to those whose hope is in him, to the one who seeks him" (V. 25).

That night, each person in our congregation represented a tangible expression of God's life-transforming love. Whatever we'd face in the years to come, as members of the interdependent body of Christ, we could rely on the Lord. And as we continue to seek Him and support one another, we can, as did Jeremiah, find our hope being ratified by faith-building memories of God's unchanging character and dependability.   *XOCHITL DIXON*

Lord, thank You for using our past to assure us our hope remains secure in Your everlasting faithfulness.

As we look ahead to the new year, let's remember that God has always been and always will be faithful.

About the Authors

Dr. **James Banks** and his wife have two adult children and live in Durham, North Carolina, where he is the pastor of Peace Church. He is the author of *The Lost Art of Praying Together*, *Praying the Prayers of the Bible*, *Prayers for Prodigals*, and *Prayers for Your Children*.

Shelly Beach is a freelance writer, public speaker, and author of *Ambushed By Grace* and 2008 Christy Award-winning novel *Hallie's Heart*. She is the founder of the Cedar Falls Christian Writers' Workshop in Cedar Falls, Iowa. Shelly and her husband, Dan, have two children and live in Sparta, Michigan.

Monica Brands is from Edgerton, Minnesota, where she grew up on a farm with seven siblings. She studied English and Theology at Trinity Christian College in Palos Heights, Illinois, and worked with children with special needs at Elim Christian Services before completing a Master of Theological Studies degree at Calvin Seminary in Grand Rapids. She treasures time with friends, family, and her awesome nieces and nephews.

If you've read articles by **Dave Branon** over the years, you know about his family and the lessons learned from father- (and now grandfather-) hood. After serving for 18 years as managing editor of *Sports Spectrum* magazine, Dave is now an editor for Discovery House. A freelance writer for many years, he has authored 15 books. Dave and his wife, Sue, love rollerblading and spending time with their children and grandchildren. Dave also enjoys traveling overseas with students on ministry trips.

Anne Cetas became a follower of Jesus in her late teens. At 19, she was given a copy of *Our Daily Bread* by a friend to help her read the Bible consistently. She also devoured Discovery Series topical study booklets. Several years later, she joined the editorial staff of *Our Daily Bread* as a proofreader. Anne began writing for the devotional booklet in September 2004 and is managing editor of the publication. Anne and her husband, Carl, enjoy walking and bicycling together and working as mentors in an urban ministry.

Poh Fang Chia never dreamed of being in a language-related profession; chemistry was her first love. The turning point came when she received Jesus as her Savior as a 15-year-old and expressed to Jesus that she would like to create books that touch lives. She serves with Our Daily Bread Ministries at the Singapore office as an editor and is also a member of the Chinese editorial review committee. Poh Fang says: "I really enjoy exploring the Scripture and finding passages that bring a fresh viewpoint, answer a question that is burning in my mind, or deal with a life issue I'm facing. My prayer is to write so that readers will see how presently alive the Bible is and will respond to the life-transforming power of the Word."

Peter Chin is a pastor, writer, speaker, and advocate for racial reconciliation. A graduate of Yale University and Fuller Seminary, he has pastored and planted churches in Los Angeles, Virginia, Washington, D.C., and Seattle, and now serves as lead pastor of Rainier Avenue Church, located in one of the most culturally diverse zip codes of the United States. He is also a blogger for *Christianity Today* and the author of *Blindsided by God*, a memoir of his wife's fight against cancer while pregnant with their third child. Peter is the husband of a courageous breast cancer survivor and the father of five wonderful children. He does nothing in his free time because as a father of five, free time does not exist!

Bill Crowder joined the Our Daily Bread Ministries staff after more than 20 years in the pastorate. Bill serves as vice president of teaching content and spends much of his time in a Bible-teaching ministry for Christian leaders around the world. He has written many booklets for the Discovery Series, and he has published several books with Discovery House. Bill and his wife, Marlene, have five children as well as several grandchildren he'd be thrilled to tell you about.

Lawrence Darmani is a Ghanaian novelist and publisher. His first novel, *Grief Child*, won the Commonwealth Writers' Prize as best first book from Africa. He is editor of *Step* magazine and CEO of Step Publishers. He is married and lives in Accra with his family. Lawrence enjoys church life and volunteers at other Christian ministry activities. He says that he derives writing ideas "out of personal experiences, reading, testimonies, and observing the world around me."

Mart DeHaan, grandson of Our Daily Bread Ministries founder, Dr. M. R. DeHaan, and son of former president, Richard W. DeHaan, has served with the ministry for more than fifty years. Mart is heard regularly on the *Discover the Word* radio program. He is also an author of many booklets for Discovery Series. He and his wife, Diane, have two grown children. Mart enjoys spending time outdoors, especially with fishing pole in hand.

Xochitl (soh-cheel) **Dixon** equips and encourages readers to embrace God's grace and grow deeper in their personal relationships with Christ and others. Serving as an author, speaker, and blogger at xedixon.com, she enjoys singing, reading, photography, motherhood, and being married to her best friend, Dr. W. Alan Dixon Sr.

Dennis Fisher received Jesus as his Savior at a church meeting in Southern California. He says, "I came under terrible conviction of sin. After receiving Christ, I felt like I had taken a shower on the inside." Dennis was a professor of evangelism and discipleship at Moody Bible Institute for 8 years. In 1998, he joined Our Daily Bread Ministries, where he served as senior research editor. He is now retired but continues to assist the ministry through writing and reviewing. Dennis has two adult children and one grandson and lives with his wife, Janet, in Sacramento, California.

Tim Gustafson writes for *Our Daily Bread* and serves as an editor for Discovery Series. As the adopted son of missionaries to Ghana, Tim has an unusual perspective on life in the West. He and his wife, Leisa, are the parents of one daughter and seven sons. Perhaps not surprisingly, his life verses say: "Father to the fatherless, defender of widows—this is God, whose dwelling is holy. God places the lonely in families; he sets the prisoners free and gives them joy" (PSALM 68:5–6 NLT).

Chek Phang (C. P.) Hia brings a distinctive flavor to *Our Daily Bread*. He and his wife, Lin Choo, reside in the island nation of Singapore. C. P. came to faith in Jesus Christ at the age of 13. During his early years as a believer, he was privileged to learn from excellent Bible teachers who instilled in him a love for God's Word. He currently serves in the Singapore office as Special Assistant to the Our Daily Bread Ministries president. He and his wife enjoy traveling and going for walks. They have a son, daughter-in-law, grandson, and granddaughter who also live in Singapore.

Kirsten Holmberg is a writer and speaker based in the Pacific Northwest. She's the author of *Advent with the Word: Approaching Christmas through the Inspired Language of God* and several Bible studies. She speaks regularly at church and parachurch events, encouraging others to step closer to Jesus and better know His love for them through His Word. Find her online at www.kirstenholm berg.com or on Facebook, Twitter, and Instagram (@kirholmberg).

In the fall of 2016, after twenty-eight years of pastoral ministry in the Chicago area, **Arthur Jackson** and his wife, Shirley, relocated to Kansas City, Kansas, where Arthur was born and raised. In addition to being a contributor to *Our Daily Bread*, Arthur serves as the Midwest region urban director for PastorServe (a ministry that cares for pastors) and as a director for Neopolis Network (a global church-planting ministry based in Chicago).

Cindy Hess Kasper served for more than 40 years at Our Daily Bread Ministries, where she was most recently the associate editor for *Our Daily Journey*. An experienced writer, she has penned youth devotional articles for more than a decade. She is a daughter of longtime senior editor Clair Hess, from whom she learned a love for singing and working with words. Cindy and her husband, Tom, have three grown children and seven grandchildren, in whom they take great delight.

Alyson Kieda has been an editor for Our Daily Bread Ministries for over a decade and has more than 35 years of editing experience. Alyson has loved writing since she was a child and is thrilled to be writing for *Our Daily Bread*. She is married with three adult children and a growing number of grandchildren. Alyson loves reading, walking in the woods, and being with family. She feels blessed to be following in her mother's footsteps— she wrote articles many years ago for another devotional.

Randy Kilgore spent most of his 20-plus years in business as a senior human resource manager before returning to seminary. Since finishing his Masters in Divinity in 2000, he has served as a writer and workplace chaplain. He writes a weekly internet devotional, and a collection of those devotionals appears in the Discovery House book *Made to Matter: Devotions for Working Christians*. Randy and his wife, Cheryl, founded Desired Haven Ministries in 2007 and work together in Massachusetts, where they live with their two children.

Born and raised in Singapore, **Leslie Koh** spent more than 15 years as a journalist in the busy newsroom of local newspaper *The Straits Times* before moving to Our Daily Bread Ministries. He's found moving from bad news to good news most rewarding, and still believes that nothing reaches out to people better than a good, compelling story. He likes eating (a lot), traveling, running, editing, and writing.

Albert Lee was director of international ministries for Our Daily Bread Ministries for many years, and he lives in Singapore. Albert's passion, vision, and energy expanded the work of the ministry around the world. He continues to oversee a number of projects for the ministry. Albert grew up in Singapore and took a variety of courses from Singapore Bible College, as well as served with Singapore Youth for Christ from 1971–1999. Albert also taught a course on youth evangelism at Taylor University in Indiana. Albert appreciates art and collects paintings. He and his wife, Catherine, have two children.

After a lengthy battle with cancer, **Julie Ackerman Link** went to be with the Lord on April 10, 2015. Since 2000, Julie has written articles each month for *Our Daily Bread.* She is a popular author with *Our Daily Bread* readers, and her insightful and inspiring articles have touched millions of lives around the world. Julie also wrote the books *Above All, Love*; *A Heart for God*; *Hope for All Seasons*; and *100 Prayers Inspired by the Psalms.*

David McCasland began writing for *Our Daily Bread* in 1995. His books *Oswald Chambers: Abandoned to God* and *Eric Liddell: Pure Gold* are published by Discovery House. David and his wife, Luann, live in Colorado Springs, Colorado. They have four daughters and six grandchildren.

Elisa Morgan has authored over fifteen books on mothering, spiritual formation, and evangelism, including *The NIV Mom's Devotional Bible* and *The Prayer Coin: Daring to Pray with Honest Abandon.* She currently authors a blog under the title *Really* (elisamorgan.com). For twenty years, Elisa served as CEO of MOPS International. Elisa is married to Evan (president of Christian University GlobalNet from Our Daily Bread Ministries), and they have two grown children and two grandchildren who live near them in Denver, Colorado.

Harold Myra is an award-winning editor, author, and publishing executive. He served as the CEO of Christianity Today International for 32 years. He also taught writing and publishing at the Wheaton College Graduate School in Wheaton, Illinois. Harold is the author of five novels, several children's and nonfiction books, and various magazine articles. He and his wife, Jeanette, live in Wheaton, Illinois.

Keila Ochoa and her husband are very busy parents of two young children. She helps Media Associates International with their training ministry for writers around the world and has written several books in Spanish for children, teens, and women. She teaches in an international school. When she has time, she enjoys reading, talking to friends over a cup of hot chocolate, and watching a good movie.

Jeff Olson is a licensed professional counselor in the State of Michigan and has worked for Our Daily Bread Ministries as a counselor and a writer since 1992. He has authored a number of Discovery Series booklets (discoveryseries.org) on such topics as addictions, grief, depression, and marital abuse. He also maintains a part-time private counseling practice in the West Michigan area. Jeff and his wife, Diane, have been married since 1986 and have raised two lovely daughters. He is an avid outdoorsman.

Amy Peterson works with the Honors program at Taylor University. She has a B.A. in English Literature from Texas A&M and an M.A. in Intercultural Studies from Wheaton College, and is completing an M.F.A. through Seattle Pacific University. Amy taught ESL for two years in Southeast Asia before returning stateside to teach in California, Arkansas, Washington, and Indiana. She is the author of *Dangerous Territory: My Misguided Quest to Save the World*. Amy enjoys reading, quilting, hiking, and experimenting in sustainable practices of living.

A teacher for twenty-five years, **Jolene Philo** now writes and speaks about caregiving. She is the author of *A Different Dream for My Child* by Discovery House, and she hosts a thriving online community for parents of children with special needs at DifferentDream.com. She and her husband have two children and live in Iowa.

Amy Boucher Pye is a writer and speaker who lives in North London. She's the author of the book *The Living Cross: Exploring God's Gift of Forgiveness and New Life* and the award-winning book *Finding Myself in Britain: Our Search for Faith, Home, and True*

Identity. She runs the Woman Alive book club in the UK and enjoys life with her family in their English vicarage. Find her at www.amy boucherpye.com or on Facebook or Twitter (@amyboucherpye).

David Roper was a pastor for more than 30 years and now directs Idaho Mountain Ministries, a retreat dedicated to the encouragement of pastoral couples. He enjoys fishing, hiking, and being streamside with his wife, Carolyn. His favorite fictional character is Reepicheep, the tough little mouse that is the soul of courage in C. S. Lewis's Chronicles of Narnia series. His favorite biblical character is Caleb—that rugged old saint who never retired, but who "died climbing."

Jennifer Benson Schuldt has been writing professionally since 1997 when she graduated from Cedarville University and began her career as a technical writer. Jennifer lives in the Chicago suburbs with her husband, Bob, and their two children. When she isn't writing or serving at home and church, she enjoys painting, reading poetry and fiction, and taking walks with her family. One of her favorite verses is Micah 6:8, "This is what He requires of you: to do what is right, to love mercy, and to walk humbly with your God" (NLT).

Julie Schwab graduated from Cornerstone University in May 2017 with her bachelor's degree in Creative Writing. Being from Kimball, Michigan, she enjoys tractor shows, playing the guitar, and writing. Julie is currently in the process of writing and editing a novel. Although she loves writing fiction, her dream and is to write full-length Bible studies. However, her goal is to glorify God through all of her writing.

You may know **Joe Stowell** as the former president of Moody Bible Institute. Currently, he serves as president of Cornerstone University in Grand Rapids, Michigan. An internationally recognized speaker, Joe's first love is Jesus Christ and preaching His Word. He has also written numerous books, including *Strength for the Journey*, *The Upside of Down*, and *Jesus Nation*. He and his wife, Martie, have 3 children and 10 grandchildren.

Sheridan Voysey is a writer, speaker, and broadcaster based in Oxford, England. Sheridan has authored several books, including *Resurrection Year: Turning Broken Dreams into New Beginnings* and *Resilient: Your Invitation to a Jesus-Shaped Life.* For many years Sheridan was the host of *Open House*, a live talk show heard around Australia every Sunday night, exploring life, faith, and culture. He speaks regularly at conferences and events around the world. He holds degrees in theology and communication, and has served in numerous church and parachurch leadership roles. He blogs and podcasts at sheridanvoysey.com, or find him on Facebook (facebook.com/sheridanvoysey) and Twitter (@sheridanvoysey).

Linda Washington received a B.A. in English/Writing from Northwestern University in Evanston, Illinois, and an MFA from Vermont College of Fine Arts in Montpelier, Vermont. She has authored or co-authored fiction and nonfiction books for kids, teens, and adults, including *God and Me* and *The Soul of C. S. Lewis.*

Marvin Williams began writing for *Our Daily Bread* in 2007. Marvin is senior teaching pastor at Trinity Church in Lansing, Michigan. Educated at Bishop College in Dallas, Texas, and Trinity Evangelical Divinity School in Deerfield, Illinois, he has also served in several pastoral positions in Grand Rapids, Michigan. He and his wife, Tonia, have three children.

Karen Wolfe is a native of Jamaica who now lives in the United States. She became a follower of Christ at the age of 26, and one of the first devotionals she read was *Our Daily Bread.* Karen enjoys teaching and writing so that she can share the truths she learns from Scripture. Her desire is to see men and women walk in the freedom that Christ has given and to see lives transformed by the Word of God. She completed her biblical studies degree at New Orleans Baptist Theological Seminary. In addition to writing, Karen loves to cook, especially when she can use locally sourced ingredients in her dishes. She is married to Joey, and they reside in Tennessee. Karen currently writes at thekarenwolfe.com.

Topic Index

About the Publisher

Our Daily Bread Ministries

Our Daily Bread Ministries is a nondenominational, nonprofit organization with more than 600 staff and 1,000 volunteers serving in 37 countries. Together we distribute more than 60 million resources every year in over 150 countries. Our mission is to make the life-changing wisdom of the Bible understandable and accessible to all.

Beginning in 1938 as a Bible class aired on a small radio station in Detroit, Michigan, USA, Our Daily Bread Ministries now offers radio programs and devotional, instructional, evangelistic, and apologetic print and digital resources. You can access our online resources at ourdailybread.org. Our signature publication, *Our Daily Bread*, is published in nearly 50 languages and is read by people in almost every country around the world.

Discovery House

Discovery House was founded in 1988 as an extension of Our Daily Bread Ministries. Our goal is to produce resources that feed the soul with the Word of God, and we do this through books, music, video, audio, greeting cards, and downloadable content. All our materials focus on the never-changing truths of Scripture, so everything we produce shows reverence for God and His Word, demonstrates the relevance of vibrant faith, and equips and encourages people in their everyday lives.

Enjoy this book? Help us get the word out!

Share a link to the book or
mention it on social media

Write a review on your blog, on a retailer site,
or on our website (dhp.org)

Pick up another copy to share with someone

Recommend this book for your
church, book club, or small group

Follow Discovery House on
social media and join the discussion

Contact us to share your thoughts:

 @discoveryhouse    @DiscoveryHouse

Discovery House
P.O. Box 3566
Grand Rapids, MI 49501 USA

Phone: 1-800-653-8333
Email: books@dhp.org
Web: dhp.org